APEX ACADEMIC RESOURCES

Property and Casualty Insurance Exam Success

5 Full-Length Exams, 600+ Practice Questions & Detailed Answer Explanations for Guaranteed First-Attempt Success

First edition

This book was professionally typeset on Reedsy.
Find out more at reedsy.com

Contents

Preface

Introduction to the Book

Welcome to your comprehensive guide to mastering the Property and Casualty Insurance License Exam! If you're reading this, chances are you're on the path to becoming a licensed insurance professional, seeking to expand your knowledge and skills in the field of property and casualty insurance. This book is designed to be your ally, providing you with the tools and insights needed to confidently approach the exam and succeed.

We understand that preparing for any exam can be daunting, especially one as crucial as the Property and Casualty Insurance License Exam. The world of insurance is complex, with its own language, principles, and regulations. That's where this book comes in. Our goal is to break down these complexities into manageable, understandable pieces, making the learning process as smooth and effective as possible.

This book isn't just a collection of facts and figures; it's structured to offer a logical progression through the various aspects of property and casualty insurance, from the foundational concepts to the nuances of state-specific regulations. Each chapter builds on the previous one, ensuring that you build a solid understanding of the material as you progress.

But we don't stop at just presenting the information. We've included features designed to reinforce your learning and prepare you for the exam format you'll face. 5 Full-Length Exams with over 600 Practice questions, real-world scenarios, and review sections are just a few of the tools at your disposal. These elements are crafted to not only test your knowledge but to also provide insights into the reasoning behind correct answers, helping you to think like an insurance professional.

This book is for you if you're aiming to not just pass the exam but to also gain a deeper understanding of property and casualty insurance's role and impact in people's lives. Whether you're new to the field or looking to refresh and update your knowledge, we've got you covered.

So, let's get started! With this book in hand, you're well-equipped to tackle the challenges ahead and move forward in your career with confidence.

How to Use This Book Effectively

Great to have you on board! Now that you're here, let's talk about how you can make the most out of this book. We've designed it not just as a study guide but as a toolkit to help you prepare for the Property and Casualty Insurance License Exam in a way that suits your personal learning style.

1. Start with a Bird's-Eye View: Before diving into the chapters, take a moment to skim through the book. Get a feel for the layout, note the chapters that might need more of your attention, and familiarize yourself with the additional resources and practice sections.

2. Set a Steady Pace: It's tempting to rush through the material, but true understanding comes from taking your time. Break down your study sessions into manageable chunks and schedule them in a way that fits your daily routine. Consistency is key.

3. Active Engagement: As you work through each chapter, engage actively with the content. Highlight key points, jot down notes, or even summarize sections in your own words. This active engagement helps reinforce what you've learned and makes it easier to recall later.

4. Practice, Practice, Practice: Take full advantage of the practice questions and mock exams included in the book. They're designed to mirror the format of the actual exam, giving you a taste of what to expect. After completing a set of questions, review the explanations for both correct and incorrect answers to deepen your understanding.

5. Lean on the Summaries and Reviews: Each chapter concludes with a summary and review section. Use these as a quick refresher before moving on to new topics or as a revision tool in the lead-up to your exam day.

6. Stay Flexible: As you progress, you might find that some strategies work better for you than others. Stay flexible and be willing to adjust your approach. The goal is to find what works best for you.

Remember, this book is more than just a study guide; it's a support system designed to help you build confidence and competence in the field of property and casualty insurance. Use it in a way that amplifies your strengths and supports you in areas where you're keen to grow. We're here to help you succeed, and we can't wait to see where this step takes you in your career.

Overview of the Property and Casualty Insurance License Exam

Alright, let's get into what the Property and Casualty Insurance License Exam is all about. This exam is a significant step for anyone looking to make their mark in the insurance industry, specifically in the areas of property and casualty insurance. It's designed to test your knowledge and understanding of a wide range of topics within this field, ensuring that you're well-equipped to serve your future clients effectively.

The exam itself covers a lot of ground. You'll find questions on the principles of insurance, types of policies, and the specifics of property and casualty insurance. This includes understanding policy coverage, terms, conditions, and exclusions. You'll also need to be familiar with the legal aspects of insurance, including state-specific laws and regulations that govern insurance practices.

Format-wise, the exam typically consists of multiple-choice questions. These questions are structured to assess not only your recall of factual information but also your ability to apply this knowledge in practical, real-world scenarios. It's as much about understanding the 'why' and 'how' as it is about the 'what.'

Now, it's important to note that the exact content and structure of the exam can vary from state to state. Each state has its own regulatory body that oversees the licensing process, and they may have slightly different requirements or focus areas. That's something to keep in mind as you prepare, especially when it comes to the legal and regulatory aspects.

Preparation is key for this exam. It's not just about memorizing facts; it's about understanding concepts deeply and being able to think critically about insurance practices and policies. This is where this book comes in handy, offering you a structured way to build up your knowledge, test your understanding, and sharpen your test-taking skills.

So, take a deep breath. You're taking a significant step towards a rewarding career in the insurance industry. With the right preparation and mindset, you're going to do great. Let's tackle this together, one chapter at a time.

I

Part I: Foundations of Property and Casualty Insurance

Chapter 1: Introduction to Insurance

Basic Principles of Insurance

Welcome to the world of insurance! At its core, insurance is a fascinating concept. It's all about managing risk and providing a safety net when unexpected events occur. Whether it's a fender bender on the way to work or a storm damaging your home, insurance is there to help cushion the impact. Let's break down the basic principles that make insurance work.

1. Pooling of Risks: Imagine you and your friends put money into a pot to help out any one of you who might face a tough situation. That's the essence of risk pooling. By bringing together a large group of people, each contributing a small amount (premiums), the financial burden of losses is spread out. This way, no one person has to bear the full brunt of a loss.

2. Transfer of Risk: When you buy an insurance policy, you're essentially transferring the risk of a financial loss to the insurance company. In exchange for your premium, the insurer agrees to take on the financial risk associated with certain events, like accidents or natural disasters.

3. Law of Large Numbers: This principle is all about predictability. The more people an insurance company covers, the more data it has. With this data, insurers can predict losses more accurately and set premiums that are fair for everyone. It's statistics in action!

4. Indemnity: This fancy term simply means "compensation for loss." Insurance policies are designed to restore you to the financial position you were in before the loss occurred, no more and no less. It's about making things right, not about profit or gain from a claim.

5. Utmost Good Faith: Insurance relies heavily on trust. When you apply for insurance, you're expected to be honest about everything that could affect your coverage. Likewise, insurance companies must be clear and honest about what the policy covers. This mutual honesty ensures that everyone is on the same page.

6. Insurable Interest: To insure something, you need to have a stake in it. For instance, you can insure your car because if something happens to it, you'd face a financial loss. This principle prevents people from insuring things they don't own or care about, which could lead to fraud.

7. Subrogation: This principle is a bit like stepping into someone else's shoes. If your insurance company pays out a claim for damages caused by someone else, they have the right to "step into your shoes" and seek reimbursement from the person responsible for the damages.

Understanding these principles is like getting the keys to the insurance kingdom. They are the foundation upon which the entire industry is built, guiding how policies are written, claims are handled, and how insurance companies operate. As we move forward, we'll see these principles in action across different types of insurance and scenarios. So, keep these concepts in mind – they're the building blocks of everything we'll cover in the chapters ahead!

The History and Development of Insurance

A Look Back at How It All Began

Have you ever wondered how the concept of insurance came to be? It's a story that goes way back, and it's pretty fascinating to see how it's evolved over time. Let's take a step back and see how insurance has grown from its humble beginnings to the complex industry it is today.

The Early Days: The roots of insurance can be traced back to ancient times. Imagine ancient traders and merchants, sailing across the unpredictable seas, knowing well that a single storm could wipe out their entire cargo. To mitigate this risk, they came up with a simple yet effective solution: they would distribute their goods across multiple ships. This way, if one ship encountered trouble, the loss would be manageable, and not all would be lost. This practice laid the groundwork for what we now understand as the pooling of risks.

Middle Ages and Beyond: Fast forward to the Middle Ages in Europe, and you'll find the concept of insurance becoming more formalized, especially among sea-faring folk. The term "insurance" itself first appeared in the 14th century, derived from the French word 'ensurer', meaning 'to make safe'. Merchants and shipowners began entering into formal agreements to protect against losses at sea, giving birth to marine insurance.

The Great Fire of London: A pivotal moment in insurance history occurred in 1666 with the Great Fire of London. The fire ravaged the city, destroying thousands of homes and buildings. In the aftermath, people saw the need for a more systematic way to protect against such catastrophic losses. This led to the creation of one of the first fire insurance companies in 1681, marking a significant evolution in the concept of property insurance.

The Birth of Modern Insurance: The 18th century saw the birth of modern insurance. In 1752, Benjamin Franklin founded the Philadelphia Contributionship for the Insurance of Houses from Loss by Fire, America's first successful insurance company. Around the same time, across the Atlantic, the famous Lloyd's of London was establishing itself as a global hub for insurance, especially marine insurance.

The Expansion and Regulation: As the industrial revolution took hold, the types of risks businesses and individuals faced became more varied and complex. This period saw the expansion of insurance to cover a wide array of risks, from life and health to property and liability. With this expansion, the need for regulation became evident. Governments began to step in, enacting laws to ensure that insurance practices were fair, reliable, and in the public's best interest.

The 20th Century and Beyond: The 20th century brought with it unprecedented technological advancements, economic shifts, and societal changes, all of which had a profound impact on the insurance industry. The introduction of computers and the internet revolutionized how insurance was sold, managed, and underwritten. Today, the industry continues to evolve with advancements in data analytics, artificial intelligence, and the ever-changing landscape of global risks.

The history of insurance is a testament to human ingenuity in the face of uncertainty. From its simplest forms in ancient times to the sophisticated and vital industry it is today, insurance has always been about finding ways to make life a little more secure. As we move forward, who knows what new chapters will be added to this ongoing story?

Types of Insurance Providers

Navigating the World of Insurance Companies

When you think about insurance, what comes to mind? A safety net, perhaps, or a promise of protection against the unpredictable. Behind this promise are the providers - the companies that offer insurance policies. But not all insurance providers are created equal. They come in different shapes and sizes, each with its own way of operating. Let's break down the main types of insurance providers you'll encounter in the industry.

1. Stock Insurance Companies: These are the ones you might be most familiar with. Stock insurance companies are owned by their shareholders. When you buy a policy from a stock company, you're purchasing a product from a business that aims to make a profit for its shareholders. They offer a wide range of insurance products, from auto and homeowners to life and health insurance.

2. Mutual Insurance Companies: Here's where things get a bit different. Mutual insurance companies are owned by the policyholders themselves. If you have a policy with a mutual company, you're not just a customer; you're an owner. These companies often focus on serving their policyholders' interests, and any profits are typically returned to policyholders in the form of dividends or reduced premiums.

3. Government Insurance Providers: Certain types of insurance are provided by government entities. Think of social security, Medicare, and workers' compensation in some states. These programs are designed to offer a safety net for specific risks, such as retirement income, healthcare for the elderly, and protection for workers injured on the job.

4. Reciprocal Exchanges: This type might sound a bit more complex. In a reciprocal exchange, policyholders insure each other. Each member is both an insurer and insured. They agree to share each other's losses and are managed by an attorney-in-fact. This setup can offer a more personalized insurance experience, often tailored to specific groups or industries.

5. Lloyd's Associations: Lloyd's of London is a famous example of this type. Lloyd's isn't an insurance company in the traditional sense but a marketplace where members (individuals or corporations) come together to pool and spread risk. These members, known as "syndicates," are the ones who provide the capital and underwrite the insurance.

6. Captive Insurance Companies: These are insurance companies created and owned by a parent company to insure the risks of its owners. Captives are a way for businesses to take control of their insurance, often resulting in cost savings and customized policies that are a perfect fit for their specific risks.

7. Reinsurance Companies: Think of reinsurers as the insurance companies for insurance companies. They provide a way for insurers to spread their own risks, ensuring that no single company is overexposed to potential losses. Reinsurance is a critical component of the global insurance ecosystem, providing stability and capacity.

Each type of provider has its own set of advantages, operating models, and focus areas. Understanding the differences can help you navigate the insurance landscape more effectively, whether you're choosing policies for yourself, advising clients, or exploring career opportunities in the industry. So, next time you come across an insurance policy, take a moment to consider the provider behind it. Their structure and approach can have a big impact on the services and benefits they offer.

Chapter 2: Understanding Risk and Insurability

Definition and Types of Risk

Let's talk about risk. It's a word we hear a lot, especially in the insurance world, but what does it really mean? In the simplest terms, risk is the possibility that something unexpected might happen, and this 'something' could lead to a loss. When it comes to insurance, understanding risk is key because it's all about managing those 'what ifs' in life.

Defining Risk: Risk is essentially uncertainty. It's not knowing what's around the corner and how it might affect us. In insurance, risks are those events or situations that can lead to a claim. Think about driving your car. There's always a risk of an accident, no matter how careful you are. That's where insurance steps in, offering a safety net.

Types of Risk: Risks can be categorized in several ways, but let's focus on two main types: 'pure' risk and 'speculative' risk.

1. **Pure Risk:** This type of risk involves situations where there are only two outcomes: something bad happening or nothing happening at all. There's no upside, only the potential for loss. Accidents, natural disasters, and theft are examples of pure risks. These are the

kinds of risks that insurance policies typically cover because they're measurable and definite.

2. **Speculative Risk:** Now, speculative risk is a bit different. It involves a chance of loss, but there's also a potential for gain. Think about investing in the stock market or gambling. You might make money, but there's also a risk you could lose. Generally, speculative risks are not insurable because they're not purely about protection; they're about taking a chance for potential reward.

Why Understanding Risk Matters: Grasping the types of risk is crucial because it helps us understand what can and can't be insured. It also sheds light on why we seek insurance for certain aspects of our lives and not others. Insurance is designed to provide peace of mind and financial security against the risks we can't afford to take on ourselves.

When it comes to insurability, not all risks are created equal. Insurers look at how likely something is to happen and how severe the consequences might be. This evaluation helps determine whether a risk can be insured and, if so, how much the coverage will cost.

So, as we delve deeper into the world of property and casualty insurance, keep these concepts of risk in mind. They're the foundation of every policy written and every premium calculated. Understanding risk not only helps us make informed decisions about insurance but also guides us in managing the uncertainties of everyday life.

The Concept of Insurability

Now that we've talked about what risk is, let's dive into something closely related: insurability. Essentially, insurability is all about whether a particular risk can be covered by insurance. Not every risk out there is insurable, and understanding why that is can be pretty eye-opening.

What Makes a Risk Insurable? For a risk to be insurable, it needs to meet certain criteria. These aren't just arbitrary rules but practical guidelines that help insurers provide coverage that's fair and financially viable. Let's break these down:

1. **Definite and Measurable:** An insurable risk must have a loss that is clear and quantifiable. This means being able to pinpoint when the loss occurred and how much it will cost to fix or replace what's lost. For instance, if a storm damages your roof, the cost to repair that damage can be calculated.

2. **Accidental and Unintentional:** The loss should be unexpected and not something that happens as a result of intentional actions. Insurance is there to protect against surprises, not things you can see coming from a mile away or things done on purpose.

3. **Large Pool of Similar Exposure Units:** This one might sound a bit technical, but it's all about spreading risk among many people. For a risk to be insurable, there needs to be a large enough group of similar risks to predict losses accurately. This is why you can get insurance for your car or home but not for a one-of-a-kind priceless artifact.

4. **Not Catastrophic:** For individual insurers, covering risks that could lead to catastrophic losses for a large number of policyholders at the same time (like widespread natural disasters) is challenging. While some of these risks can be insured, they often require special arrangements, like reinsurance, to be viable.

5. **Economically Feasible Premium:** The cost of insuring a risk must make sense for both the insurer and the insured. If the premium you'd have to pay is so high that it's not practical, then the risk might not be considered insurable.

Why It Matters Understanding what makes a risk insurable helps you see insurance from the insurer's perspective. It's not just about whether they want to provide coverage but whether they can do so in a way that makes sense for everyone involved. This is crucial when you're evaluating insurance policies or considering what risks you want to insure in your life or business.

Insurability is a key concept in the insurance world, and it shapes everything from the types of policies available to the premiums we pay. By grasping this concept, you're better equipped to make informed decisions about your insurance needs and understand the protections available to you.

Risk Management Strategies

So, we've talked about what risk is and what makes it insurable. Now, let's shift gears a bit and look at how we can handle these risks. This is where risk management comes into play. Think of risk management as your personal toolkit for dealing with the uncertainties that life throws your way. It's not just about avoiding risks but about knowing how to approach them smartly.

1. Risk Avoidance: The first tool in your kit is avoidance. Sometimes, the best way to deal with a risk is to steer clear of it altogether. If something poses too high a risk with no significant benefit, avoiding it might be your best bet. For instance, if you're considering an investment that's way too volatile, it might be wise to pass on it.

2. Risk Reduction: Avoiding all risks isn't always possible or practical. That's where risk reduction comes in. This strategy is all about taking steps to minimize the likelihood or impact of a risk. Regular maintenance on your vehicle to prevent breakdowns or installing a security system in your home are examples of risk reduction.

3. Risk Sharing: Sharing risk is another effective strategy. This can involve entering into agreements where the risk is distributed among several parties. In a business context, this might look like forming partnerships or alliances where risks and rewards are shared. It's all about not having all your eggs in one basket.

4. Risk Retention: Sometimes, you might choose to keep certain risks on your plate, especially if they're minor or if the cost of transferring or avoiding them is too high. This is known as risk retention. It's like deciding to bear the cost of minor car repairs yourself instead of making an insurance claim to keep your premium low.

5. Risk Transfer: Insurance falls into this category. Risk transfer is about shifting the financial burden of a risk to another party. By purchasing an insurance policy, you're transferring the financial risk of certain events (like accidents or natural disasters) to the insurance company in exchange for a premium.

Crafting Your Risk Management Plan: Effective risk management often involves a mix of these strategies. It's about assessing each risk you face and deciding which tool or combination of tools is the best fit for managing it. The goal is to protect yourself, your assets, and your financial well-being without being overly cautious or taking unnecessary risks.

Remember, risk management is a dynamic process. As your life changes, so will your risk profile and the strategies you'll need to manage them. Regularly reviewing and adjusting your approach to risk management is key to staying ahead of the game.

So, as we move forward, think of risk management as an essential skill in your personal and professional life. It's not just about dealing with the risks you currently face but also about being prepared for whatever comes your way in the future.

Chapter 3: Insurance Contracts

Elements of an Insurance Contract

Diving into the world of insurance contracts can feel a bit like learning a new language. But don't worry, it's not as daunting as it seems. At their heart, insurance contracts are about making a promise: you pay a premium, and the insurance company agrees to cover certain risks. To make this promise clear and enforceable, every insurance contract is built on a few fundamental elements. Let's break these down.

1. Offer and Acceptance: Every contract starts with an offer and acceptance. You (the policyholder) apply for insurance, which is the offer. The insurance company then reviews your application and decides whether to insure you. Their agreement to provide you insurance, often by issuing a policy, is the acceptance. This mutual agreement is what kicks off the contract.

2. Consideration: In the world of contracts, 'consideration' refers to what each party gives and gets. In an insurance contract, your consideration is the premium you pay. In return, the insurance company's consideration is the commitment to pay for certain losses covered by the policy. It's this exchange that binds the contract.

3. Competent Parties: For a contract to be valid, both parties entering into the agreement must be legally capable of doing so. This means they must be of legal age and sound mind, and they must not be under the influence of substances or coerced into the agreement. Essentially, everyone needs to be on the same page and able to make informed decisions.

4. Legal Purpose: An insurance contract must be for a legal purpose. This means it can't provide coverage for illegal activities. The purpose of the contract must be in line with the law and public policy. It's all about ensuring that the contract promotes lawful and ethical behavior.

5. Insurable Interest: This is a big one. You must have an insurable interest in whatever you're insuring. In other words, you need to suffer a financial loss if the insured event occurs. For example, you have an insurable interest in your own car because you'd be out of pocket if it were damaged. This principle prevents people from insuring things they have no financial stake in, which could lead to fraudulent claims.

Understanding These Elements: Grasping these core elements can shed a lot of light on how insurance contracts work and why they're structured the way they are. It's not just about legal formalities; it's about creating a clear, fair, and enforceable agreement that outlines the promise between you and the insurance company.

So, next time you're looking at an insurance policy, remember these key elements. They're the backbone of the contract, ensuring that the coverage you're counting on is solid and stands on firm ground.

Declarations, Insuring Agreements, Exclusions, and Conditions

When you hold an insurance policy in your hands, you're looking at more than just paper and ink. You're looking at a carefully crafted document designed to spell out the nitty-gritty of your coverage. Among its pages, you'll find sections like declarations, insuring agreements, exclusions, and conditions. Let's unpack these so you know exactly what you're dealing with.

Declarations: Think of the declarations page as the ID card of your insurance policy. It's where you'll find the who, what, when, and how much of your coverage. This includes your name and address, a description of what's being insured (like your car or home), the policy term (how long the coverage lasts), and the amount of coverage and deductibles. It's the go-to section for the specifics about your policy.

Insuring Agreements: This part is the heart of the policy. It outlines exactly what the insurance company promises to do. The insuring agreement details the covered perils (the events or situations that could lead to a claim) and the scope of coverage. It's essentially the insurance company saying, "Here's what we'll cover and under what circumstances."

Exclusions: Now, exclusions are just as crucial as the coverage itself. This section clarifies what's not covered by the policy. Understanding exclusions helps set realistic expectations about your coverage. It's the insurance company's way of saying, "We've got you covered, but here are the scenarios where your policy won't apply." Common exclusions might include intentional damage or normal wear and tear.

Conditions: Conditions are the rules of the road for your insurance policy. They outline what you and the insurer must do to keep the contract in good standing. This can include paying premiums on time, notifying the insurer about changes or losses, and cooperating in the event of a claim. Conditions are all about maintaining a transparent and fair relationship between you and the insurance company.

Why They Matter: Understanding these sections of your insurance contract is like knowing the rules of a game. It helps you play your part well and makes the whole process smoother if you ever need to make a claim. More importantly, it empowers you to make informed decisions about your insurance needs and how best to protect what matters to you.

So next time you review your policy, take a closer look at these sections. They hold the key details that define your coverage and ensure you know exactly where you stand with your insurance protection.

Endorsements and Riders

Have you ever wished you could tweak your insurance policy a bit to make it fit your needs perfectly? Well, that's where endorsements and riders come into play. These handy tools allow you to customize your insurance policy without having to rewrite the whole thing. Let's dive into what they are and how they work.

Endorsements: Think of an endorsement as a mini-update to your insurance policy. It's a document that gets attached to your policy to modify it in some way. Endorsements can add, delete, or change the coverage or terms of the policy. For example, if you've just built a fancy new deck on your house and want to make sure it's covered, you could add an endorsement to your homeowners policy specifically for that deck.

Endorsements are super flexible and can be used for all sorts of adjustments, big and small. They ensure your policy keeps up with changes in your life or property without starting from scratch.

Riders: Riders are essentially the same as endorsements but are more commonly used with certain types of insurance, like life insurance. A rider adds a specific benefit to the policy that wasn't included in the original agreement. For instance, you might add a rider to your life insurance policy to provide additional coverage in case of accidental death.

Why Use Them? Endorsements and riders give you the power to tailor your insurance coverage to your exact needs. Life changes, and your insurance should be able to change with it. Maybe you've acquired some valuable jewelry, started a home business, or upgraded your car. With endorsements and riders, you can adjust your coverage to protect these new assets or cover additional risks.

Things to Keep in Mind: While endorsements and riders are incredibly useful, there are a couple of things to remember. First, they usually mean a change in your premium, so it's essential to discuss the financial impact with your insurance provider. Second, not every situation or item can be covered with an endorsement or rider, so it's crucial to understand the limitations and exclusions.

Endorsements and riders are like the personalization features of your insurance policy. They let you tweak and adjust your coverage to make sure it's just right for you. Whether it's adding coverage for new risks or ensuring new assets are protected, these tools ensure your insurance policy remains relevant and effective, no matter what life throws your way.

II

Part II: Types of Property and Casualty Insurance Policies

Chapter 4: Homeowners Insurance

Coverage Types (HO-1 through HO-8)

When it comes to protecting your home, one size doesn't fit all. That's where different types of homeowners insurance policies come in, each with its own level of coverage. These policies are commonly referred to as HO-1 through HO-8. Let's break down what each of these coverage types offers so you can figure out which one might be the best fit for your home sweet home.

HO-1: Basic Form The HO-1 policy is the most basic type of homeowners insurance. It covers your home against a short list of specific perils, such as fire, lightning, and windstorms. Because it's so limited, many insurance companies no longer offer this type of policy. It's like the bare bones of home insurance coverage.

HO-2: Broad Form Taking it up a notch, the HO-2 policy covers everything in HO-1 plus additional perils, such as falling objects and damage from the weight of ice, snow, or sleet. It's a broader policy that provides a bit more peace of mind without going all out.

HO-3: Special Form The HO-3 policy is where things start to get more comprehensive. This is the most commonly purchased homeowners policy because it offers a solid level of coverage. It protects your home against all perils except those explicitly excluded in the policy, like floods or earthquakes. It's a good middle ground for many homeowners.

HO-4: Contents Broad Form (Renters Insurance) Though not for homeowners per se, HO-4 is essential for renters. It covers personal property against the same perils as the HO-2 policy. It also includes liability coverage, which can be crucial if someone is injured in your rented space.

HO-5: Comprehensive Form The HO-5 policy is like the HO-3 but with even more coverage. It offers broader coverage for personal property, often covering all perils unless specifically excluded. If you have high-value items or want the peace of mind of more extensive coverage, this might be the way to go.

HO-6: Unit-Owners Form (Condo Insurance) For condo owners, the HO-6 policy is tailored to fit the unique needs of condo living. It covers personal property, liability, and specific parts of the condo unit that the owner might be responsible for, under the condo association's rules.

HO-7: Mobile Home Form Mobile homes have specific needs, and the HO-7 policy is designed to meet those. It's similar to the HO-3 policy but is tailored for mobile or manufactured homes, covering them against a broad range of perils.

HO-8: Modified Coverage Form The HO-8 policy is for older homes where the cost to rebuild might be higher than the market value. It covers the same perils as HO-1 but pays out on an actual cash value basis, which means depreciation is taken into account.

Choosing the Right Coverage: Picking the right type of homeowners insurance depends on various factors, like the value of your home, your personal belongings, and your appetite for risk. It's worth having a chat with an insurance agent to discuss your specific situation and needs.

Remember, the goal is to strike a balance between being adequately covered and not overpaying for insurance you don't need.

Policy Components and Endorsements

Diving into a homeowners insurance policy can feel a bit like exploring a new city. There's a lot to see and understand, but knowing the key landmarks can make all the difference. In insurance terms, these landmarks are the core components of your policy, each playing a crucial role in providing the protection you need. And just like a city has options to enhance your experience, insurance policies have endorsements to tailor your coverage. Let's navigate through these essential elements.

Core Components of Your Policy:

1. **Dwelling Coverage:** This is like the foundation of your home insurance policy. It covers the physical structure of your home, from the walls and roof right down to the floors and built-in appliances. If a covered peril damages your home, dwelling coverage helps pay for the repairs or rebuilding.
2. **Other Structures Coverage:** Think of this as the coverage for the "extras" on your property - like a detached garage, a garden shed, or a fence. Even though they might not be attached to your main home, they're still important and need protection.
3. **Personal Property Coverage:** This part covers all the stuff you own, from your furniture and clothes to your gadgets and kitchen appliances. If your belongings are stolen or damaged by a covered peril, this coverage can help replace them.
4. **Liability Protection:** Liability coverage is your financial safeguard if someone gets hurt on your property or if you (or someone in your family) accidentally damages someone else's property. It can cover legal fees, medical bills, and more, protecting your wallet from unexpected hits.

5. **Additional Living Expenses (ALE):** If a covered peril makes your home uninhabitable, ALE coverage can be a lifesaver. It helps pay for temporary housing and living expenses, ensuring you're comfortable while your home is being repaired.

Enhancing Your Coverage with Endorsements:

Endorsements are like the customizations you make to your policy to ensure it fits your needs perfectly. Here are a few common ones:

- **Scheduled Personal Property Endorsement:** For those high-value items that exceed the typical personal property coverage limits (like fine jewelry, art, or high-end electronics), this endorsement can provide the additional coverage you need.
- **Water Backup and Sump Pump Overflow Endorsement:** Standard policies usually don't cover damage from water backup or sump pump failures. This endorsement adds that layer of protection, offering peace of mind from these specific risks.
- **Home Business Endorsement:** If you run a business from your home, this endorsement can extend your coverage to include business-related equipment and liabilities, bridging gaps that a standard policy might leave.

Understanding the core components of your homeowners insurance policy and knowing how endorsements can enhance your coverage is key to building a safety net that fully protects your home and everything in it. Think of your policy as a customizable map, with core components guiding you through the basics and endorsements allowing you to add detail and depth where you need it most.

Claims Process

Facing damage to your home or property can be stressful, but knowing how to navigate the claims process can make a world of difference. It's like having a roadmap in an unfamiliar city; it can guide you through each step, ensuring you reach your destination smoothly. Let's walk through the typical claims process for homeowners insurance, so you know exactly what to do if you ever need to file a claim.

Step 1: Assess the Situation First things first, ensure everyone's safety and take any immediate action needed to prevent further damage (if it's safe to do so). For example, if you have a leak, try to contain it to minimize water damage.

Step 2: Document the Damage Grab your camera or smartphone and start documenting. Take photos or videos of the damage from different angles. This visual evidence can be invaluable when you file your claim, providing a clear picture of the extent of the damage.

Step 3: Review Your Policy Before you pick up the phone, take a moment to review your insurance policy. Understanding your coverage, deductibles, and any specific reporting requirements can help set your expectations and prepare you for the conversation with your insurer.

Step 4: Get in Touch with Your Insurance Company Now it's time to reach out to your insurance company. Most insurers have a 24/7 claims center, so don't hesitate to call as soon as you're able. When you do, explain what happened and provide all the necessary details. They'll walk you through the next steps and what information they'll need from you.

Step 5: Fill Out Claim Forms Your insurer will likely send you some claim forms to fill out. Be as detailed and accurate as possible when describing the damage and the circumstances around the event. If you have any doubts or questions, your insurance agent can help guide you through the process.

Step 6: Prepare for the Adjuster's Visit The insurance company will send an adjuster to assess the damage in person. This is where your earlier documentation comes in handy. Show the adjuster all the damage and provide any photos, videos, or lists of damaged items you've compiled. The more information the adjuster has, the better they can evaluate your claim.

Step 7: Review the Settlement Offer Once the adjuster has reviewed the damage, the insurance company will present you with a settlement offer based on your policy coverage and the adjuster's assessment. Review this offer carefully. If it seems fair and covers the damages, you may choose to accept it. However, if you feel the offer is too low, you have the right to negotiate or dispute the amount.

Step 8: Complete Repairs and Settle the Claim After agreeing on a settlement, you can proceed with the repairs. Depending on your policy, you might get reimbursed for expenses or the insurer might pay the contractors directly. Once the repairs are completed to your satisfaction, the claim is settled.

Remember, the claims process is designed to help you restore your home and property after a loss. Knowing what steps to take and what to expect can make the experience as smooth as possible, helping you get back on your feet faster.

Chapter 5: Auto Insurance

Liability Coverage

When it comes to auto insurance, liability coverage is the cornerstone. It's the part of your policy that kicks in when you're responsible for an accident, covering the costs associated with the damage and injuries you may have caused to others. Think of it as your financial safety net, ensuring that a momentary mistake behind the wheel doesn't lead to a significant financial burden.

Understanding Liability Coverage:
Liability coverage is typically split into two main components: bodily injury liability and property damage liability. Let's break these down:

1. **Bodily Injury Liability:** This part of your coverage is there to cover the costs if someone is injured in an accident where you're at fault. It can help pay for medical expenses, lost wages, and even legal fees if you're sued. It's not just about covering the driver; it can also extend to passengers, pedestrians, or cyclists involved in the accident.

2. **Property Damage Liability:** Accidents often result in more than just physical injuries; there's usually some property damage involved, whether it's to another vehicle, a fence, or a streetlight. Property damage liability helps cover the repair or replacement costs of anything you damage in an at-fault accident, excluding your own vehicle.

Why It's Essential:

In most places, carrying liability coverage is not just a good idea; it's the law. The minimum required limits can vary from one location to another, but it's often recommended to consider limits beyond the legal minimum. Why? Because accidents can be expensive, and if the damages exceed your coverage limits, you could be on the hook for the difference.

Choosing Your Coverage Limits:

When selecting your liability coverage limits, you'll typically see them represented by three numbers, for example, 100/300/50. Here's what those numbers mean:

- The first number (100) represents the maximum amount (in thousands) your insurer will pay for bodily injury per person in an accident you cause.
- The second number (300) is the maximum amount your insurer will pay for all bodily injuries per accident.
- The third number (50) indicates the maximum amount your insurer will pay for property damage per accident.

A Word of Caution:

While it might be tempting to go for the minimum coverage to save on premiums, consider the potential long-term costs. If you're involved in a serious accident, the actual costs could quickly surpass your coverage limits, leaving you to cover the remainder. It's a balancing act between protecting your financial well-being and managing your insurance costs.

Liability coverage is a critical part of your auto insurance policy, providing essential protection if you're at fault in an accident. It's not just about complying with the law; it's about ensuring that an unexpected incident doesn't derail your financial security. So, when reviewing your auto insurance options, give liability coverage the attention it deserves, ensuring it aligns with your needs and risks.

Physical Damage Coverage

When it comes to protecting your vehicle itself, physical damage coverage is where it's at. This part of your auto insurance policy is all about covering damages to your car, whether from a collision with another vehicle or other mishaps like hitting a tree or having a run-in with a deer. It's divided into two main types: collision coverage and comprehensive coverage. Let's dive into what each of these covers and why they're crucial for your peace of mind on the road.

Collision Coverage: As the name suggests, collision coverage is focused on damages to your car resulting from a collision, whether it's with another vehicle, a lamppost, or a fence. It doesn't matter who's at fault; if your car takes a hit, collision coverage steps in to help cover the repair costs. It's like having a safety net that ensures your car can bounce back from bumps and bruises it might encounter on the road.

Comprehensive Coverage: Now, comprehensive coverage is the broader protector of the two. It covers almost everything else that could happen to your car outside of a collision. We're talking about events like theft, vandalism, fire, natural disasters (think hail storms or floods), and yes, even if an animal decides to make a dent in your car. It's your car's shield against the unexpected, the things you just can't predict.

Why Physical Damage Coverage Matters: Investing in a car is a big deal, and for many, it's essential for daily life, getting you from point A to point B. Physical damage coverage helps protect that investment. It ensures that if something happens to your car, you're not left footing the entire bill for repairs or replacement, which can be a significant relief, especially if your vehicle is newer or has a high value.

Choosing Your Deductibles: Both collision and comprehensive coverage typically come with deductibles, which is the amount you agree to pay out of pocket before your insurance kicks in. Choosing the right deductible is a bit of a balancing act. A higher deductible can lower your insurance premiums, but it means you'll pay more upfront if you file a claim. On the other hand, a lower deductible reduces what you'll pay for a claim but might increase your monthly premiums. It's all about finding what works best for your budget and peace of mind.

Physical damage coverage is your car's best friend, offering a layer of protection against the many mishaps it could face on and off the road. Whether you're dealing with the aftermath of a fender bender or the surprise of a fallen tree branch, this coverage helps ensure that your vehicle can be repaired or replaced, keeping your daily life on track. So, when reviewing your auto insurance options, consider how collision and comprehensive coverage can contribute to your overall financial protection plan.

Uninsured and Underinsured Motorist Coverage

Imagine you're driving home, minding your own business, when suddenly another car collides with yours. It's not your fault, but to your dismay, you find out the other driver either doesn't have insurance (uninsured) or doesn't have enough insurance to cover the damages (underinsured). That's where uninsured and underinsured motorist coverage comes into the picture, providing you with peace of mind in these frustrating scenarios.

Uninsured Motorist Coverage (UM): This part of your auto insurance policy steps in when you're involved in an accident where the other party is at fault and doesn't have any liability insurance. It can help cover your medical bills, lost wages, and even pain and suffering. Some policies also cover damage to your vehicle, depending on the state and the specific policy details.

Underinsured Motorist Coverage (UIM): Underinsured motorist coverage kicks in under similar circumstances as UM coverage, but in this case, the at-fault driver has insurance, just not enough to cover all your costs. UIM coverage can make up the difference, ensuring you're not left out of pocket for someone else's mistake.

Why They Matter: You might wonder why you need UM and UIM coverage if you already have health insurance or collision coverage. The truth is, while those policies can cover some of your expenses, they might not cover everything, like lost wages or pain and suffering. Plus, relying solely on collision coverage to repair your vehicle could mean paying a deductible, which UM or UIM coverage might help avoid.

State Requirements and Recommendations: It's worth noting that requirements for UM and UIM coverage vary by state. Some states require all drivers to carry it, while in others, it's optional. Even if it's not required in your state, it's a coverage worth considering to protect yourself against the unpredictable.

Choosing Your Coverage Limits: Like other parts of your auto insurance policy, you'll choose limits for your UM and UIM coverage. These limits are the maximum amounts your insurer will pay for a covered claim. It's generally recommended to match these limits to your liability coverage limits, providing a balanced level of protection.

Uninsured and underinsured motorist coverage provides an essential safety net, ensuring that an accident with an uninsured or underinsured driver doesn't lead to significant financial hardship for you. As you prepare for the Property and Casualty Insurance License Exam, understanding the nuances of UM and UIM coverage will not only help you pass the test but also equip you to better serve your future clients, guiding them through the complexities of auto insurance with confidence and clarity.

Chapter 6: Commercial Insurance

Commercial Property Insurance

For any business, large or small, the physical assets are the backbone that supports operations day in and day out. From the building that houses your business to the equipment and inventory inside, these assets are crucial for your success. That's where commercial property insurance comes into play, offering a safety net to protect these assets from a variety of risks. Understanding this coverage is key for anyone preparing for the Property and Casualty Insurance License Exam, as it's a fundamental component of commercial insurance.

What It Covers: Commercial property insurance is designed to protect the physical assets of a business from losses due to a wide range of perils, including fires, storms, theft, and vandalism. It's not just about the structure itself but extends to the contents, such as office furniture, computers, machinery, and even important documents. Some policies may also cover loss of income or increase in expenses that result from property damage, helping a business recover more smoothly after a setback.

Key Features to Understand:

1. **Named Perils vs. All-Risk Policies:** Commercial property policies can be structured in two main ways: named perils, which only cover the risks specifically listed in the policy, and all-risk (or open

perils) policies, which cover all risks except those explicitly excluded. Understanding the distinction is crucial, as it determines the breadth of protection a policy offers.

2. **Replacement Cost vs. Actual Cash Value:** When it comes to settling a claim, policies can offer compensation based on replacement cost (the cost to replace or repair the damaged property with new materials) or actual cash value (replacement cost minus depreciation). The choice between these two can significantly impact the amount a business recovers after a loss.

3. **Business Interruption Coverage:** An important aspect to consider is business interruption coverage, which can be included in or added to a commercial property policy. This coverage helps a business cover lost income and ongoing expenses when operations are halted due to covered property damage, ensuring the business's financial stability during recovery.

Customizing Coverage: Every business is unique, and so are its insurance needs. Commercial property insurance can be customized with various endorsements to address specific risks unique to a business's operations or industry. For example, a restaurant might need spoilage coverage for perishable goods, while a manufacturer might require equipment breakdown coverage.

For Exam Preparation:

When preparing for the exam, focus on understanding the types of risks commercial property insurance covers, the key features and options within these policies, and how they can be tailored to meet the specific needs of different businesses. Real-world scenarios or case studies can be particularly helpful in grasping how this coverage applies in practical business settings.

Commercial property insurance is a cornerstone of business protection, safeguarding the physical and financial assets against a wide array of risks.

A thorough understanding of this coverage is not only vital for passing the Property and Casualty Insurance License Exam but also for providing valuable advice and solutions to business clients in your future career in insurance.

Commercial Liability Insurance

In the bustling world of business, commercial liability insurance stands as a guardian, shielding businesses from the financial fallout of claims related to bodily injury, property damage, and more, that can occur during business operations. It's a critical component of a business's insurance portfolio, ensuring that a moment's mishap doesn't lead to a mountain of debt.

Understanding the Coverage:

Commercial liability insurance is designed to protect businesses from the risks of liabilities imposed by lawsuits and similar claims. It covers legal costs and payouts that the insured would be found liable for, within the policy limits. Here are the key areas it typically covers:

1. **Bodily Injury:** If a customer slips and falls in your store or an employee accidentally injures a client during a service, commercial liability insurance can cover the medical expenses and legal fees if your business is found liable.
2. **Property Damage:** If your business activities cause damage to someone else's property, this insurance can help cover the repair or replacement costs. For example, if a contractor accidentally damages a client's home, this coverage can help make things right.
3. **Personal and Advertising Injury:** Beyond physical harm, businesses can face liabilities related to defamation, slander, copyright infringement, and more from their advertising. This coverage helps protect against these types of claims.

Why It's Essential:

In today's litigious society, any business can find itself on the wrong end of a lawsuit, regardless of its size or industry. Legal defense and settlement costs can quickly escalate, potentially crippling a business financially. Commercial liability insurance provides a safety net, ensuring that these unforeseen expenses don't derail your business operations.

Choosing the Right Coverage:

Selecting the appropriate level of coverage is pivotal. It involves assessing your business's specific risks based on its operations, industry, and the legal environment in which it operates. A local bakery will have different liability risks compared to a construction company, necessitating tailored coverage for each.

For Exam Preparation:

When studying for the Property and Casualty Insurance License Exam, focus on understanding the breadth of commercial liability insurance, including the types of risks it covers and the factors influencing coverage needs. Familiarize yourself with policy structures, common exclusions, and how coverage limits are determined. Real-life examples can be particularly helpful in illustrating how this insurance applies in various business scenarios.

Commercial liability insurance is a cornerstone of risk management for businesses, providing critical protection against a wide range of liability risks. A deep understanding of this coverage is essential not only for passing the licensing exam but also for advising business clients effectively in your future role as an insurance professional.

Business Owners Policy (BOP)

When it comes to safeguarding small to medium-sized businesses, a Business Owners Policy (BOP) is like a Swiss Army knife, combining several essential coverages into one convenient package. This bundled approach not only simplifies the insurance landscape for business owners but often provides a cost-effective solution for their core coverage needs.

What's in a BOP?

A typical BOP weaves together three main strands of protection:

1. **Commercial Property Insurance:** This is the shield for your physical assets, covering your business premises, equipment, inventory, and sometimes even the loss of income due to business interruption. Whether it's a fire, theft, or other covered disasters, this component ensures your business can recover and rebuild.

2. **General Liability Insurance:** This aspect provides defense against the slings and arrows that businesses might face, such as claims of bodily injury, property damage, or personal and advertising injury that occur on your premises or as a result of your operations. It's your safeguard against the legal vulnerabilities that come with running a business.

3. **Business Interruption Insurance:** Often integrated with the property insurance component, this coverage helps keep the financial wheels of your business turning if you're forced to close temporarily due to a covered event. It can cover lost income and ongoing expenses, helping your business weather the storm and bounce back.

Who Benefits from a BOP?

BOPs are tailor-made for small to medium-sized businesses that face common risks and have physical assets to protect. They're particularly popular among retail stores, small restaurants, and service-based businesses. However, they might not be the right fit for larger businesses or those in specialized industries with unique risks that require more customized insurance solutions.

Customizing Your BOP:

While BOPs offer a solid foundation of coverage, they're also flexible. You can often add endorsements or riders to address specific risks unique to your business or industry. For example, a restaurant might add spoilage coverage, while a retail store might include coverage for outdoor signs.

For Exam Preparation:

As you gear up for the Property and Casualty Insurance License Exam, understanding the structure, common components, and applicability of BOPs is crucial. Focus on the synergies created by bundling these coverages and how they can offer a comprehensive risk management solution for small to medium-sized businesses. Be prepared to explain how a BOP can be customized with additional endorsements to meet a business's unique needs.

A Business Owners Policy (BOP) provides a streamlined, cost-effective way for small to medium-sized businesses to secure the essential insurance coverages they need. Grasping the nuances of BOPs is not only vital for passing your licensing exam but will also be invaluable in advising small business clients in your future insurance career.

Chapter 7: Workers' Compensation and Employers Liability

Workers' Compensation Basics

Navigating the waters of Workers' Compensation can seem daunting at first glance, but it's a pivotal aspect of both employee welfare and business operations. At its core, Workers' Compensation is a form of insurance providing wage replacement and medical benefits to employees injured in the course of employment. Let's unpack the essentials of this system to understand its impact and importance.

The Foundation of Workers' Compensation:
   Workers' Compensation operates under a no-fault principle, meaning employees can receive benefits regardless of who was at fault for their injury. This system creates a safety net for employees while also protecting employers from potential lawsuits. It's a balance designed to benefit both parties in the event of workplace injuries.

Coverage Scope:
   Workers' Compensation covers a range of assistance for injured employees, including:

- Medical care for the injury or illness.

- Replacement income for lost wages.
- Costs for retraining or rehabilitation.
- Compensation for any permanent injuries.
- Benefits to survivors if the employee is killed on the job.

Employer Responsibilities:

For employers, carrying Workers' Compensation insurance is not just a good practice; it's a legal requirement in most jurisdictions. This insurance helps ensure that employees receive the support they need if they're injured on the job, while also safeguarding the business against the financial burden of these incidents.

Employee Eligibility:

To be eligible for benefits, the injury or illness must be related to the employee's job duties. Whether it's a sudden accident or a condition developed over time due to work-related activities, Workers' Compensation is designed to address the health and financial implications for the employee.

The Claims Process:

When an injury occurs, prompt reporting is crucial. Employees should inform their employer about the injury as soon as possible, and employers must then file a claim with their Workers' Compensation insurance carrier. The insurer will assess the claim to determine eligibility and the extent of benefits to be provided.

For Exam Preparation:

As you prepare for the Property and Casualty Insurance License Exam, focus on understanding the principles of Workers' Compensation, the types of injuries and illnesses it covers, and the process for filing and approving claims. Be aware of the variations in laws and requirements from state to state, as Workers' Compensation is governed at the state level, leading to differences in coverage and procedures across jurisdictions.

Workers' Compensation plays a crucial role in the workplace, providing essential protections for employees while offering employers a structured system to manage the risks associated with workplace injuries. A thorough understanding of Workers' Compensation is not only key to passing your licensing exam but also to providing valuable guidance and support to businesses in your future career in insurance.

Employers Liability Insurance

While Workers' Compensation is a critical safety net for employees, Employers Liability Insurance serves as a vital layer of protection for businesses. It's a part of the Workers' Compensation policy but addresses a different set of risks, focusing on the employer's legal liability beyond the scope of Workers' Compensation benefits. Understanding this coverage is essential for a well-rounded approach to workplace safety and risk management.

The Role of Employers Liability Insurance:

Workers' Compensation typically covers employee injuries without regard to fault, providing benefits like medical expenses and lost wages. However, there are instances where an employee might claim that employer negligence contributed to their injury. This is where Employers Liability Insurance comes into play, covering legal fees, court costs, and settlements for such claims.

What It Covers:

Employers Liability Insurance kicks in for various situations not covered by Workers' Compensation, including:

- Third-party over actions: If an employee is injured due to equipment provided by a third party, and they sue the third party, that third party might then sue the employer.
- Loss of consortium: Family members of the injured employee might claim loss of companionship and sue the employer.

- Dual-capacity suits: If an employee is injured by a product the employer manufactures, and they sue the employer in their capacity as a manufacturer.

Why It's Important:

This insurance is a crucial component for businesses because it helps protect against potentially significant financial losses from lawsuits not covered by Workers' Compensation. It ensures that a business can defend itself while maintaining financial stability.

Tailoring Coverage to Your Business:

Just like any other insurance policy, Employers Liability Insurance can be customized to fit the unique needs of your business. The limits of coverage, exclusions, and endorsements should be carefully selected to ensure they align with your risk profile and business operations.

For Exam Preparation:

When preparing for the Property and Casualty Insurance License Exam, pay close attention to the distinctions between Workers' Compensation and Employers Liability Insurance. Understand the types of incidents each covers, the protection they offer to businesses, and the typical exclusions and limitations of Employers Liability Insurance. Real-life scenarios can help illustrate these points and deepen your understanding.

Employers Liability Insurance is an essential counterpart to Workers' Compensation, providing businesses with a crucial shield against legal liabilities that arise from workplace injuries. A deep understanding of this coverage will not only help you succeed in your licensing exam but also equip you to advise businesses on protecting their operations and their employees effectively.

State-Specific Regulations

When diving into the world of Workers' Compensation and Employers Liability, it's crucial to recognize that the rules of the game can vary significantly from state to state. Just like each state has its own flavor and character, they also have distinct regulations governing Workers' Compensation. Understanding these nuances is key, not only for passing the Property and Casualty Insurance License Exam but also for effectively guiding businesses in managing their workforce risks.

Why State Regulations Matter:

Workers' Compensation is largely regulated at the state level, meaning each state can set its own rules regarding coverage requirements, benefits, and procedures. This state-specific approach ensures that the system aligns with local labor markets and legal environments.

Common Variations Across States:

1. **Coverage Requirements:** One of the most significant differences lies in who must carry Workers' Compensation insurance. While most states mandate coverage for almost all businesses, some have exceptions based on the number of employees, type of business, or employment status (like independent contractors).
2. **Benefits Provided:** The scope and duration of benefits can vary. For instance, some states might have higher wage replacement rates or longer durations for certain benefits. The process for calculating these benefits can also differ.
3. **Choice of Provider:** Some states allow employees to choose their healthcare provider for work-related injuries, while others require them to use a provider selected by the employer or the insurance carrier.
4. **Exemptions and Inclusions:** Certain types of workers (like agricultural or domestic workers) may be excluded from mandatory coverage in some states but included in others. Similarly, the treatment of

42

independent contractors can vary.

5. **Experience Rating System:** States might use different methods for calculating premiums based on a business's claim history. Understanding how these experience ratings work can be crucial for advising businesses on managing their Workers' Compensation costs.

Navigating State Regulations:

For anyone preparing for the Property and Casualty Insurance License Exam, it's important to familiarize yourself with the general principles of Workers' Compensation and Employers Liability, as well as the specifics of the state where you'll be practicing. This might involve studying:

· The particular nuances of your state's Workers' Compensation laws.
· The procedural aspects of filing claims and appealing decisions in your state.
· State-specific requirements for employers, like posting notices and keeping records.

State-specific regulations in Workers' Compensation and Employers Liability are a critical piece of the puzzle. As you prepare for your exam, focus on understanding both the broad principles that apply across the board and the unique rules that apply in your state. This dual understanding will be invaluable in your future role, enabling you to provide accurate, relevant advice to businesses navigating the complexities of Workers' Compensation in their specific locale.

Chapter 8: Miscellaneous Policies

Umbrella and Excess Liability Policies

In a world where lawsuits can skyrocket and claims can exceed basic policy limits, umbrella and excess liability policies act as a financial safety net, providing an additional layer of protection. These policies are the reinforcements that step in when your standard insurance policies have reached their limits, ensuring that one massive claim doesn't spell disaster for your financial stability.

Umbrella Liability Policies:
Think of an umbrella policy as an overarching layer of security that provides extra coverage beyond the limits of your underlying policies, like homeowners, auto, or watercraft insurance. But it doesn't just add more coverage to existing limits; it can also broaden the scope of what's covered, filling in some of the gaps that might exist in your primary policies. Key points about umbrella policies include:

- **Additional Coverage:** They kick in when the liability limits of your other policies have been reached, offering an extra cushion of protection.
- **Wider Protection:** Umbrella policies can cover a broader range of scenarios, potentially including claims like libel, slander, and false arrest.
- **Peace of Mind:** They provide significant coverage amounts, often

starting at $1 million, offering substantial protection against large claims.

Excess Liability Policies:

Excess liability policies are similar to umbrella policies in that they provide additional coverage beyond your primary policy limits. However, they're more like a direct extension of your existing policy, increasing the coverage limit without expanding the coverage scope. Key aspects of excess liability policies include:

- **Extended Limits:** They add on to the limits of an existing policy, such as a commercial liability policy, without altering the terms or coverage types.
- **Specific to One Policy:** Excess liability is usually tied to a single underlying policy and follows its coverage terms closely.
- **Situational Use:** These policies are often used in business contexts where higher coverage limits are needed for specific risks.

Why They Matter:

In an era where litigation is common and settlements can be substantial, having an umbrella or excess liability policy can mean the difference between a manageable situation and a financial crisis. For individuals and businesses alike, these policies offer an extra layer of security, safeguarding assets against unforeseen claims that exceed primary policy limits.

For Exam Preparation:

When studying for the Property and Casualty Insurance License Exam, focus on understanding the distinctions between umbrella and excess liability policies, their roles in risk management, and how they complement primary insurance policies. Be prepared to discuss scenarios where these policies could be beneficial and how they contribute to a comprehensive risk management strategy.

Umbrella and excess liability policies are crucial tools in the risk management arsenal, providing additional coverage that can protect against potentially ruinous financial losses. Understanding these policies is not only key to passing your licensing exam but also essential for advising clients on creating a robust insurance protection plan.

Professional Liability Insurance

In the intricate tapestry of the insurance world, Professional Liability Insurance stands out as a critical safeguard for individuals and businesses that offer professional services. This type of insurance, often known as Errors and Omissions (E&O) Insurance, is designed to protect professionals against claims arising from errors, omissions, or negligence in the provision of their services. Let's delve into the essentials of Professional Liability Insurance and its significance.

The Essence of Professional Liability Insurance:
Professional Liability Insurance addresses a niche yet vital area of risk. It's about covering the financial fallout when professional advice or services don't go as planned, leading to a financial loss for a client. This could be an architect whose design error causes a construction flaw or an accountant who makes a significant mistake on a tax return.

Key Features to Understand:

- **Claims-Made Coverage:** Unlike some other types of insurance, Professional Liability policies typically operate on a claims-made basis. This means coverage is only effective if the policy is active both when the alleged incident occurred and when the claim is filed, highlighting the importance of continuous coverage.
- **Defense Costs:** These policies usually cover legal defense costs, which can be substantial even if the allegations are unfounded. It's a layer of financial defense that ensures professionals can protect their reputation and continue their practice without the crippling costs of legal

battles.

· **Settlements and Judgments:** Should a claim against a professional be successful, Professional Liability Insurance helps cover the settlement or judgment amount, up to the policy limits, ensuring that a single mistake doesn't lead to financial ruin.

Tailoring Coverage:

Given the diverse nature of professional services, from legal and medical to tech and creative fields, Professional Liability Insurance can and should be tailored to fit the specific risks and needs of the profession in question. It's not a one-size-fits-all solution but rather a customizable shield against the unique vulnerabilities professionals face.

For Exam Preparation:

When gearing up for the Property and Casualty Insurance License Exam, it's crucial to grasp the nuances of Professional Liability Insurance. Understand its role in risk management for professionals, the intricacies of claims-made coverage, and the types of claims typically covered. Real-world examples can provide clarity on how this insurance works in practice and the impact it can have in protecting professionals against the financial consequences of errors or omissions in their work.

Professional Liability Insurance is an indispensable part of the risk management strategy for anyone providing professional services. It not only protects professionals from the financial implications of claims related to their work but also safeguards the trust and confidence that are the foundation of professional relationships. A thorough understanding of this coverage is essential, not just for passing your licensing exam, but for advising professional clients on how to protect their careers and livelihoods effectively.

Specialized Policies (Flood, Earthquake, etc.)

In the world of insurance, while standard policies cover a broad range of risks, there are certain events that require specialized coverage due to their unique nature. Among these, flood and earthquake insurance stand out as essential protections for individuals and businesses in susceptible areas. Let's delve into these specialized policies and their significance.

Flood Insurance:

Despite the common misconception, standard homeowners and commercial property policies typically do not cover flood damage. Flood insurance is a specialized policy that fills this gap, providing protection against loss due to flooding. Here's what you need to know:

- **Availability:** Flood insurance is often provided through government programs, such as the National Flood Insurance Program (NFIP) in the United States, as well as through some private insurers.
- **Coverage:** These policies typically cover the structure of the building and its contents from water damage due to flooding, but there are often specific definitions and exclusions that apply.
- **Importance:** For those in flood-prone areas, this insurance is not just a safety measure but a crucial financial safeguard, given the potentially devastating cost of flood damage.

Earthquake Insurance:

Like flood insurance, standard policies usually exclude earthquake damage, making earthquake insurance a vital consideration for those in seismically active regions.

- **Coverage:** Earthquake policies can cover damage to the building, personal property, and may also include additional living expenses if the home is uninhabitable after an earthquake.
- **Deductibles:** These policies often come with high deductibles, calcu-

lated as a percentage of the home's replacement value, which is an important factor to consider when purchasing coverage.

- **Considerations:** The cost and necessity of earthquake insurance can vary significantly based on geographic location and the construction standards of the building in question.

For Exam Preparation:

As you prepare for the Property and Casualty Insurance License Exam, it's important to understand the role of specialized policies like flood and earthquake insurance. Focus on the types of risks they cover, how they differ from standard policies, and the mechanisms through which they are provided, such as government programs or private insurers. Being able to distinguish these policies and their applications is crucial for advising clients accurately and effectively.

Specialized policies such as flood and earthquake insurance play a critical role in risk management, particularly for those in high-risk areas. These policies provide targeted protection against specific, potentially catastrophic events that are not covered under standard insurance policies. Understanding these specialized coverages is essential for anyone entering the field of property and casualty insurance, ensuring you can offer comprehensive guidance to those who rely on your expertise.

III

Part III: Policy Provisions, Underwriting, and Rating

Chapter 9: Policy Provisions and Options

Standard Policy Provisions and Their Implications

Diving into the world of insurance policies can sometimes feel like navigating a maze with its myriad of terms and conditions. Standard policy provisions, however, are the signposts that guide you through, providing a framework for the coverage, rights, and responsibilities within an insurance contract. Let's unravel these standard provisions and understand the implications they have for policyholders and insurers alike.

The Building Blocks of an Insurance Policy:

Standard policy provisions lay the groundwork for how an insurance policy operates. While specific terms can vary across different types of insurance and between insurers, certain foundational provisions are commonly found in many policies.

1. **Deductibles:** This is the amount the policyholder agrees to pay out of pocket before the insurance coverage kicks in. Deductibles can significantly impact the overall cost of a claim and the premium of the policy. Higher deductibles typically lead to lower premiums, as the policyholder assumes more financial responsibility.
2. **Policy Limits:** These define the maximum amount an insurer will pay for a covered loss. Understanding policy limits is crucial, as it determines the extent of protection provided and the potential out-

of-pocket expenses in the event of a claim.

3. **Premiums:** The premium is the price you pay for your insurance coverage, determined by various factors including risk levels, coverage amounts, and policy terms. It's the financial commitment made by the policyholder to keep the insurance active.

4. **Exclusions:** These are specific conditions or circumstances that are not covered by the policy. Exclusions are critical to understand because they delineate the boundaries of the policy's protection, highlighting scenarios where the policyholder won't receive benefits.

5. **Grace Period:** Most policies include a grace period, allowing policyholders a certain timeframe to pay their premium after the due date without losing coverage. This provision offers a safety net, ensuring temporary financial hiccups don't result in immediate loss of protection.

6. **Cancellation and Renewal:** These provisions outline the conditions under which a policy can be canceled or renewed, either by the policyholder or the insurer. Understanding these terms is vital for maintaining continuous coverage and managing insurance needs effectively.

Implications for Policyholders and Insurers:

Standard policy provisions create a clear, mutual understanding between the insurer and the policyholder. For policyholders, they highlight the scope of protection, financial obligations, and the process for filing claims. For insurers, these provisions help manage risk, ensure financial stability, and set clear guidelines for policy administration.

For Exam Preparation:

When studying for the Property and Casualty Insurance License Exam, focus on grasping the standard provisions commonly found in insurance policies, their functions, and their implications for both policyholders and insurers. Be prepared to discuss how these provisions affect the underwriting process, premium calculation, and claims handling.

Standard policy provisions form the backbone of insurance contracts, defining the coverage landscape and establishing the rules of engagement between insurers and policyholders. A thorough understanding of these provisions is essential for anyone entering the field of insurance, ensuring you can navigate policy details effectively and provide accurate advice to clients.

Policy Options and Customization

Just as every individual is unique, with specific needs and preferences, insurance policies too can be tailored to fit the unique requirements of each policyholder. This customization is achieved through a variety of policy options and endorsements, allowing for a personalized insurance experience. Let's explore how these options work and their importance in crafting a policy that aligns perfectly with the policyholder's needs.

Tailoring Your Coverage:

1. **Endorsements:** Endorsements, also known as riders, are amendments to the standard insurance policy that can add, remove, or alter coverage. They are the primary tools for customization, enabling policyholders to adjust their coverage to match their specific risk exposure. For example, a homeowner in an area prone to earthquakes might add an earthquake endorsement to their standard homeowners policy.
2. **Flexible Deductibles:** Choosing the right deductible is a balancing act between manageable premium costs and acceptable out-of-pocket expenses in the event of a claim. Higher deductibles typically lead to lower premiums, but it's important to ensure the deductible is not so high that it becomes a financial burden in itself.
3. **Coverage Limits:** Policyholders can often choose the limits of their coverage, which is the maximum amount an insurer will pay for a covered loss. Adjusting these limits provides flexibility in managing

protection levels and can influence premium costs.

4. **Policy Exclusions:** While standard policies come with certain exclusions, policyholders may have the option to add coverage for typically excluded risks through endorsements, or conversely, to accept additional exclusions in exchange for lower premiums.

The Importance of Customization:

Customizing an insurance policy ensures that the coverage closely matches the policyholder's lifestyle, assets, and risk profile. This tailored approach helps avoid over-insurance, where premiums are unnecessarily high for coverage that exceeds the policyholder's needs, and under-insurance, where the coverage is insufficient to protect against potential losses.

Navigating Policy Options:

Understanding the available policy options and how they impact coverage and cost is crucial. Policyholders should consider:

- The specific risks they face, based on their location, lifestyle, and the assets being insured.
- The financial impact of various deductibles and coverage limits.
- The cost-benefit analysis of adding endorsements for additional protection.

For Exam Preparation:

When preparing for the Property and Casualty Insurance License Exam, focus on understanding the different types of policy options, endorsements, and customization strategies available. Be prepared to discuss how these options can be used to tailor a policy to a policyholder's specific needs and the implications of these choices on coverage and premiums.

Policy options and customization play a vital role in the insurance process, allowing policyholders to fine-tune their coverage to fit their unique needs.

A deep understanding of these options is essential for anyone entering the insurance field, enabling them to provide valuable advice and solutions to clients seeking the right balance of protection and affordability.

Chapter 10: Underwriting Principles

The Underwriting Process

At the heart of the insurance industry lies the underwriting process, a critical step where the magic of assessing risk and determining insurability happens. It's like the backstage of a theater, where all the essential work is done to ensure the show goes smoothly. Understanding this process is key for anyone stepping into the world of insurance, especially when preparing for the Property and Casualty Insurance License Exam.

Step-by-Step Through the Underwriting Process:

1. **Application Review:** The process kicks off when an application for insurance is submitted. This is the underwriter's first glimpse into who the applicant is and what risks might be involved. The application contains vital information, including personal details, the type of coverage sought, and any specific risks that need to be evaluated.
2. **Risk Assessment:** This is where underwriters really put on their detective hats. They assess the level of risk associated with insuring the applicant, looking at factors such as the likelihood of a claim being made and what that claim might cost. This step might involve reviewing past claims, financial records, or conducting inspections.
3. **Information Verification:** Accuracy is key in underwriting. Under-writers may verify the information provided in the application through

various means, such as credit checks, background checks, or previous insurance records. This helps ensure they have a clear and accurate picture of the risk involved.

4. **Rating and Pricing:** Based on the risk assessment, underwriters then determine the premium, or the cost of the insurance. This involves using actuarial data and risk models to price the policy in a way that covers potential claims but is also competitive and fair to the applicant.

5. **Policy Issuance:** Once the underwriting process is complete and the premium is set, the policy can be issued. This final step solidifies the contract between the insurer and the insured, outlining the terms, coverage, and premiums.

Why the Underwriting Process Matters:

The underwriting process is crucial for several reasons. It ensures that risks are thoroughly evaluated and priced appropriately, maintaining the insurer's financial stability. It also helps in the fair treatment of applicants, ensuring that premiums reflect their individual risk profiles.

For Exam Preparation:

When studying for your exam, focus on understanding each step of the underwriting process, the factors considered in risk assessment, and the methods used to verify information and determine premiums. Be prepared to discuss how underwriting principles apply to different types of insurance policies and the role of technology in modern underwriting practices.

The underwriting process is the backbone of insurance operations, ensuring that policies are issued on a sound financial basis and that risks are adequately assessed and managed. A thorough understanding of this process is essential for anyone entering the field of insurance, providing the foundation needed to navigate the complexities of risk and coverage.

Factors Affecting Insurability and Premiums

When it comes to insurance, not all risks are created equal. The insurability of an individual or a business and the premiums they pay are influenced by a myriad of factors, each telling a part of their risk story. Understanding these factors is like piecing together a puzzle, providing a clear picture of the risk involved. Let's explore the key elements that underwriters consider when assessing insurability and determining premiums.

1. Risk Type: At the core, insurance is about managing risk, and the type of risk plays a pivotal role in the underwriting process. Whether it's the risk of a car accident, a house fire, or a professional liability claim, each type of risk has its own characteristics and likelihood of occurrence, which are crucial in assessing insurability and setting premiums.

2. Loss History: Past behavior can often predict future outcomes, at least in the world of insurance. An individual's or business's history of claims provides valuable insights into their risk level. Frequent claims can indicate higher risk, leading to higher premiums, while a clean history can be advantageous for insurability and cost.

3. Location: Location can significantly impact risk exposure. For example, properties located in flood-prone areas or regions susceptible to natural disasters may face higher premiums due to the increased risk of damage. Similarly, auto insurance premiums can vary depending on local traffic conditions and accident rates.

4. Age and Condition: In the case of property and auto insurance, the age and condition of the insured item play a crucial role. Newer, well-maintained properties and vehicles are generally considered lower risk, while older, poorly maintained ones may attract higher premiums due to the increased likelihood of claims.

5. Occupation and Activities: For personal and professional liability insurance, the insured's occupation and activities can influence risk assessment. High-risk professions or hobbies that increase the likelihood of injury or liability claims can result in higher premiums.

6. Credit History: Many insurers use credit history as an indicator of risk, based on statistical correlations between credit behavior and the likelihood of filing insurance claims. A strong credit history can lead to more favorable premium rates, while poor credit can increase costs.

7. Policy Options and Deductibles: The choices policyholders make about their coverage, including the limits and deductibles, also affect premiums. Higher coverage limits and lower deductibles offer more protection but come at a higher cost, whereas accepting a higher deductible can reduce premium expenses.

For Exam Preparation:

When preparing for the Property and Casualty Insurance License Exam, focus on understanding how these factors contribute to the assessment of risk and the determination of premiums. Be able to discuss how underwriters weigh these elements during the underwriting process and the impact of policyholder choices on insurability and insurance costs.

A wide range of factors influences insurability and premiums, reflecting the complex nature of risk in the insurance landscape. A deep understanding of these factors is crucial for effectively navigating the underwriting process and for providing informed advice to clients seeking insurance coverage.

Underwriting Tools and Technologies

In the dynamic world of insurance, underwriting tools and technologies play a pivotal role in streamlining the process, enhancing accuracy, and ultimately shaping the decisions that underwriters make. As we delve into this high-tech toolbox, it becomes clear how these innovations are transforming the landscape of risk assessment and policy issuance.

Advanced Data Analytics: Data is the lifeblood of the underwriting process, and advanced analytics tools are the heart that pumps it. These technologies sift through vast amounts of data to identify patterns, trends, and insights that might not be visible to the human eye. By leveraging data analytics, underwriters can make more informed decisions, predict potential risks more accurately, and tailor policies to fit the unique risk profiles of policyholders.

Risk Assessment Models: Sophisticated risk assessment models use algorithms to evaluate the probability and potential impact of risks. These models take into account various factors, from historical claims data to new and emerging risk trends. By applying these models, underwriters can assess risks more consistently and efficiently, ensuring that policies are priced fairly and accurately.

Geographic Information Systems (GIS): GIS technology has become an invaluable tool in underwriting, especially for property insurance. By analyzing geographic data, underwriters can assess environmental risks such as flood zones, earthquake fault lines, or wildfire-prone areas. This spatial analysis helps in determining the insurability of properties and in setting appropriate premiums based on location-specific risks.

Telematics: In the realm of auto insurance, telematics technology is revolutionizing the way underwriters assess driver risk. By collecting data on driving behavior, such as speed, braking patterns, and time of day driven, insurers can gain a more nuanced understanding of individual risk profiles. This allows for more personalized pricing and encourages safer driving habits among policyholders.

Artificial Intelligence and Machine Learning: AI and machine learning are at the forefront of underwriting innovation. These technologies can process and analyze data at an unprecedented scale, learning and adapting over time. From automating routine tasks to predicting future trends, AI enhances the efficiency and effectiveness of the underwriting process.

For Exam Preparation:

When preparing for the Property and Casualty Insurance License Exam, it's essential to understand the role and impact of these tools and technologies in modern underwriting. Be familiar with how they contribute to risk assessment, the benefits they offer, and the challenges they may present. Real-world examples of their application can provide valuable context and deepen your comprehension of these concepts.

Underwriting tools and technologies are reshaping the insurance industry, offering new ways to assess and manage risk. As these innovations continue to evolve, they not only improve the underwriting process but also contribute to more customized and equitable insurance solutions. A solid grasp of these tools and their applications is crucial for anyone looking to excel in the insurance field, providing the knowledge needed to navigate the future of underwriting.

Chapter 11: Rating and Insurance Premiums

How Premiums Are Determined

Understanding how insurance premiums are determined is like unlocking a puzzle where each piece represents a different factor influencing the overall picture. It's a blend of art and science, where actuaries and underwriters play a crucial role in setting prices that are fair, competitive, and sufficient to cover the risks. Let's break down this process to understand the key elements that come into play.

Risk Assessment: At the core of premium determination is the assessment of risk. Insurers look at the likelihood of a claim being made and the potential cost of that claim. This involves analyzing historical data, current trends, and individual risk factors. For example, in auto insurance, factors like driving history, vehicle type, and usage can significantly impact the risk assessment and, consequently, the premium.

Actuarial Tables: Actuaries use statistical tables and models to predict the likelihood of certain events, such as accidents or natural disasters. These tables help insurers estimate the expected costs associated with different risks, forming the basis for premium calculations. The more precise these predictions are, the more accurately insurers can price their policies.

Rating Factors: Several rating factors are considered when determining premiums. These can include the insured's age, location, credit history, and for businesses, the industry type and size. Each factor is weighted based on its impact on the likelihood and cost of potential claims, with higher risk factors leading to higher premiums.

Policy Options and Coverage Limits: The choices policyholders make regarding their coverage also influence premiums. Opting for higher coverage limits, lower deductibles, or additional endorsements can increase the premium, as these choices expand the insurer's obligation in the event of a claim.

Competition and Market Conditions: The insurance market is competitive, and insurers must price their policies in a way that is attractive to consumers while still covering costs and ensuring profitability. Market conditions, such as the availability of reinsurance and legal and regulatory environments, can also impact premium levels.

Loss Experience: An insurer's past loss experience with similar policies plays a crucial role in premium determination. If an insurer has experienced higher than expected claims for a particular type of policy, this may lead to adjustments in premiums for that category to mitigate future financial risk.

For Exam Preparation:

When studying for the Property and Casualty Insurance License Exam, it's important to grasp the multi-faceted approach to determining premiums. Be prepared to discuss the role of risk assessment, actuarial tables, rating factors, and how policy options influence the final premium. Understanding these components not only helps in passing the exam but is also essential for providing accurate advice and explanations to clients regarding their insurance costs.

Determining insurance premiums is a complex process that balances the assessment of risk with the need to offer competitive and fair prices. This process ensures that policyholders are charged appropriately for the coverage they receive, reflecting their individual risk profiles and the insurer's need to manage financial exposure.

Rating Agencies and Their Role

In the intricate world of insurance, rating agencies stand as pivotal beacons, guiding both insurers and policyholders through the complexities of financial strength and stability. These agencies evaluate and rate insurance companies based on their ability to meet policyholder obligations, playing a crucial role in maintaining transparency and trust within the industry. Let's delve into the role of these agencies and how they impact the insurance landscape.

The Function of Rating Agencies:

Rating agencies assess the financial health of insurance companies, providing ratings that indicate the insurer's ability to pay claims, manage its investments, and maintain overall financial stability. These ratings are based on comprehensive analyses of the insurer's financial statements, business model, risk management practices, and market position.

Key Rating Agencies:

Several prominent rating agencies specialize in evaluating insurance companies, including A.M. Best, Standard & Poor's, Moody's, and Fitch Ratings. Each agency has its own rating scale and criteria, but their core mission is the same: to provide an independent assessment of an insurer's financial strength.

Impact on Insurers and Policyholders:

For insurers, a strong rating from these agencies can be a powerful tool in attracting and retaining policyholders. It serves as a badge of financial health and reliability, essential in a competitive market. For policyholders, these ratings offer an objective measure to assess the risk of their chosen insurer, aiding in informed decision-making.

Ratings and Premiums:

While the primary focus of rating agencies is on financial strength, rather than premium levels, there's an indirect relationship between the two. Insurers with higher ratings may have more efficient operations and risk management practices, potentially leading to more competitive premium rates. Conversely, insurers facing financial difficulties might need to adjust their premiums to mitigate risk.

For Exam Preparation:

When preparing for the Property and Casualty Insurance License Exam, it's important to understand the role of rating agencies in the insurance industry. Be familiar with the major rating agencies, their rating scales, and how these ratings influence the perceptions and decisions of insurers and policyholders alike. Discussing the impact of financial ratings on an insurer's market position and premium strategy can also provide valuable insights.

Rating agencies play a vital role in the insurance industry, offering an independent assessment of insurers' financial strength and stability. These ratings help ensure transparency and trust, guiding both insurers and policyholders in their decision-making processes. Understanding the function and impact of these agencies is crucial for anyone looking to navigate the insurance industry successfully.

The Impact of Claims on Premiums

In the realm of insurance, the relationship between claims and premiums is akin to a dance, where each step by one partner leads to a responsive move by the other. Understanding how claims impact premiums is crucial for anyone navigating the insurance landscape, whether you're a policyholder trying to make sense of your premium adjustments or an aspiring insurance professional preparing for the Property and Casualty Insurance License Exam.

Claims and Risk Perception:

At its heart, insurance is a risk-sharing mechanism. When a policyholder files a claim, it's an indication that a loss has occurred, which could alter the insurer's perception of the risk associated with that policyholder or the covered asset. Frequent or severe claims can signal higher risk, prompting insurers to adjust premiums to adequately compensate for this increased risk exposure.

Premium Adjustments:

After a claim, policyholders might see adjustments in their premiums at renewal time. This is because insurers use historical claims data as one of the factors to project future claims likelihood and costs. A history of claims can lead to higher premiums, reflecting the insurer's need to collect sufficient funds to cover potential future payouts.

No-Claim Discounts and Surcharge Schedules:

Many insurers offer no-claim discounts as a reward for claim-free periods, recognizing lower risk with lower premiums. Conversely, surcharge schedules may be applied after claims, incrementally increasing premiums to account for the heightened risk. These mechanisms aim to balance risk and reward, encouraging policyholders to manage risks proactively.

The Nature and Size of Claims:

Not all claims impact premiums equally. The nature and size of a claim can influence its effect on premiums. Small, infrequent claims might have a minimal impact, especially if they're covered by deductibles. However, large or multiple claims within a short period can significantly affect premiums, reflecting the increased cost to the insurer.

Loss Mitigation and Premiums:

Insurers often consider policyholders' efforts to mitigate future losses when adjusting premiums post-claim. Implementing measures to prevent future losses, such as installing security systems or undertaking safety training, can positively influence premium adjustments, showcasing a commitment to reducing risk.

For Exam Preparation:

When preparing for your exam, it's important to understand the nuanced relationship between claims and premiums. Be able to discuss how claims can influence an insurer's risk assessment and the mechanisms insurers use to adjust premiums in response to claims. Examples and scenarios can help illustrate these concepts and their practical implications in real-world insurance settings.

The impact of claims on premiums is a fundamental aspect of insurance that reflects the dynamic nature of risk assessment and management. A thorough understanding of this relationship is essential for anyone involved in the insurance industry, ensuring informed decisions and effective risk management strategies.

IV

Part IV: Regulatory Environment and Legal Aspects

Chapter 12: State and Federal Insurance Regulations

Licensing Requirements for Agents and Brokers

Stepping into the world of insurance as an agent or broker is akin to embarking on a new career path, where the first milestone is obtaining the right license. This licensing process is not just a formality but a crucial step in ensuring that insurance professionals are well-equipped with the knowledge and ethical standards needed to serve their clients effectively. Let's navigate through the licensing requirements for agents and brokers, shedding light on this essential aspect of the regulatory environment.

Understanding the Licensing Landscape:

The requirements for obtaining an insurance license can vary significantly from state to state, reflecting the decentralized nature of insurance regulation in the United States. Despite these variations, certain core requirements are commonly found across most jurisdictions.

1. **Pre-Licensing Education:** Most states require prospective agents and brokers to complete a certain number of hours of pre-licensing education. This education covers the fundamentals of insurance, state-specific regulations, and the ethical obligations of insurance professionals. The goal is to ensure that all licensees have a solid

foundation of knowledge before they begin advising clients.

2. **Licensing Examination:** After completing the pre-licensing education, candidates must pass a licensing examination. These exams test knowledge of insurance concepts, state laws governing insurance, and the practical aspects of selling insurance and handling claims. The exams are designed to ensure that agents and brokers have the necessary expertise to operate effectively within the regulatory framework.

3. **Application Process:** With education and examination requirements met, candidates can then submit an application for a license to the state insurance regulatory authority. This application process often includes a background check to ensure the candidate's suitability for a role that involves financial trust and personal integrity.

4. **Continuing Education:** Obtaining a license is not the end of the educational journey for insurance professionals. Most states require agents and brokers to complete continuing education courses on a regular basis. This requirement ensures that insurance professionals stay current with changes in laws, regulations, and industry best practices.

The Role of Regulatory Bodies:

State insurance departments or commissions are the primary regulatory bodies overseeing the licensing of agents and brokers. They set the requirements, administer the examinations, and monitor compliance with continuing education mandates. These bodies also play a critical role in enforcing ethical standards and consumer protection laws within the industry.

For Exam Preparation:

When preparing for the Property and Casualty Insurance License Exam, it's important to not only focus on the insurance concepts and policies but also to understand the regulatory framework that governs the profession. Familiarize yourself with the licensing process, the role of state regulatory bodies, and the importance of continuing education in maintaining professional standards.

The licensing requirements for insurance agents and brokers serve as the gateway to the profession, ensuring that those who enter the field are equipped with the knowledge, skills, and ethical grounding needed to serve their clients effectively. Understanding these requirements is crucial for anyone aspiring to embark on a career in insurance.

Regulatory Bodies and Their Functions

Navigating the complex landscape of insurance requires understanding the guardians of this realm: the regulatory bodies. These entities play a pivotal role in shaping the insurance industry, ensuring fairness, solvency, and consumer protection. Let's delve into the functions of these regulatory bodies, shedding light on their crucial role in maintaining the integrity and stability of the insurance market.

State Insurance Departments:

At the state level, insurance is regulated by state insurance departments or divisions. Each state has its own department that operates under the leadership of an Insurance Commissioner, who may be appointed or elected depending on the state's laws.

Core Functions:

1. **Licensing:** State insurance departments are responsible for licensing insurance companies, agents, and brokers within their jurisdiction. This ensures that only qualified and ethical professionals and organizations can offer insurance products and services.
2. **Regulation and Compliance:** These bodies enforce state insurance laws and regulations, overseeing the practices of insurance providers to ensure they comply with legal and ethical standards. This includes

reviewing policy forms, setting standards for financial stability, and conducting audits and examinations.

3. **Consumer Protection:** Protecting policyholders and insurance consumers is a key mandate of state insurance departments. They provide resources and assistance for consumers, handle complaints, and offer guidance on insurance matters to ensure consumers are treated fairly and have access to the information they need to make informed decisions.

4. **Market Conduct:** Regulatory bodies monitor the behavior of insurance companies in the marketplace, ensuring that they engage in fair competition and do not engage in practices that could harm consumers or the integrity of the insurance market.

National Association of Insurance Commissioners (NAIC):

While insurance is primarily regulated at the state level, the NAIC plays a crucial role in standardizing regulations and promoting best practices among states. The NAIC is a collective organization of state insurance regulators that develops model laws and regulations, provides education and resources, and facilitates coordination and cooperation among states.

Federal Oversight:

Although insurance regulation is predominantly a state responsibility, certain aspects of insurance are subject to federal oversight. For example, the Federal Insurance Office (FIO) monitors the insurance industry's health and its systemic risk potential, and laws like the Health Insurance Portability and Accountability Act (HIPAA) and the Affordable Care Act (ACA) set federal standards for specific insurance sectors.

For Exam Preparation:

When preparing for the Property and Casualty Insurance License Exam, it's essential to understand the role and functions of these regulatory bodies. Be familiar with the regulatory framework at both state and federal levels, the key responsibilities of state insurance departments, and the role of the

NAIC in shaping insurance regulation.

Regulatory bodies are the backbone of the insurance industry's regulatory framework, ensuring that the industry operates fairly, ethically, and in the best interest of consumers. A thorough understanding of these entities and their functions is crucial for anyone looking to navigate the insurance industry effectively.

Key Insurance Laws and Regulations

In the tapestry of the insurance industry, laws and regulations form the threads that hold everything together, ensuring order, fairness, and protection for all stakeholders. From landmark federal acts to pivotal state regulations, these legal frameworks shape the operations of insurance companies, the work of professionals, and the rights of policyholders. Let's explore some of the key insurance laws and regulations that are essential knowledge for anyone venturing into the field of insurance.

McCarran-Ferguson Act (1945): A cornerstone of insurance regulation, the McCarran-Ferguson Act established that insurance regulation is primarily a state responsibility. It allows states to regulate insurance within their borders while also providing a federal antitrust exemption for insurance activities that are regulated by state law.

National Association of Insurance Commissioners (NAIC) Model Laws: While not laws themselves, the NAIC's model laws and regulations serve as templates to promote uniformity across state insurance regulations. States often adopt or adapt these models, covering areas such as life and health insurance standards, property and casualty insurance, and market conduct.

State Insurance Codes: Each state has its own set of insurance codes, which are comprehensive laws governing all aspects of insurance within the state. These codes cover licensing requirements, solvency standards, consumer protections, and the operations of insurance companies and professionals.

Gramm-Leach-Bliley Act (GLBA) (1999): At the federal level, the GLBA is significant for its provisions on financial privacy and consumer protection. It requires financial institutions, including insurance companies, to explain their information-sharing practices to consumers and to safeguard sensitive data.

Health Insurance Portability and Accountability Act (HIPAA) (1996): HIPAA is a critical law in the health insurance sector, providing standards for protecting sensitive patient health information. It ensures the confidentiality and security of healthcare information and outlines the rights of individuals to their health information.

Affordable Care Act (ACA) (2010): The ACA brought significant changes to health insurance, including provisions for expanding healthcare coverage, consumer protections (such as preventing denial of coverage based on pre-existing conditions), and establishing health insurance marketplaces.

State Guaranty Associations: While not a single law, state guaranty associations are a crucial regulatory feature, providing a safety net for policyholders if an insurance company becomes insolvent. Funded by the insurance industry, these associations ensure that claims are paid even if an insurer fails.

For Exam Preparation:

When preparing for the Property and Casualty Insurance License Exam, it's vital to familiarize yourself with these key laws and regulations. Understanding their implications on the insurance landscape, both at the federal and state levels, is crucial for navigating the legal and regulatory aspects of the industry effectively.

A myriad of laws and regulations govern the insurance industry, ensuring its orderly and ethical operation. A solid grasp of these legal foundations is essential for anyone looking to make their mark in the insurance field, ensuring that they can operate within the bounds of the law while providing the best service to their clients.

Chapter 13: Ethics in Insurance

Ethical Responsibilities of Insurance Professionals

In the intricate web of the insurance industry, the ethical responsibilities of insurance professionals stand as the cornerstone of trust and integrity. These ethical standards guide professionals in their interactions with policyholders, colleagues, and the broader community, ensuring that their actions uphold the highest principles of honesty and fairness. Let's explore the core ethical responsibilities that are fundamental to the practice of insurance.

Honesty and Transparency: At the heart of ethical conduct is a commitment to honesty and transparency. Insurance professionals must ensure that all communications with clients and stakeholders are clear, accurate, and truthful. This includes providing complete and straightforward information about policy terms, coverage limitations, and any associated risks or exclusions.

Confidentiality and Privacy: Respecting the confidentiality and privacy of clients is paramount. Insurance professionals are often privy to sensitive personal and financial information. It is their duty to protect this information, only using it in ways that serve the client's interests and comply with applicable privacy laws and regulations.

Conflict of Interest Management: Insurance professionals must vigilantly identify and manage conflicts of interest that may compromise their ability to act in the best interests of their clients. This involves disclosing any potential conflicts to clients and taking steps to mitigate them, ensuring that professional judgment is not unduly influenced by personal gain.

Professional Competence: Maintaining professional competence through continuous learning and adherence to industry standards is essential. Insurance professionals should only offer advice and services in areas where they have adequate knowledge and expertise, and they should commit to ongoing education to keep their skills and knowledge up to date.

Fair Treatment: Ethical responsibility includes the fair treatment of all clients, without discrimination. This means providing equal access to insurance products and services regardless of a client's background, and ensuring that underwriting and claims decisions are based on fair and objective criteria.

For Exam Preparation:

When preparing for the Property and Casualty Insurance License Exam, understanding the ethical responsibilities of insurance professionals is crucial. Be prepared to discuss scenarios that may pose ethical dilemmas and how to navigate them in accordance with ethical standards. Familiarize yourself with the principles of honesty, confidentiality, conflict of interest management, professional competence, and fair treatment, as these form the basis of ethical conduct in the insurance industry.

The ethical responsibilities of insurance professionals are foundational to building and maintaining trust in the insurance industry. Upholding these standards ensures that professionals act in the best interests of their clients and the public, fostering a culture of integrity and respect. A thorough grasp of these ethical principles is essential for anyone aspiring to make a positive impact in the field of insurance.

Handling Conflicts of Interest

In the nuanced world of insurance, conflicts of interest can arise, casting shadows on the clarity and fairness expected in professional conduct. Handling these conflicts with integrity is paramount for insurance professionals, ensuring that their actions always align with the best interests of their clients and uphold the ethical standards of the industry. Let's explore effective strategies for identifying and managing conflicts of interest.

Recognizing Conflicts of Interest:

The first step in handling conflicts of interest is recognizing when they occur. A conflict of interest arises when an insurance professional's personal interests, relationships, or financial gains could potentially influence, or appear to influence, their professional judgment or actions. This could involve situations where an agent has a financial interest in a particular policy or where personal relationships might affect policy recommendations.

Disclosure:

Transparency is key when managing conflicts of interest. Insurance professionals should disclose any potential conflicts to their clients and relevant parties as soon as they are identified. This disclosure should be clear, complete, and made well in advance of any decision-making, allowing clients to fully understand the situation and how it might affect their insurance choices.

Mitigation and Management:

Once a conflict of interest is disclosed, steps should be taken to mitigate or manage it. This might involve removing oneself from decision-making processes related to the conflict, seeking guidance from supervisors or ethics committees, or in some cases, transferring the client's account to another professional who does not have the same conflict.

Creating a Culture of Integrity:

Insurance organizations can play a significant role in handling conflicts of interest by fostering a culture of integrity and transparency. This can be achieved through clear policies and procedures for identifying and managing conflicts, regular training on ethical issues, and mechanisms for reporting and addressing potential conflicts without fear of reprisal.

For Exam Preparation:

When studying for the Property and Casualty Insurance License Exam, it's important to understand the ethical implications of conflicts of interest and the best practices for handling them. Be prepared to discuss examples of potential conflicts and the appropriate steps for disclosure, mitigation, and management, demonstrating a thorough understanding of how to maintain ethical standards in complex situations.

Effectively handling conflicts of interest is crucial for maintaining trust and integrity in the insurance industry. By recognizing, disclosing, and managing conflicts, insurance professionals can ensure that their actions are always guided by the best interests of their clients and the ethical principles that underpin their profession. This commitment to ethical conduct is essential for anyone looking to build a successful and respected career in insurance.

Consumer Protection and Privacy Laws

In the intricate landscape of insurance, consumer protection and privacy laws serve as vital safeguards, ensuring that the rights and personal information of policyholders are securely protected. These laws not only fortify trust in the insurance process but also uphold the dignity and respect of every individual seeking insurance coverage. Let's delve into the essence of these laws and their significance in the ethical practice of insurance.

Foundation of Consumer Protection:

Consumer protection laws in the insurance sector are designed to prevent unfair practices, promote transparency, and ensure that policyholders are treated with fairness and respect. These laws cover a wide range of practices, from clear and honest advertising of insurance products to the fair handling of claims and the provision of accurate policy information.

Privacy Laws and Confidentiality:

Privacy laws play a critical role in protecting the sensitive personal and financial information that policyholders share with their insurance providers. Laws such as the Health Insurance Portability and Accountability Act (HIPAA) and the Gramm-Leach-Bliley Act (GLBA) set stringent standards for how this information must be handled, ensuring it is used appropriately and safeguarded against unauthorized access.

Key Aspects of Privacy Protection:

1. **Data Security:** Insurance companies are required to implement robust security measures to protect policyholders' data from breaches and cyber threats.
2. **Consent and Disclosure:** Policyholders must be informed about how their information is used and must consent to its use, particularly when sensitive information is involved.
3. **Access and Correction:** Individuals have the right to access their personal information held by insurance companies and to request corrections to any inaccuracies.

Ethical Implications for Insurance Professionals:

For insurance professionals, adhering to consumer protection and privacy laws is not just a legal obligation but an ethical duty. It involves:

- Ensuring that all interactions with policyholders are conducted with honesty and integrity.
- Providing clear and accurate information about insurance products and

policies.
- Respecting the privacy and confidentiality of policyholder information at all times.
- Addressing any concerns or complaints from policyholders promptly and fairly.

For Exam Preparation:

When preparing for the Property and Casualty Insurance License Exam, it's crucial to understand the principles of consumer protection and privacy laws relevant to the insurance industry. Be prepared to discuss how these laws influence the practices of insurance professionals and the measures taken to comply with them, demonstrating a comprehensive understanding of their ethical and legal implications.

Consumer protection and privacy laws are cornerstone principles in the ethical practice of insurance, ensuring that policyholders are treated with fairness, respect, and dignity. A thorough grasp of these laws is essential for anyone aspiring to uphold the highest standards of integrity and professionalism in the insurance industry.

V

Part V: Exam Preparation and Strategies

Chapter 14: Study Strategies and Tips

Effective Study Habits and Schedules

Embarking on the path to mastering the content for the Property and Casualty Insurance License Exam requires not just dedication, but also a strategic approach to studying. Establishing effective study habits and a well-organized schedule is akin to laying a strong foundation for a building—it's essential for ensuring the structure stands firm. Let's explore some strategies to cultivate these habits and create a schedule that maximizes your study efficiency.

Setting Realistic Goals: Begin by setting clear, achievable goals for your study sessions. Whether it's mastering a particular concept or completing a chapter, having a specific target in mind can keep you focused and motivated. Break down the exam content into manageable sections, and set goals for each to track your progress.

Creating a Study Schedule: Design a study schedule that fits your lifestyle and commitments. Consistency is key, so aim to allocate regular, dedicated time slots for studying each day. Remember, shorter, consistent study sessions are often more effective than occasional marathon sessions.

Balanced Study Blocks: Divide your study time into blocks dedicated to different topics or types of study activities, such as reading, practicing questions, or reviewing notes. This variety can keep your study sessions engaging and cover the material more comprehensively.

Active Learning Techniques: Engage with the material actively rather than passively reading or listening. This could involve teaching concepts to someone else, discussing topics with peers, or applying theories to practical scenarios. Active engagement helps deepen understanding and retention.

Prioritizing Difficult Topics: Identify areas where you feel less confident and prioritize these in your study schedule. Tackling challenging subjects first, when your mind is fresher, can make your study sessions more productive.

Scheduled Breaks: Incorporate short breaks into your study sessions to prevent burnout and maintain focus. The Pomodoro Technique, which involves studying for 25 minutes followed by a 5-minute break, is a popular method that can enhance concentration and stamina.

Self-Assessment: Regularly assess your understanding through practice tests or quizzes. This not only familiarizes you with the exam format but also helps identify areas that need further review.

For Exam Preparation:
   When preparing for the Property and Casualty Insurance License Exam, remember that a well-structured study plan is your blueprint for success. Adapt these strategies to fit your personal preferences and circumstances, and be flexible—adjust your plan as needed based on your progress and comprehension of the material.

Cultivating effective study habits and a thoughtful schedule is essential for exam preparation. By setting realistic goals, engaging actively with the material, and maintaining a balanced and consistent study routine, you'll be well-equipped to tackle the Property and Casualty Insurance License

Exam with confidence.

Memory Aids and Note-Taking Techniques

Mastering the vast array of concepts required for the Property and Casualty Insurance License Exam can feel overwhelming, but with the right memory aids and note-taking techniques, the information can become more manageable and easier to recall. These strategies are like tools in a toolbox, each with a specific purpose to help construct a strong foundation of knowledge. Let's explore some effective methods to enhance memory retention and make note-taking more efficient.

Memory Aids:

1. **Mnemonics:** Mnemonics are creative ways to remember lists or complex information. They can take the form of acronyms, phrases, or even songs. For example, creating an acronym from the first letters of a list of principles can make them easier to recall during the exam.
2. **Visualization:** Transforming information into visual formats such as charts, graphs, or mind maps can help in understanding and remembering complex concepts. Visual cues are often easier to recall than text-heavy notes.
3. **Storytelling:** Turning information into a narrative can make it more memorable. By weaving facts and concepts into a story, you create a context that makes the information more relatable and easier to recall.

Note-Taking Techniques:

1. **The Cornell Method:** This system involves dividing your note page into three sections: cues, notes, and summary. The notes section is for traditional note-taking during study sessions or lectures, the cues section is for keywords or questions based on the notes, and the summary at the bottom helps consolidate and review the main ideas.

2. **Outlining:** Organizing notes in a structured format, with main topics and subtopics, can help in understanding the relationships between concepts and in creating a clear, hierarchical structure of the material.

3. **Active Note-Taking:** Instead of passively copying text, engage with the material by paraphrasing, summarizing, and questioning the content as you take notes. This active engagement helps deepen understanding and retention.

4. **Digital Tools:** Utilizing digital note-taking apps and tools can offer flexibility and efficiency. Features like searchability, tagging, and cloud storage make organizing and revisiting notes easier.

For Exam Preparation:

When preparing for the Property and Casualty Insurance License Exam, experiment with these memory aids and note-taking techniques to find what works best for you. Incorporating these strategies into your study routine can enhance memory retention, making it easier to navigate the vast amount of material covered in the exam.

Effective memory aids and note-taking techniques are invaluable allies in the journey to exam success. By making information more memorable and notes more organized, these strategies can significantly enhance your study efficiency and confidence as you prepare for the Property and Casualty Insurance License Exam.

Utilizing Online Resources and Study Groups

In today's digital age, the world of learning and exam preparation has expanded far beyond traditional textbooks and classroom settings. Online resources and study groups have emerged as powerful tools in the arsenal of those preparing for the Property and Casualty Insurance License Exam. Let's look into how these modern study aids can enhance your preparation and lead you towards success.

Online Resources:

1. **Educational Platforms:** Websites and platforms dedicated to insurance education offer a wealth of knowledge, from fundamental concepts to complex policy details. These platforms often feature interactive courses, video tutorials, and practice exams tailored to the Property and Casualty Insurance License Exam.

2. **Regulatory Bodies and Professional Associations:** State insurance department websites and professional insurance associations provide valuable resources, including regulatory updates, industry news, and professional standards that can enrich your understanding of the insurance landscape.

3. **Digital Libraries and Publications:** Access to online libraries and industry publications can keep you informed about the latest trends, studies, and best practices in insurance. Staying current with industry developments can give you an edge in both exam preparation and your future career.

Study Groups:

1. **Collaborative Learning:** Joining or forming a study group with fellow exam takers can foster a collaborative learning environment. Group discussions can clarify complex topics, offer new perspectives, and reinforce your understanding through teaching and explaining concepts to others.

2. **Accountability and Motivation:** Study groups create a sense of accountability, encouraging consistent study habits and keeping motivation levels high. Regular meetings and shared goals can help maintain focus and momentum throughout the preparation process.

3. **Sharing Resources and Strategies:** Within a study group, members can share valuable resources, study tips, and test-taking strategies they've discovered. This collective pool of knowledge and experience can benefit all group members and provide a diverse array of study

aids.

For Exam Preparation:

When preparing for the Property and Casualty Insurance License Exam, actively seek out and utilize online resources that resonate with your learning style. Consider joining study groups, either locally or online, to tap into the benefits of collaborative learning and shared experiences.

Leveraging online resources and engaging with study groups can significantly enhance your exam preparation. These modern study aids offer a dynamic and interactive approach to learning, providing access to a broad spectrum of information and the support of a like-minded community. Embracing these tools can not only aid in passing the exam but also in laying a solid foundation for a successful career in the insurance industry.

Chapter 15: Test-Taking Strategies

Understanding the Exam Format

As you stand at the threshold of taking the Property and Casualty Insurance License Exam, one of the most empowering steps you can take is to familiarize yourself thoroughly with the exam format. Knowing what to expect not only alleviates anxiety but also enables you to strategize your study and test-taking approach effectively. Let's demystify the exam format to set a solid groundwork for your preparation.

Exam Structure:

The Property and Casualty Insurance License Exam typically comprises a series of multiple-choice questions, designed to assess your knowledge across a broad spectrum of topics within the property and casualty insurance domain. Understanding the breakdown of these topics and the weight each section carries can help you prioritize your study efforts.

Question Types:

While multiple-choice questions are the standard, it's essential to recognize that they can vary in complexity:

- **Direct Questions:** These may ask for specific facts or definitions and tend to be straightforward.
- **Scenario-Based Questions:** These questions present a scenario or case

study, asking you to apply your knowledge to a practical situation. They test your ability to use your understanding in a real-world context.

- **Best Answer Questions:** Sometimes, multiple answers may seem correct, but your task is to choose the 'best' one based on the nuances of the question.

Time Allocation:

Each section of the exam will have a time limit. Familiarizing yourself with these limits and the average time you can spend on each question is crucial. This understanding will help you pace yourself during the exam, ensuring that you have adequate time to thoughtfully consider each question.

Format Nuances:

Be aware of any specific rules or nuances of the exam format, such as:

- Are you penalized for incorrect answers, or is it better to guess if you're unsure?
- Can you mark questions for review and return to them later?
- What identification or materials are you allowed to bring into the exam room?

For Exam Preparation:

As part of your exam preparation, take the time to review official exam guides or resources provided by the licensing authority in your jurisdiction. These often contain detailed information about the exam format, including the number of questions, the duration of the exam, and the passing criteria.

Additionally, consider taking practice exams that mimic the format of the actual test. This practice can acclimate you to the exam's timing and pressure, making the actual exam experience feel more familiar and manageable. This book provides 5 full length practice exams that can be used.

A deep understanding of the exam format is a crucial component of your test-taking strategy. By familiarizing yourself with the structure, types of questions, and time management aspects of the exam, you can approach test day with confidence and a clear plan for success.

Techniques for Multiple-Choice Questions

Facing a series of multiple-choice questions in the Property and Casualty Insurance License Exam can seem daunting, but with the right techniques, you can navigate through them effectively and boost your chances of success. These questions are not just about what you know; they're also about how well you can apply strategic thinking to eliminate wrong answers and zero in on the right one. Let's explore some proven techniques to tackle multiple-choice questions with confidence.

Read Questions Carefully: Start by reading each question thoroughly, paying close attention to what is being asked. Look out for key terms and phrases that might hint at the correct answer. Be on the lookout for qualifiers like "always," "never," "only," or "except," as they can significantly alter the meaning of a question.

Understand Before Answering: Ensure you understand the question before scanning the answer choices. Sometimes, formulating an answer in your mind before looking at the options can prevent you from being swayed by misleading choices.

Eliminate Clearly Wrong Answers: Use the process of elimination to narrow down your choices. Discard any options that are clearly incorrect or irrelevant to the question. This increases your chances of selecting the correct answer from the remaining options.

Watch for Absolute Words: Be cautious of answers with absolute words such as "all," "none," "always," or "never." These options are less likely to be correct, as they leave no room for exceptions. Conversely, options with words like "usually," "often," or "may" might be more plausible since they allow for flexibility.

Consider "All of the Above" and "None of the Above": If "all of the above" is an option and you're certain that more than one of the other answers is correct, it's likely the right choice. Similarly, if you're confident that multiple answers are incorrect and "none of the above" is an option, it might be the correct answer.

Best Answer Questions: For questions where more than one option seems correct, look for the "best" answer. Consider the specifics of the question and the context of the answers to determine which one most fully or accurately addresses the question.

Answer Every Question: Unless there is a penalty for incorrect answers, make sure to answer every question, even if you have to guess. An educated guess, especially after eliminating one or two options, has a better chance of being correct than leaving a question blank.

Review Your Answers: If time permits, review your answers, particularly for questions you were unsure about. Re-reading the questions and answers with a fresh perspective might reveal clues you missed initially.

For Exam Preparation:

Incorporate these techniques into your practice sessions to become more adept at handling multiple-choice questions. Familiarity with these strategies can reduce anxiety and improve your performance on the actual exam day.

Mastering multiple-choice questions involves a combination of solid knowledge and strategic thinking. By carefully reading questions, eliminating wrong answers, and applying logical reasoning, you can enhance your ability to choose the correct answers more consistently. These techniques are invaluable tools in your test-taking arsenal, helping you to approach the Property and Casualty Insurance License Exam with greater confidence and skill.

Managing Time and Stress During the Exam

Tackling the Property and Casualty Insurance License Exam is not just a test of knowledge; it's also a test of your ability to manage time and keep stress at bay. Efficient time management and stress reduction techniques are key to unlocking your full potential and ensuring a calm, focused approach to the exam. Let's dive into strategies that can help you navigate the pressures of exam day with ease.

Time Management Tips:

1. **Familiarize Yourself with the Exam Structure:** Knowing the number of questions and the total time allotted can help you pace yourself effectively. Determine how much time you can afford to spend on each question and try to stick to that limit.
2. **Prioritize Questions:** Begin with questions that you find easier or are more confident about. This approach not only secures marks early on but also builds confidence as you proceed.
3. **Keep Track of Time:** Regularly check the clock or use a watch (if allowed) to keep track of your time without becoming obsessive. Being aware of the time can help you adjust your pace as needed.
4. **Allocate Time for Review:** If possible, save some time towards the end to review your answers, especially those you were unsure about or had marked for review.

Stress Reduction Techniques:

1. **Deep Breathing:** Practice deep, slow breathing to calm your nerves

before and during the exam. This can help reduce anxiety and maintain focus.

2. **Positive Visualization:** Visualize a positive outcome before the exam starts. Imagine yourself answering questions confidently and success-fully completing the exam.

3. **Stay Hydrated and Nourished:** Ensure you're well-hydrated and have eaten a light, nutritious meal before the exam. Physical well-being can significantly influence mental state and performance.

4. **Take Brief Mental Breaks:** If you feel overwhelmed, pause for a moment, close your eyes, and take a few deep breaths. A short mental break can help reset your focus and reduce stress.

5. **Maintain Perspective:** Remind yourself that while the exam is impor-tant, it's not the sole determinant of your future. Keeping the exam in perspective can help reduce fear and anxiety.

For Exam Preparation:

Incorporate time management and stress reduction practices into your study routine well before exam day. Practice exams under timed conditions and experiment with different stress-relief techniques to find what works best for you.

Effectively managing time and stress during the Property and Casualty Insurance License Exam can significantly enhance your performance. By approaching the exam with a clear strategy for time management and equipped with techniques to maintain calm and focus, you can navigate the challenges of exam day with confidence and poise. Remember, preparation is key—not just in mastering the content but also in mastering the exam experience itself.

VI

Part VI: Full Length Practice Exams

Practice Exam 1 (Total: 124 Questions)

Insurance Basics (Total: 18 Questions)

Principles of insurance: 6 questions

1) What is the principle of indemnity in insurance?

- A) Insuring only high-risk individuals
- B) Providing benefits beyond the actual loss
- C) Compensating for the loss no more than the insured's economic loss
- D) Sharing risk among all policyholders

2) Which principle describes the sharing of loss by all members of a group?

- A) Contribution
- B) Subrogation
- C) Risk pooling
- D) Utmost good faith

3) The principle of utmost good faith requires which of the following?

- A) The insurer to compensate for losses promptly
- B) Both parties to enter into the insurance contract in good faith
- C) The insured to pay a premium

· D) The insurer to cover all declared risks

4) What does the principle of subrogation enable an insurer to do?

· A) Increase the premium after a claim
· B) Refuse to pay out in the event of fraud
· C) Pursue a third party that caused an insurance loss to the insured
· D) Share the loss with other insurers

5) Which principle prevents the insured from profiting from insurance?

· A) Insurable interest
· B) Indemnity
· C) Contribution
· D) Subrogation

6) Insurable interest must exist at which time?

· A) Only at the time of the contract's inception
· B) Only at the time of the loss
· C) At the time of the contract's inception and at the time of the loss
· D) At the time the premium is paid

Types of insurers: 4 questions

7) Which type of insurer is owned by its policyholders?

· A) Stock insurer
· B) Mutual insurer
· C) Captive insurer
· D) Reinsurer

8) What is a stock insurance company?

- A) A company that insures stocks and bonds
- B) A company owned by shareholders
- C) A company owned by its policyholders
- D) A company that only provides insurance to stock market companies

9) Which insurer operates on a non-profit basis by returning surplus funds to its policyholders?

- A) Stock insurer
- B) Mutual insurer
- C) Captive insurer
- D) Lloyd's of London

10) A captive insurance company is primarily established for what purpose?

- A) To insure the general public
- B) To insure the risks of its parent company
- C) To offer reinsurance
- D) To operate in the stock market

Policy renewals and cancellations: 8 questions

11) What is a policy renewal?

- A) Changing the terms of an insurance policy
- B) Continuing an existing insurance policy term without changes
- C) Canceling an existing insurance policy
- D) Increasing the premium of an insurance policy

12) Which of the following reasons might an insurer cancel an insurance policy?

- A) The insured has moved to a new state
- B) The insured has filed a single claim
- C) Non-payment of premium
- D) The insured has obtained another insurance policy

13) What is the grace period in an insurance policy?

- A) The time after a policy expires during which coverage is still effective
- B) A period during which all premiums are waived
- C) A specified period after a missed payment during which the policy remains in force
- D) The time frame an insurer has to approve or deny a claim

14) Under what circumstance can a short-rate cancellation occur?

- A) When the insurer cancels the policy
- B) When the insured decides to cancel the policy before its expiration date
- C) When the policy reaches its natural expiration
- D) When a policy is canceled due to non-payment of premium

15) Which term describes the automatic renewal of a policy for a new term?

- A) Conversion
- B) Endorsement
- C) Non-renewal
- D) Evergreen

16) What must an insurer provide to an insured if they decide not to renew a policy?

- A) A renewal premium discount

- B) Written notice of non-renewal within a specified time frame before the policy expires
- C) A justification for every claim denied during the policy period
- D) An offer to renew under adjusted terms and conditions

17) In the context of insurance, what does 'pro-rata cancellation' mean?

- A) The insurer cancels the policy and returns the unused premium on a proportional basis
- B) The insured is penalized for early cancellation
- C) The insurer retains the full premium regardless of when the policy is canceled
- D) The insured receives a full refund of the premium

18) What is the primary reason an insurer might non-renew a policy?

- A) The insured inquired about the possibility of filing a claim
- B) The risk profile of the insured has significantly changed
- C) The insured has reached the age of retirement
- D) The insurer is exiting the market altogether

Property Insurance (Total: 32 Questions)

Dwelling policies: 8 questions

19) What is a dwelling policy primarily used to insure?

- A) Commercial properties
- B) Personal vehicles
- C) Residential properties not typically covered by standard homeowners policies
- D) Agricultural lands

20) Which of the following is NOT covered under a basic dwelling policy?

- A) Fire
- B) Theft
- C) Lightning
- D) Internal explosion

21) Dwelling Policy Program offers how many coverage forms?

- A) One
- B) Two
- C) Three
- D) Four

22) What does DP-1, or Basic Form Dwelling Policy, typically cover?

- A) Fire, lightning, and internal explosion only
- B) All risks of physical loss
- C) Named perils including windstorm, hail, and vandalism
- D) Comprehensive coverage including accidental direct physical loss

23) Which Dwelling Policy form provides the broadest coverage?

- A) DP-1
- B) DP-2
- C) DP-3
- D) They all provide the same level of coverage

24) In dwelling policies, 'Other Structures' coverage is:

- A) Automatically included at 10% of the dwelling coverage amount
- B) Only available through endorsement
- C) Not available under any circumstances

- D) Included at 50% of the dwelling coverage amount

25) What is the primary difference between DP-2 and DP-3 coverage forms?

- A) DP-2 covers named perils, while DP-3 offers open perils coverage
- B) DP-2 is for commercial properties, while DP-3 is for residential
- C) DP-2 offers liability coverage, while DP-3 does not
- D) There is no difference; they are interchangeable

26) Which peril is typically covered by a DP-2 (Broad Form) dwelling policy but NOT by a DP-1 (Basic Form)?

- A) Fire
- B) Lightning
- C) Theft
- D) Falling objects

Homeowners policies: 10 questions

27) Which of the following is NOT a type of coverage typically provided by a homeowners policy?

- A) Dwelling
- B) Personal Property
- C) Automobile
- D) Loss of Use

28) What does Coverage A in a standard homeowners policy insure?

- A) The main dwelling
- B) Other structures on the property
- C) Personal property

- D) Liability protection

29) Personal Liability coverage in a homeowners policy protects the insured against claims for:

- A) Bodily injury to others
- B) Property damage caused by the insured
- C) Both A and B
- D) Damage to the insured's own property

30) Which homeowners policy form is specifically designed for renters?

- A) HO-2
- B) HO-4
- C) HO-6
- D) HO-8

31) The 'open perils' coverage in a homeowners policy means the policy covers:

- A) Only named perils listed in the policy
- B) All perils except those specifically excluded
- C) All perils with no exclusions
- D) Perils that are open for negotiation at the time of a claim

32) Which of the following is typically excluded from a standard home-owners policy?

- A) Fire
- B) Theft
- C) Earth movement
- D) Windstorm

33) What is the purpose of 'Medical Payments to Others' coverage in a homeowners policy?

- A) To cover the medical expenses of the homeowner
- B) To pay for medical expenses of guests injured on the property, regardless of fault
- C) To cover medical expenses for injuries the homeowner causes off the property
- D) To reimburse the homeowner for health insurance deductibles

34) HO-6 insurance policies are designed specifically for:

- A) Single-family homes
- B) Condominium owners
- C) Renters
- D) Mobile homes

35) In a homeowners policy, 'Other Structures' coverage (Coverage B) typically covers:

- A) Structures attached to the dwelling
- B) The personal property inside detached structures
- C) Structures on the property not attached to the dwelling, like a detached garage
- D) Landscaping and trees

36) Which coverage in a homeowners policy would cover the insured in case of a lawsuit for accidentally injuring someone off their property?

- A) Medical Payments to Others
- B) Personal Property
- C) Dwelling
- D) Personal Liability

Commercial property policies: 8 questions

37) What is the primary purpose of commercial property insurance?

- A) To protect the personal property of employees
- B) To cover the business against liability claims
- C) To insure the business's physical assets against loss or damage
- D) To provide health insurance for employees

38) Which of the following is typically NOT covered under a standard commercial property policy?

- A) Inventory
- B) Customer data
- C) Office furniture
- D) The building itself

39) The 'Building and Personal Property Coverage Form' in a commercial property policy covers:

- A) Only the building structure
- B) The building and permanently installed fixtures
- C) Business personal property on premises
- D) B and C

40) What does 'Coinsurance' in a commercial property policy require?

- A) The policyholder to share in the risk by insuring the property to a specified percentage of its value
- B) The insurer to cover all damages without considering the policy limit
- C) The policyholder to pay a fixed percentage of all loss amounts
- D) Multiple insurers to share the risk on a single property

41) 'Business Income Coverage' in a commercial property policy is designed to:

- A) Replace lost income during a period of restoration following a covered loss
- B) Compensate for the income lost due to employee theft
- C) Cover the salaries of employees during business interruptions
- D) Insure against loss of income due to fluctuations in the market

42) Which of the following would be covered under 'Extra Expense Coverage' in a commercial property policy?

- A) Costs to repair damaged property
- B) Expenses to relocate temporarily following a covered loss
- C) Legal fees resulting from a lawsuit
- D) Debts owed to creditors

43) The 'Cause of Loss – Basic Form' in a commercial property policy typically includes coverage for:

- A) Earthquakes and floods
- B) Fire, lightning, and explosion
- C) Theft and vandalism
- D) Business interruption

44) What is the purpose of the 'Builders Risk Coverage Form' in commercial property insurance?

- A) To cover the liability of contractors and builders
- B) To insure buildings under construction against specified perils
- C) To provide liability coverage for property owners
- D) To cover the cost of building materials stored off-site

Business interruption: 6 questions

45) What is the primary purpose of business interruption insurance?

- A) To cover the cost of physical repairs to the business premises
- B) To compensate for lost income during a period of restoration after a covered loss
- C) To provide liability protection for businesses
- D) To insure against theft of business assets

46) Business interruption insurance typically covers income lost due to:

- A) Voluntary closure for remodeling
- B) A natural disaster that damages the insured property
- C) A planned strike by employees
- D) Economic downturns

47) Which of the following is typically required for a business interruption claim to be valid?

- A) The interruption must result from a direct physical loss or damage to the property
- B) The business must be located in a disaster-prone area
- C) The interruption must last more than 30 days
- D) The business must have been profitable for the last three fiscal years

48) What does the 'period of restoration' refer to in a business interruption policy?

- A) The time it takes for the business to fully recover its lost market share
- B) The duration for which the business receives compensation under the policy

- C) The time from the occurrence of the damage until the property should be repaired, rebuilt, or replaced
- D) The grace period given to the business to file a claim after a loss

49) 'Extra Expense' coverage in a business interruption policy is designed to:

- A) Compensate for expenses beyond normal operating expenses that a business incurs to continue operation during restoration
- B) Cover additional expenses not covered by the primary business interruption policy
- C) Reimburse for extravagant expenses incurred by the business owner
- D) Pay for overtime wages and hiring temporary workers

50) Which factor is NOT considered when calculating the amount of business interruption coverage needed?

- A) Historical profit margins
- B) The cost of moving to a temporary location
- C) Projected revenue growth over the next fiscal year
- D) The physical size of the business premises

Casualty Insurance (Total: 34 Questions)

Auto insurance: 8 questions

51) What does Liability coverage in an auto insurance policy provide?

- A) Protection for the policyholder's vehicle from damage
- B) Coverage for injuries or damages the policyholder causes to others
- C) Coverage for theft of the vehicle
- D) Protection against damage from natural disasters

52) Under an auto insurance policy, what is 'Medical Payments' coverage designed to do?

- A) Pay for the medical expenses of the policyholder and passengers regardless of fault
- B) Cover the healthcare costs of pedestrians injured by the policyholder
- C) Reimburse the policyholder for lost wages due to injury
- D) Pay for long-term care and rehabilitation

53) What does Comprehensive coverage in an auto insurance policy typically include?

- A) Damage to the vehicle from a collision
- B) Liability for bodily injury
- C) Damage to the vehicle from non-collision incidents
- D) Legal fees in the event of a lawsuit

54) 'Collision' coverage in an auto insurance policy specifically covers:

- A) Damage to your vehicle when it hits, or is hit by, another vehicle or object
- B) Damage to another person's vehicle for which you are at fault
- C) Personal injury in the event of an accident
- D) Damage to the vehicle from vandalism or theft

55) What is the primary purpose of 'Uninsured Motorist' coverage?

- A) To cover repairs to your vehicle if damaged in a hit-and-run
- B) To protect against damage from drivers without sufficient insurance coverage
- C) To provide coverage in states with no-fault insurance laws
- D) To increase the liability coverage beyond standard limits

56) Which type of coverage would pay for damage to your car from a hail storm?

- · A) Collision
- · B) Comprehensive
- · C) Liability
- · D) Medical Payments

57) In auto insurance, 'Personal Injury Protection' (PIP) coverage is:

- · A) Mandatory in all states
- · B) Optional in no-fault states
- · C) Required only for commercial vehicles
- · D) Designed to cover medical expenses and lost wages, regardless of fault

58) What does the 'Property Damage Liability' portion of an auto insurance policy cover?

- · A) Damage to your own vehicle
- · B) Damage you cause to someone else's property with your vehicle
- · C) Personal property stolen from your vehicle
- · D) Damage to attached vehicle accessories

Workers compensation: 8 questions

59) What is the primary purpose of workers' compensation insurance?

- · A) To protect employers from personal injury lawsuits by employees
- · B) To provide benefits to employees for injuries or illnesses related to work
- · C) To cover the cost of legal representation for employees in labor disputes

- D) To insure the employer's property against damages caused by employees

60) Which of the following is typically covered under workers' compensation insurance?

- A) Injuries sustained while commuting to work
- B) Stress-related illnesses not specific to work
- C) Occupational diseases contracted as a result of work environment
- D) Injuries sustained during voluntary, off-duty social activities

61) What is the 'exclusive remedy' provision in workers' compensation law?

- A) Employees can only receive medical treatment from providers approved by the employer
- B) Workers' compensation benefits are the sole remedy for employees injured on the job, barring most lawsuits against employers
- C) Employers are exclusively responsible for determining the benefits an injured employee receives
- D) Only workers' compensation insurance can be used to cover workplace injuries, excluding health insurance

62) How are workers' compensation premiums typically calculated for an employer?

- A) Based on the overall profitability of the company
- B) According to the number of employees the company has
- C) Based on the company's past claims history and payroll amount
- D) Fixed rates set by the state regardless of the business type

63) What does 'Temporary Total Disability' (TTD) benefits in workers' compensation provide?

- A) A permanent settlement to workers who cannot return to their previous employment
- B) Compensation for the time an employee is completely unable to work on a temporary basis
- C) A lump-sum payment for minor injuries requiring short-term care
- D) Ongoing medical benefits without wage replacement

64) Under workers' compensation, the 'Waiting Period' refers to:

- A) The time an employee must wait before becoming eligible for insurance coverage
- B) The duration an injured worker must wait after an injury before benefits begin
- C) The amount of time an employer has to file a claim after an incident
- D) The probationary period before new employees can claim benefits

65) 'Permanent Partial Disability' (PPD) benefits are intended for employees who:

- A) Can return to work but with permanent restrictions due to their injury
- B) Are temporarily unable to work and are expected to recover fully
- C) Have fully recovered and can return to work without restrictions
- D) Are permanently unable to work in any capacity

66) Which of the following injuries would typically NOT be covered by workers' compensation?

- A) An injury sustained while using company equipment during work hours
- B) A car accident occurring while commuting from home to the workplace
- C) An illness developed due to exposure to toxic chemicals at work

- D) A back injury from lifting heavy objects as part of job duties

Liability insurance: 12 questions

67) What is the primary purpose of liability insurance?

- A) To cover damages to the insured's property
- B) To protect the insured against claims for bodily injury or property damage to others
- C) To provide life insurance coverage
- D) To insure against natural disasters

68) 'Bodily Injury Liability' coverage in an auto insurance policy covers:

- A) Medical expenses for injuries the policyholder sustains
- B) Injuries sustained by passengers in the policyholder's car
- C) Injuries the policyholder causes to someone else
- D) All medical expenses, regardless of fault

69) Which of the following is typically covered by a 'General Liability Insurance' policy?

- A) Employee theft from the business
- B) Damage to the insured business's own property
- C) Claims of false advertising
- D) Professional errors and omissions

70) 'Property Damage Liability' coverage is intended to:

- A) Repair or replace the policyholder's damaged property
- B) Cover damage policyholders cause to someone else's property
- C) Cover natural disaster damage
- D) Pay for personal property stolen from the insured's premises

71) What does 'Personal and Advertising Injury' coverage in a General Liability policy include?

- A) Injuries sustained during personal and advertising activities
- B) Damage to the insured's reputation due to slander or libel
- C) Physical injuries caused by advertising signs
- D) Injuries to actors during commercial shoots

72) The 'Medical Payments' coverage in a General Liability policy:

- A) Covers all medical expenses of the insured
- B) Pays for medical expenses of third parties injured on the insured's property, regardless of fault
- C) Is only applicable to employees of the insured
- D) Reimburses the medical expenses of the insured's family members only

73) What is a 'Combined Single Limit' (CSL) in liability insurance?

- A) A limit that combines property damage and bodily injury payments into one total available limit
- B) A policy that combines general liability and professional liability into a single policy
- C) The maximum amount payable for a single incident of property damage
- D) The total amount of coverage available for all claims during the policy period

74) An 'Umbrella Policy' in liability insurance:

- A) Provides coverage only for rain-related damage
- B) Extends the limits of underlying liability policies
- C) Covers only the excess amount not covered by primary policies

- D) Is a stand-alone policy with no underlying coverage requirements

75) 'Employers Liability Insurance' is part of which policy?

- A) Workers' Compensation
- B) Commercial Property
- C) Professional Liability
- D) Commercial Auto

76) Which of the following best describes 'Products Liability' insurance?

- A) It covers damage caused by products sold or manufactured by the insured
- B) It insures against injuries sustained by the use of a product
- C) It covers the theft of products from a business
- D) A and B

77) 'Cyber Liability Insurance' primarily covers:

- A) Physical damage to computers and hardware
- B) Liability for data breaches and loss of digital information
- C) The cost of recovering lost data
- D) Penalties for violating online copyright laws

78) In liability insurance, 'Duty to Defend' refers to:

- A) The insured's obligation to defend their property
- B) The insurer's obligation to provide legal defense for the insured against covered claims
- C) The court's duty to defend the rights of the injured party
- D) The police's responsibility to defend businesses

Umbrella policies: 6 questions

79) What is the primary purpose of an umbrella policy?

- · A) To provide additional health insurance benefits
- · B) To extend liability coverage beyond the limits of an underlying policy
- · C) To cover property damage that exceeds the limits of a homeowner's policy
- · D) To insure items not covered by standard insurance policies

80) An umbrella policy typically provides coverage for:

- · A) Personal liability only
- · B) Business liabilities
- · C) Both personal and business liabilities, depending on the policy
- · D) Property damage only

81) Which of the following is NOT typically covered by an umbrella policy?

- · A) Bodily injury liability
- · B) Property damage liability
- · C) Personal injury liability
- · D) Professional services liability

82) How does an umbrella policy work in conjunction with underlying policies?

- · A) It replaces the underlying policy when its limits are exhausted
- · B) It provides primary coverage, with the underlying policy covering excess claims
- · C) It only covers claims denied by the underlying policy
- · D) It provides additional coverage after the limits of the underlying policy are reached

83) What is typically required to purchase an umbrella policy?

- A) A minimum amount of liability coverage on underlying policies
- B) A specific net worth
- C) Ownership of a business
- D) A commercial driver's license

84) Which scenario would likely trigger coverage under an umbrella policy?

- A) A covered loss under a homeowner's policy that exceeds its liability limits
- B) A medical expense claim that exceeds health insurance limits
- C) A claim that is covered entirely by the auto insurance policy's limits
- D) A professional malpractice lawsuit

Package Policies (Total: 14 Questions)

Business Owners Policy (BOP): 7 questions

85) What is a Business Owners Policy (BOP)?

- A) A policy offering only liability protection for businesses
- B) A packaged policy combining property and liability insurance for small businesses
- C) A health insurance package for business owners and their employees
- D) Insurance covering only the vehicles used by a business

86) Which type of business is typically eligible for a BOP?

- A) Large manufacturing plants
- B) Small to medium–sized retail stores
- C) International corporations

- D) Financial institutions

87) What does the property insurance portion of a BOP cover?

- A) Damage to the business's vehicles
- B) Personal property of the business owner
- C) Damage to the business premises and its contents
- D) Damage to rented or leased equipment

88) BOP liability coverage protects a business against claims involving:

- A) Employee injuries at work
- B) Damage to business-owned vehicles
- C) Bodily injury or property damage caused to others
- D) Professional errors and omissions

89) Which of the following is NOT typically covered by a BOP?

- A) Business interruption losses
- B) Professional liability claims
- C) Property damage from a fire
- D) Customer injury on business premises

90) Business Interruption Insurance included in a BOP covers:

- A) The cost of relocating to a new business location permanently
- B) Losses resulting from the business having to temporarily close or relocate due to covered property damage
- C) Decreased business income due to market fluctuations
- D) Penalties for not delivering services on time due to an interruption

91) What additional coverage can often be added to a BOP?

- A) Auto liability insurance for personal vehicles
- B) Workers' compensation
- C) Data breach/ cyber liability insurance
- D) Health insurance for the business owner

Commercial package policy: 7 questions

92) What is a Commercial Package Policy (CPP)?

- A) A policy exclusively for industrial businesses
- B) A bundled insurance policy that combines various commercial coverages for businesses
- C) A policy that packages personal and commercial auto insurance
- D) An insurance policy for commercial property only

93) Which of the following coverages can typically be included in a CPP?

- A) Personal auto insurance
- B) Homeowners insurance
- C) Commercial property insurance
- D) Health insurance for employees

94) The primary advantage of a CPP over purchasing separate policies is:

- A) Lower deductibles for claims
- B) Coverage for personal assets
- C) The flexibility and potential cost savings from bundling coverages
- D) Automatic coverage for international incidents

95) Which statement is true regarding the customization of a CPP?

- A) CPPs are pre-determined by the insurer and cannot be customized
- B) Businesses can choose specific coverages to meet their unique needs

- C) All CPPs include workers' compensation by default
- D) Customization is limited to choosing the policy limits

96) 'Business Interruption' coverage in a CPP is designed to:

- A) Cover the cost of relocating a business after a disaster
- B) Compensate for lost income when business operations are disrupted due to a covered cause of loss
- C) Provide ongoing income to employees during periods of business closure
- D) Insure against interruptions in utility services

97) 'Commercial General Liability' (CGL) insurance within a CPP protects a business against claims of:

- A) Property damage caused by the company's operations
- B) Employee injuries on the job
- C) Damage to the business's own property
- D) Financial losses due to poor investment decisions

98) What does 'Commercial Property' insurance cover in a CPP?

- A) Damage to vehicles used for business purposes
- B) Personal property of the business owner
- C) Damage to the business premises and its contents due to covered perils
- D) Property owned by third parties

State-Specific Regulations (Total: 10 Questions)

Licensing requirements: 3 questions

99) What is the primary purpose of licensing requirements for property and casualty insurance agents?

- A) To increase revenue for the state
- B) To ensure agents have the necessary knowledge and skills to serve the public effectively
- C) To limit the number of agents in the market
- D) To standardize insurance policies across states

100) Which entity typically regulates the licensing of property and casualty insurance agents?

- A) The Federal Insurance Office (FIO)
- B) The National Association of Insurance Commissioners (NAIC)
- C) State insurance departments or commissions
- D) The Insurance Regulatory Authority (IRA)

101) Pre-licensing education for property and casualty insurance agents usually includes:

- A) Courses in finance and accounting only
- B) Training in sales techniques and customer service
- C) Education on state-specific insurance laws, policies, and ethics
- D) A mandatory internship with an insurance company

State laws governing insurance practices: 4 questions

102) What entity typically enforces state laws governing insurance practices?

- A) The Federal Insurance Office (FIO)

- B) The National Association of Insurance Commissioners (NAIC)
- C) State Insurance Departments or Commissions
- D) The U.S. Department of Insurance

103) Which of the following is a primary focus of state laws governing insurance practices?

- A) Setting federal insurance standards
- B) Regulating insurance rates and policy forms
- C) Overseeing international insurance treaties
- D) Directly managing insurance companies' daily operations

104) State laws governing insurance practices typically require insurers to:

- A) Obtain a federal license before operating
- B) Submit rates and forms for approval before use
- C) Share proprietary pricing algorithms with competitors
- D) Offer the same products nationwide

105) The purpose of 'solvency regulations' under state insurance laws is to:

- A) Ensure that insurance companies maintain sufficient reserves to cover future claims
- B) Standardize premiums across states
- C) Mandate uniform policy forms across all states
- D) Eliminate competition among insurers

Ethical practices and the regulatory environment: 3 questions

106) What is the primary purpose of ethical practices in the insurance industry?

- A) To ensure maximum profitability for insurance companies
- B) To protect the interests of shareholders
- C) To foster trust and fairness between insurers, agents, and policy-holders
- D) To simplify regulatory compliance

107) Which entity is primarily responsible for regulating the insurance industry and ensuring ethical practices?

- A) The Federal Trade Commission (FTC)
- B) State Insurance Departments or Commissions
- C) The National Association of Insurance Commissioners (NAIC)
- D) The Better Business Bureau (BBB)

108) Confidentiality in handling client information is a key ethical practice because it:

- A) Allows for targeted marketing strategies
- B) Protects the personal and financial information of policyholders
- C) Enables insurers to assess risks more accurately
- D) Helps in setting competitive premium rates

Insurance Operations (Total: 10 Questions)

Underwriting principles: 4 questions

109) What is the primary purpose of underwriting in the insurance industry?

- A) To maximize the insurer's profit by increasing premiums
- B) To determine the risk of insuring a potential client and set appropriate premiums
- C) To deny coverage to high-risk individuals and businesses
- D) To simplify the claims process

110) Which factor is NOT typically considered during the underwriting process for property and casualty insurance?

- A) The insured's past claim history
- B) The physical condition of the property to be insured
- C) The insured's credit score
- D) The insured's educational background

111) 'Risk Classification' in underwriting refers to:

- A) Categorizing applicants based on their level of education
- B) Grouping risks according to their potential impact on society
- C) The process of assigning potential insureds into groups based on perceived risk levels
- D) Classifying businesses by their industry type only

112) How does 'moral hazard' influence the underwriting process?

- A) It refers to the use of morals and ethics to guide underwriting decisions
- B) It is a factor that increases the likelihood of a loss due to the insured's behavior or character

- C) It involves evaluating the legal implications of insuring a risk
- D) It is disregarded as it has no impact on actual risk assessment

Rate making: 3 questions

113) What is the primary goal of rate making in insurance?

- A) To ensure that the insurance company makes a substantial profit
- B) To set premiums that are fair, adequate, and not unfairly discrimi-natory
- C) To minimize the payout for claims
- D) To maximize the number of policyholders

114) Which factor is NOT typically considered in the rate-making process for property and casualty insurance?

- A) The insured's age and gender
- B) The likelihood of a claim being made
- C) The potential cost of a claim
- D) The operational costs of the insurer

115) 'Experience rating' in the context of rate making refers to:

- A) The use of historical data from the insured's own experience to determine premiums
- B) The rating given to an insurance company based on customer reviews
- C) A method of rating based solely on the age of the insured
- D) Assessing the insurer's experience in the industry

Risk management: 3 questions

116) What is the primary goal of risk management in the context of property and casualty insurance?

- A) To generate the highest possible profit for insurance companies
- B) To eliminate all risks associated with property and casualty
- C) To identify and mitigate potential losses through various strategies
- D) To ensure that all claims are paid out in minimum time

117) Which of the following best describes 'risk avoidance' in risk management?

- A) Investing in security systems to deter theft
- B) Choosing not to engage in activities that carry risk of loss
- C) Transferring risk to another party through insurance
- D) Setting aside funds to cover potential losses

118) 'Risk transfer' is a strategy that typically involves:

- A) Moving potential risks to different areas of the business
- B) Physical relocation of high-risk assets
- C) Purchasing insurance to shift financial responsibility of losses to the insurer
- D) Distributing risks evenly across all departments within a company

Miscellaneous Coverages (Total: 6 Questions)

Flood insurance: 2 questions

119) What entity is primarily responsible for underwriting flood insurance policies in the United States?

- A) The National Association of Insurance Commissioners (NAIC)
- B) The National Flood Insurance Program (NFIP)
- C) State-run flood insurance pools
- D) Individual private insurance companies without federal involvement

120) Which of the following properties would typically be eligible for flood insurance under the NFIP?

- A) A beachfront vacation home
- B) A property located in a community that does not participate in the NFIP
- C) Commercial properties in a high-risk flood zone
- D) Only residential properties in low-risk flood zones

Earthquake insurance: 2 questions

121) What does earthquake insurance typically cover?

- A) Only structural damage to the building
- B) Structural damage and personal property inside the building, but not land movement
- C) Damage caused by floods resulting from an earthquake
- D) Only aftershocks occurring within 72 hours of the initial quake

122) Which of the following is a common feature of earthquake insurance policies?

- A) A low deductible to encourage prompt repairs
- B) Coverage for vehicles damaged during an earthquake
- C) High deductibles as a percentage of the property's replacement value
- D) Automatic coverage inclusion in all standard homeowners policies

Crime insurance policies: 2 questions

123) What is the primary purpose of crime insurance policies?

- A) To protect individuals from personal liability in the event of com-
mitting a crime
- B) To provide coverage for businesses against losses due to criminal
activities
- C) To cover legal fees associated with the prosecution of criminals
- D) To reimburse victims of crimes for their personal losses

**124) Which of the following is typically covered under a commercial crime
insurance policy?**

- A) Losses due to natural disasters
- B) Employee theft of company assets
- C) Accidental damage to property
- D) Personal injury claims from customers

Practice Exam 2 (Total: 120 Questions)

Insurance Basics (Total: 16 Questions)

Principles of insurance: 5 questions

1) What is proximate cause in insurance?

- · A) The closest insurance office
- · B) The first event in a chain of events leading to a loss
- · C) The most significant cause of a loss
- · D) The event directly leading to a loss without the intervention of any other event

2) Which principle allows insurers to divide their liability with other insurers?

- · A) Subrogation
- · B) Contribution
- · C) Indemnity
- · D) Proximate cause

3) What best defines the principle of contribution?

- · A) Policyholders must contribute to a pool of funds

- B) Insurers must contribute to losses according to their liability
- C) Losses are divided among all policyholders
- D) Insured must contribute to their losses by paying a deductible

4) How does the principle of indemnity affect the insurance payout?

- A) It ensures that policyholders receive a payout above the loss value
- B) It limits the payout to the actual value of the loss
- C) It increases the payout based on the policyholder's premiums
- D) It decreases the payout if the policyholder is found at fault

5) Which of the following best describes 'risk pooling'?

- A) Collecting sufficient premiums to cover the insurer's operational costs
- B) Combining various types of insurance into one policy
- C) Distributing losses among a large group of people
- D) Investing the premiums collected from policyholders

Types of insurers: 5 questions

6) Which of the following is known for its syndicates that insure unique and specialized risks?

- A) Mutual insurer
- B) Captive insurer
- C) Lloyd's of London
- D) Stock insurer

7) What type of insurer is typically formed under the laws of countries outside the United States to provide tax advantages and regulatory ease?

- A) Domestic insurer

- B) Foreign insurer
- C) Alien insurer
- D) Offshore insurer

8) Which of the following best describes a reinsurance company?

- A) Insures high-net-worth individuals exclusively
- B) Provides insurance to insurance companies
- C) Offers insurance directly to the public
- D) Operates only within the stock market

9) A fraternal benefit society primarily provides insurance to who?

- A) Its shareholders
- B) Members of a particular profession
- C) Members based on religious, social, or fraternal ties
- D) Employees of a specific company

10) What distinguishes a mutual insurance company from a stock insurance company?

- A) Mutual insurance companies are not allowed to issue life insurance policies.
- B) Stock insurance companies do not return profits to their policyholders.
- C) Mutual insurance companies exclusively operate in the United States.
- D) Stock insurance companies provide insurance without premiums.

Policy renewals and cancellations: 6 questions

11) Which of the following best defines a cancellation provision in an insurance policy?

- A) A clause that outlines the conditions under which a policy may be continued without changes
- B) A statement specifying the insurer's right to terminate the policy before its expiration date under certain conditions
- C) A guarantee that the policy will not be canceled by the insurer
- D) A promise from the insurer to automatically renew the policy

12) How does the 'notice of cancellation' benefit the insured?

- A) It allows the insured to cancel the policy without any penalties
- B) It provides the insured with a premium refund
- C) It gives the insured time to find alternative coverage before the policy is terminated
- D) It guarantees renewal of the policy under the same terms

13) What action can an insured take if they disagree with a cancellation decision?

- A) Accept the decision without recourse
- B) Seek arbitration to reverse the decision
- C) Immediately switch to another insurer without providing notice
- D) File a lawsuit for breach of contract

14) A policy that is set to expire without being renewed is subject to what?

- A) Automatic renewal
- B) Lapse
- C) Binding arbitration
- D) Reinstatement

15) Which of the following is true about a policy lapse?

- A) It occurs when the policy is canceled by the insurer

- B) It signifies the automatic renewal of the policy
- C) It happens when the policy is not renewed or the premium is not paid
- D) It is a term used to describe the transition period between old and new policies

16) When can an insurer legally cancel an auto insurance policy?

- A) At any time, without providing a reason
- B) Only after providing notice within a specified period as required by state law
- C) After the insured has filed more than three claims in a policy year
- D) If the insured decides to purchase a new vehicle

Property Insurance (Total: 30 Questions)

Dwelling policies: 7 questions

17) Personal Property coverage in a dwelling policy is:

- A) Included at 50% of the dwelling coverage limit by default
- B) Excluded entirely from dwelling policies
- C) Optional and requires additional premium
- D) Automatically included at 100% of the dwelling coverage limit

18) What does the 'Fair Rental Value' coverage in a dwelling policy provide?

- A) Compensation to landlords for upgrades to rental properties
- B) Reimbursement for lost rental income if a covered peril makes the rental portion of the dwelling uninhabitable
- C) Coverage for tenants' personal property
- D) Insurance for rental disputes with tenants

19) Which of the following is typically excluded from all dwelling policy forms?

- · A) Windstorm
- · B) Theft
- · C) Earth movement
- · D) Smoke

20) The 'automatic increase in insurance' endorsement in a dwelling policy is designed to:

- · A) Automatically increase the policy limits annually in line with inflation
- · B) Increase the premium automatically every year
- · C) Cover any new structures added to the property without notifying the insurer
- · D) Automatically extend coverage to neighboring properties

21) Under a dwelling policy, the coverage for 'Additional Living Expense' is:

- · A) Included as a standard part of all policy forms
- · B) Available only through a specific endorsement
- · C) Only included in DP-3 policy forms
- · D) Not available under dwelling policies

22) A DP-3 policy form is sometimes referred to as:

- · A) Basic Form
- · B) Broad Form
- · C) Special Form
- · D) Comprehensive Form

23) Which of the following would NOT be covered under the 'Personal Liability Supplement' in a dwelling policy?

- A) Bodily injury to a visitor caused by a fall on the insured property
- B) Property damage caused by the insured at a neighbor's house
- C) Damages due to intentional acts of violence by the insured
- D) Medical payments to others injured on the insured property

Homeowners policies: 9 questions

24) Which coverage in a homeowners policy would cover the insured in case of a lawsuit for accidentally injuring someone off their property?

- A) Medical Payments to Others
- B) Personal Property
- C) Dwelling
- D) Personal Liability

25 What does the 'Loss of Use' coverage in a homeowners policy provide?

- A) Compensation for damage to the home that decreases its value
- B) Reimbursement for living expenses if the home is uninhabitable due to a covered loss
- C) Coverage for lost income if a home-based business is interrupted
- D) Payment for loss of personal property use within the home

26) HO-3 homeowners policies provide broad coverage for the dwelling and personal property against:

- A) Named perils only
- B) All perils except those specifically excluded
- C) Open perils for the dwelling and named perils for personal property
- D) Open perils for both the dwelling and personal property

27) Which type of homeowners policy is often purchased for older homes where replacement costs far exceed the market value?

- A) HO-2
- B) HO-3
- C) HO-5
- D) HO-8

28) The 'Replacement Cost' coverage in a homeowners policy means the insurer will:

- A) Pay the actual cash value of a lost item
- B) Pay to repair or replace the damaged property without deduction for depreciation
- C) Only replace items with those of like kind and quality
- D) Reimburse based on the purchase price of the item

29) A homeowners policy with 'Actual Cash Value (ACV)' settlement will compensate losses based on:

- A) The replacement cost at the time of loss
- B) The item's purchase price
- C) The replacement cost minus depreciation
- D) A predetermined fixed amount

30) Which coverage component of a homeowners policy covers injuries to a guest in your home, regardless of fault?

- A) Dwelling
- B) Personal Liability
- C) Medical Payments to Others
- D) Personal Property

31) Water damage from a sewer backup is typically:

- A) Covered under standard homeowners policies
- B) Excluded from standard homeowners policies, but can be covered with an endorsement
- C) Covered only under flood insurance policies
- D) Always included without need for endorsement

32) 'Scheduled Personal Property Endorsement' on a homeowners policy is used to:

- A) Increase coverage limits on specific high-value items
- B) Schedule maintenance for personal property
- C) Cover personal property not usually included in a homeowners policy
- D) Exclude certain personal properties from coverage

Commercial property policies: 9 questions

33) In commercial property insurance, the 'Agreed Value' option means:

- A) The insurer and insured agree on the value of the property at policy inception, suspending the coinsurance clause
- B) The value of a claim is agreed upon after a loss occurs
- C) The policy automatically adjusts the property value annually
- D) The insured agrees to value the property based on its current market value

34) Which condition must be met for 'Replacement Cost' coverage to apply in a commercial property policy?

- A) The property must be insured for its actual cash value
- B) The damaged property must be repaired or replaced before payment is made

- C) The property must be insured for a minimum of 50% of its replacement cost
- D) The loss must exceed a certain percentage of the property's value

35) 'Inland Marine Insurance' under a commercial property policy is designed to cover:

- A) Marine vessels and their cargo
- B) Property in transit over land
- C) Property located near bodies of water
- D) Flood damage for properties located inland

36) What is a 'Bailee's Customer Policy' in commercial property insurance?

- A) A policy covering the personal property of the business's employees
- B) Insurance for customers that leave property in the care of the business
- C) Liability insurance for customer injuries on the business premises
- D) Property insurance for leased commercial buildings

37) 'Ordinance or Law Coverage' in a commercial property policy covers:

- A) Fines and penalties for law violations
- B) Increased costs due to enforcing building codes after a covered loss
- C) Legal fees for disputes over ordinances or laws
- D) Losses resulting from changes in market laws

38) The 'Spoilage Coverage' endorsement in a commercial property policy is intended to protect against loss of:

- A) Electronic data
- B) Perishable goods due to power outages or equipment breakdown

- C) Inventory not sold in a timely manner
- D) Business income due to supply chain disruptions

39) Which of the following best describes 'Vacancy Permit Coverage' in commercial property insurance?

- A) Allows for temporary vacancy of the property without loss of coverage
- B) Provides coverage for properties that are habitually vacant
- C) Covers the costs associated with obtaining a permit for occupancy
- D) Insures vacant properties against vandalism and theft

40) A 'Condominium Commercial Unit-Owners' Coverage Form' is designed specifically for:

- A) Owners of residential condominium units
- B) Commercial tenants leasing space in a condominium building
- C) Owners of commercial condominium units
- D) Condominium associations

41) What does the 'Leasehold Interest Coverage' protect in commercial property insurance?

- A) The interest rates on property leases
- B) The value of the lease in case the leased premises become unusable due to a covered loss
- C) Damage to property caused by tenants
- D) Losses incurred from leasing equipment for business use

Business interruption: 5 questions

42) How is the indemnity period in a business interruption policy defined?

- A) The maximum time that the insurer will make payments for a covered loss
- B) The deductible period before coverage begins
- C) The time it takes to process and pay a claim
- D) The duration of the insurance policy term

43) What is typically excluded from business interruption insurance coverage?

- A) Losses due to a fire on the premises
- B) Income lost due to a mandatory evacuation
- C) Losses resulting from broken machinery
- D) Losses from pandemics or infectious diseases, unless specifically included

44) 'Contingent Business Interruption' insurance covers losses resulting from:

- A) Damage to the insured's own premises
- B) Damage to a supplier's or customer's premises that directly affects the insured's business
- C) General economic downturns
- D) Strikes and labor disputes affecting the industry

45) The 'extended period of indemnity' option in a business interruption policy:

- A) Extends coverage indefinitely until the business recovers
- B) Provides coverage only for the first 30 days after reopening

- C) Extends coverage beyond the period of restoration for a specified duration
- D) Automatically increases the limit of insurance during high-risk periods

46) Which of the following best describes 'gross earnings' under a business interruption policy?

- A) Total revenue from sales before any deductions
- B) Net income after taxes and other deductions
- C) Revenue minus the cost of goods sold
- D) The sum of net profit and fixed costs

Casualty Insurance (Total: 35 Questions)

Auto insurance: 9 questions

47) How does 'Actual Cash Value' (ACV) affect a claim under an auto insurance policy?

- A) It ensures replacement of the vehicle with a new one of similar make and model
- B) It represents the amount needed to repair the vehicle
- C) It is the insurer's valuation of the vehicle at the time of the loss, considering depreciation
- D) It guarantees the policyholder receives the purchase price of the vehicle

48) What is typically NOT covered under a standard auto liability insurance policy?

- A) Bodily injury to others
- B) Property damage to others

- C) Damage to the policyholder's own vehicle
- D) Legal defense costs

49) 'Gap Insurance' in auto policies is designed to:

- A) Cover the gap between medical expenses and PIP limits
- B) Pay the difference between the vehicle's ACV and what is still owed on the loan or lease
- C) Provide temporary insurance coverage when switching policies
- D) Extend coverage to rental vehicles

50) Which scenario would likely be covered under 'Comprehensive' but not 'Collision' coverage?

- A) Your car is damaged in a parking lot hit-and-run
- B) You accidentally back into a light pole
- C) A tree falls on your car during a storm
- D) You collide with another vehicle at an intersection

51) 'Deductibles' in auto insurance policies are:

- A) The maximum amount paid out for a claim
- B) A fixed amount the policyholder must pay before insurance coverage begins
- C) The percentage of the claim that the policyholder is responsible for
- D) Paid by the insurance company to the policyholder after a claim

52) Which of the following would typically be excluded from coverage under an auto insurance policy?

- A) Mechanical breakdown
- B) Theft of the vehicle
- C) Damage from a collision with another vehicle

- D) Damage from a fallen tree branch

53) 'Rental Reimbursement' coverage in auto insurance policies:

- A) Covers the cost of renting a car while your vehicle is being repaired for any reason
- B) Is automatically included in all comprehensive policies
- C) Covers the cost of renting a car if your vehicle is stolen
- D) Only applies when renting a car for vacation

54) What determines the premium for an auto insurance policy?

- A) The make and model of the vehicle only
- B) The policyholder's driving history, age, type of vehicle, and coverage selected
- C) The color of the vehicle
- D) The policyholder's credit score only

55) 'Underinsured Motorist' coverage is intended to:

- A) Cover the gap between your liability coverage and the actual cost of damages
- B) Provide protection when the at-fault driver's insurance is insuffi-cient
- C) Substitute for collision coverage
- D) Increase your liability limits for bodily injury

Workers compensation: 9 questions

56) The 'Second Injury Fund' under workers' compensation is designed to:

- A) Compensate workers for a second injury unrelated to work

- B) Encourage the hiring of previously injured workers by limiting employer liability for subsequent injuries
- C) Provide additional benefits for injuries that occur outside of the workplace
- D) Cover the costs of injuries that are not reported in a timely manner

57) 'Experience Modification Rate' (EMR) affects an employer's workers' compensation premium by:

- A) Decreasing premiums for businesses with more employees
- B) Adjusting rates based on the company's claim history relative to others in the industry
- C) Offering discounts for employers who provide safety training
- D) Increasing premiums for new businesses with no claims history

58) In workers' compensation, 'Vocational Rehabilitation' benefits are provided to:

- A) Compensate employers for training costs of injured workers
- B) Help injured workers return to their previous job with modifications
- C) Assist employees in finding new employment if they cannot return to their previous job due to injury
- D) Support employees with part-time work during their recovery

59) Which statement about workers' compensation insurance is FALSE?

- A) It provides coverage for intentional injuries inflicted by the employer
- B) It includes medical care for work-related injuries and illnesses
- C) It compensates for lost wages while an employee is unable to work
- D) It may offer death benefits to dependents of workers who die from job-related causes

60) 'Death Benefits' in a workers' compensation policy are designed to:

- A) Compensate the deceased worker's family for future earnings lost
- B) Cover the funeral and burial expenses of the deceased worker
- C) Provide a lump-sum payment to the employer
- D) A and B

61) Which type of workers' compensation benefit is designed to cover medical and rehabilitation costs?

- A) Disability benefits
- B) Medical benefits
- C) Death benefits
- D) Supplemental benefits

62) The principle of 'no-fault' in workers' compensation means:

- A) Employees are not covered if they are at fault for their injury
- B) Employers cannot be sued for work-related injuries as long as they provide benefits
- C) Benefits are paid regardless of who is at fault for the injury
- D) Fault is determined by a special workers' compensation court

63) 'Employers Liability Insurance', often part of workers' compensation policies, covers:

- A) Injuries to customers and visitors at the workplace
- B) Damage to the employer's property
- C) The employer against lawsuits for work-related injuries not covered under workers' compensation
- D) The legal costs of defending against false claims of injury

64) What is the role of a 'Workers' Compensation Board' or 'Commission'?

- A) To negotiate insurance premiums with providers
- B) To oversee the investment of the workers' compensation funds
- C) To adjudicate disputes over benefits and eligibility
- D) To directly provide medical care to injured workers

Liability insurance: 11 questions

65) What is 'Directors and Officers (D&O)' liability insurance designed to protect?

- A) The personal assets of corporate directors and officers in the event of legal action against them for corporate activities
- B) The corporation's assets from mismanagement
- C) Employees from the actions of directors and officers
- D) Shareholders from losses due to decisions made by directors and officers

66) 'Professional Liability Insurance' is also known as:

- A) General Liability Insurance
- B) Errors and Omissions Insurance
- C) Product Liability Insurance
- D) Employment Practices Liability Insurance

67) Which scenario would NOT typically be covered under a standard Commercial General Liability (CGL) policy?

- A) A customer slips and falls in a store
- B) An employee's personal property is stolen from their office
- C) A defective product causes injury to a user
- D) Damage to a client's property while in the insured's care

68) 'Host Liquor Liability' insurance is designed to cover:

- A) Bars and restaurants that sell alcohol
- B) Individuals hosting parties where alcohol is served
- C) Liquor stores for theft and damage
- D) Manufacturers of alcoholic beverages

69) The 'Pollution Exclusion' in a liability insurance policy:

- A) Covers all pollution-related incidents
- B) Excludes coverage for pollution, unless coverage is specifically added by endorsement
- C) Provides limited coverage for sudden and accidental pollution incidents
- D) Is mandatory for all businesses that handle hazardous materials

70) Which type of liability insurance would cover a business against claims of discrimination or wrongful termination?

- A) Commercial Property Insurance
- B) Workers' Compensation Insurance
- C) Employment Practices Liability Insurance (EPLI)
- D) Directors and Officers (D&O) Liability Insurance

71) 'Completed Operations Coverage' in a CGL policy is intended to:

- A) Cover operations that are in progress
- B) Insure the business against liabilities arising from completed work or services
- C) Provide coverage for operations completed by subcontractors
- D) Cover the cost of completing operations that were interrupted

72) 'Liquor Liability Insurance' is most important for businesses that:

- A) Manufacture alcoholic beverages

- B) Serve or sell alcohol
- C) Host occasional company parties where alcohol is served
- D) Are involved in the transportation of alcohol

73) What distinguishes 'Claims-Made' from 'Occurrence' policies in liability insurance?

- A) The geographical area covered
- B) The type of claims covered
- C) The time period in which a claim must be made or occur for coverage to apply
- D) The limit of insurance provided

74) 'Non-Owned Auto Liability Insurance' is particularly important for businesses that:

- A) Own a fleet of vehicles
- B) Do not own vehicles but have employees who use their personal vehicles for business purposes
- C) Lease all their business vehicles
- D) Operate in the transportation industry

75) 'Tenant's Legal Liability' coverage is designed to protect against claims arising from:

- A) Damage to rented premises caused by the tenant's negligence
- B) Injuries sustained by the tenant within the rented premises
- C) Damage to the tenant's personal property
- D) Legal fees associated with disputes between the tenant and landlord

Umbrella policies: 6 questions

76) 'Personal Injury' coverage in an umbrella policy includes protection against:

- A) Physical injuries to the policyholder
- B) Claims of slander, libel, and invasion of privacy
- C) Injuries sustained in a car accident
- D) Personal injuries of employees

77) Umbrella policies typically include coverage for:

- A) Expected or intentional injury caused by the insured
- B) Business operations and professional services
- C) Certain legal defense costs outside the limits of the policy
- D) Damage to the insured's personal property

78) Which of the following best describes the coverage provided by an umbrella policy?

- A) Specific, named perils only
- B) All risks, with no exclusions
- C) Broad coverage for various liabilities not specifically excluded
- D) Coverage identical to that of underlying policies

79) An umbrella policy may provide coverage for claims that are:

- A) Not covered by any underlying policies due to exclusions
- B) Fully covered by the limits of the underlying policies
- C) Less than the deductible of the underlying policy
- D) Covered by health insurance

80) The limits of an umbrella policy typically:

- A) Match the limits of the underlying policies
- B) Are lower than the limits of the underlying policies
- C) Are higher than the limits of the underlying policies
- D) Do not have defined limits

81) What factor is NOT typically used to determine the premium of an umbrella policy?

- A) The limits of the umbrella policy
- B) The insured's credit score
- C) The coverage limits of the underlying policies
- D) The number and type of vehicles owned by the insured

Package Policies (Total: 15 Questions)

Business Owners Policy (BOP): 8 questions

82) The liability insurance included in a BOP typically covers:

- A) Penalties for breach of contract
- B) Lawsuits related to employment practices
- C) Third-party claims of bodily injury and property damage
- D) Pollution liability

83) A BOP may exclude coverage for:

- A) Fire damage to the business premises
- B) Flood or earthquake damage
- C) Theft of business personal property
- D) Customer injuries due to a fall at the business

84) Which feature is a common benefit of purchasing a BOP?

- A) Simplified policy management with combined coverage
- B) Unlimited coverage limits
- C) Coverage for international transactions
- D) Automatic coverage for all types of liability

85) How does 'Coinsurance' work within the context of a BOP?

- A) It divides the liability equally between the business and the insurer
- B) It requires the business to insure the property to a specified percentage of its value
- C) It allows businesses to coinvest in the insurance company
- D) It covers the coinsurance deductibles of health policies for employees

86) The 'Named Perils' coverage in a BOP specifies that:

- A) Only perils named in the policy are covered
- B) All perils are covered except those specifically excluded
- C) Coverage applies to all names listed on the policy
- D) Perils are named after the policyholder

87) What type of business property is typically excluded from a BOP?

- A) Buildings owned by the business
- B) Business interruption expenses
- C) Outdoor signs not attached to the building
- D) Inventory stored within insured buildings

88) In a BOP, the 'Deductible' refers to:

- A) The amount deducted from the policy limit for each covered peril
- B) The percentage of the claim that the business must pay out of pocket
- C) The amount the business pays before the insurance coverage begins
- D) A reduction in premiums for high-value policies

89) 'Business Income Insurance' within a BOP is designed to:

- A) Compensate the business owner for personal income lost due to business interruption
- B) Cover ongoing expenses and lost income during temporary closure due to a covered loss
- C) Insure against income lost due to employee theft
- D) Replace lost income due to fluctuations in the market

Commercial package policy: 7 questions

90) In a CPP, 'Crime Coverage' protects against losses from:

- A) Customer theft
- B) Employee dishonesty and theft
- C) Cybercrime only
- D) Vandalism caused by the public

91) Which coverage is NOT typically available in a CPP?

- A) Equipment breakdown
- B) Professional liability
- C) Personal life insurance for the business owner
- D) Commercial auto

92) 'Equipment Breakdown' coverage in a CPP would cover:

- A) The cost of renting temporary equipment while repairs are made
- B) Losses from business interruption due to equipment breakdown
- C) Only mechanical breakdowns, not electrical issues
- D) A and B

93) The 'Declarations Page' of a CPP includes all of the following EXCEPT:

- A) The insured's name and address
- B) A list of the covered perils
- C) The policy period
- D) The personal credit score of the business owner

94) How does 'Inland Marine' insurance within a CPP differ from 'Commercial Property' insurance?

- A) It covers goods in transit over land, as well as certain moveable property
- B) It only covers marine-related businesses
- C) It is specifically for international shipping
- D) It covers stationary property only

95) A CPP 'Conditions' section would typically outline:

- A) The premium payment schedule
- B) The responsibilities of the insured and insurer in the event of a loss
- C) Detailed descriptions of covered property
- D) Specific exclusions from coverage

96) Which type of business would MOST benefit from including 'Liquor Liability' in their CPP?

- A) A bookstore
- B) A manufacturing plant
- C) A restaurant that serves alcohol
- D) An IT consulting firm

State-Specific Regulations (Total: 12 Questions)

Licensing requirements: 4 questions

97) The property and casualty insurance license exam typically tests on:

- A) Personal financial planning
- B) Insurance laws, principles, coverages, and state-specific regulations
- C) Advanced mathematics and statistics
- D) Medical knowledge for assessing injuries

98) Continuing education for licensed property and casualty insurance agents is required to:

- A) Ensure agents remain competitive in the job market
- B) Fulfill yearly sales quotas set by insurance companies
- C) Keep agents up-to-date with changes in laws and industry practices
- D) Increase the agents' salaries over time

99) Which of the following might disqualify someone from obtaining a property and casualty insurance license?

- A) Lack of a college degree
- B) A history of bankruptcy
- C) Past criminal convictions, particularly involving fraud or dishonesty
- D) Previous employment outside the insurance industry

100) The process of obtaining a property and casualty insurance license generally includes:

- A) Passing a physical fitness test
- B) Completion of a specified number of college credits
- C) Passing a written examination and a background check
- D) A recommendation from a current licensed agent

State laws governing insurance practices: 5 questions

101) State laws governing insurance practices often include provisions for:

- A) The direct appointment of insurance commissioners by the NAIC
- B) Consumer protection and the handling of claims and complaints
- C) Federal oversight of insurance marketing practices
- D) The nationalization of insurance companies

102) Which is an example of a state-specific regulation that may affect insurance practices?

- A) A requirement for all policies to be written in English only
- B) Mandates for minimum levels of property and casualty insurance coverage
- C) A ban on all forms of digital insurance policies
- D) Uniform pricing for all insurance products within the state

103) How do state laws typically regulate the use of credit information in underwriting insurance policies?

- A) By prohibiting the use of credit information altogether
- B) Allowing unrestricted use of credit information by insurers
- C) Setting guidelines on how credit information can be used and ensuring consumer rights are protected
- D) Requiring federal approval for any use of credit information

104) State regulations regarding insurance rebates and inducements generally:

- A) Encourage insurers to offer rebates as a marketing tool
- B) Prohibit the offering of rebates and inducements to avoid unfair

discrimination
- C) Mandate that all insurers provide rebates to policyholders annually
- D) Allow unlimited inducements to attract new customers

105) What role do state laws play in regulating insurance agent licensing and conduct?

- A) Defining ethical standards and educational requirements for licen-sure
- B) Delegating the responsibility of licensing to the federal government
- C) Allowing insurers to set their own standards for agents
- D) Eliminating the need for licenses in the digital age

Ethical practices and the regulatory environment: 3 questions

106) An insurance agent recommending coverage options that are not in the best interest of the client, but generate higher commissions, is an example of:

- A) A common industry practice
- B) An ethical dilemma
- C) A conflict of interest
- D) Compliant behavior under state regulations

107) In the context of ethical practices, 'fiduciary responsibility' refers to:

- A) The obligation to manage company funds wisely
- B) The duty to act in the best interest of the client
- C) The responsibility to maximize shareholder value
- D) The task of following only those laws that directly benefit the company

108) Which of the following actions is considered unethical in the insurance industry?

- · A) Using confidential client information for personal gain
- · B) Comparing different insurance products to find the best fit for a client
- · C) Reporting suspected insurance fraud to the authorities
- · D) Following all state regulations regarding licensing and continuing education

Insurance Operations (Total: 9 Questions)

Underwriting principles: 3 questions

109) In underwriting, the term 'adverse selection' refers to:

- · A) Selecting only those risks that are most likely to result in a loss
- · B) The tendency of higher-risk individuals to seek or maintain insurance coverage more often than lower-risk individuals
- · C) The process of deselecting or rejecting high-risk applications
- · D) Choosing adverse or unfavorable terms for the insurance contract

110) 'Exposure' in the context of underwriting principles means:

- · A) The insured's tendency to expose themselves to risky situations
- · B) The potential frequency and severity of loss associated with a particular risk
- · C) The amount of information the insured exposes to the insurer
- · D) The level of public awareness about a particular type of insurance

111) Which is an example of a 'physical hazard' in property insurance underwriting?

- A) A wood-burning stove in a home
- B) The insured's previous claims for water damage
- C) A homeowner's poor credit score
- D) The neighborhood's high crime rate

Rate making: 3 questions

112) How does 'loss frequency' impact rate making for property and casualty insurance?

- A) Policies with higher loss frequency typically have lower premiums
- B) Loss frequency is unrelated to premium calculations
- C) Higher loss frequency can lead to higher premiums for the insured
- D) Only the size of the loss, not the frequency, affects premiums

113) 'Class rating' is a rate-making technique that:

- A) Applies a single rate to all policyholders regardless of risk
- B) Groups policyholders with similar risk characteristics and assigns rates based on the group's overall loss experience
- C) Is used exclusively for rating commercial properties
- D) Assigns unique rates to each policyholder based on personal interviews

114) In rate making, 'catastrophe modeling' is used to:

- A) Predict the impact of catastrophic events on policy renewals
- B) Estimate the potential losses from catastrophic events for setting premiums
- C) Model the financial impact of a catastrophe on the insurance company's profits
- D) Determine the geographic locations where catastrophes are most likely to occur

Risk management: 3 questions

115) In risk management, 'risk retention' refers to:

- A) Avoiding any form of insurance
- B) Accepting the financial consequences of risk internally
- C) Retaining a risk management consultant for advice
- D) Keeping detailed records of all identified risks without action

116) What role does 'risk assessment' play in the risk management process?

- A) It determines the premium rates for insurance policies
- B) It identifies and evaluates potential risks to prioritize management efforts
- C) It assesses the financial health of the insurance company
- D) It solely focuses on assessing risks associated with natural disasters

117) Which of the following is NOT a common risk management technique?

- A) Risk pooling
- B) Risk speculation
- C) Risk reduction
- D) Risk diversification

Miscellaneous Coverages (Total: 3 Questions)

Flood insurance: 1 question

118) What does the flood insurance policy cover in terms of property damage?

- A) Only the building's structure and not its contents
- B) Both the building's structure and its contents, though contents coverage is optional
- C) Losses due to moisture or mildew that could have been avoided by the homeowner
- D) Damage caused by wind-driven rain entering through a window left open during a storm

Earthquake insurance: 1 question

119) Why might homeowners in low-risk areas still consider purchasing earthquake insurance?

- A) Earthquakes are unpredictable and can cause significant damage even in areas not known for seismic activity
- B) It is a mandatory requirement for mortgage approval in all states
- C) Premiums are significantly lower in low-risk areas, making it a cost-effective precaution
- D) Federal disaster assistance is only available to homeowners with earthquake insurance

Crime insurance policies: 1 question

120) 'Fidelity Bonds' provided as part of crime insurance policies protect against losses from:

- A) Employee dishonesty and fraudulent acts
- B) Stock market fluctuations affecting company assets
- C) Customers stealing merchandise from a business
- D) Cyber-attacks on company financial records

Practice Exam 3 (Total: 120 Questions)

Insurance Basics (Total: 20 Questions)

Principles of insurance: 7 questions

1) Utmost good faith is a mutual obligation requiring which of the following from the insured?

- A) Disclosure of all relevant facts
- B) Payment of all premiums on time
- C) Avoidance of risky behaviors
- D) Regular updates on the insured property's condition

2) What role does the principle of subrogation play in preventing?

- A) Over-insurance
- B) The insured from profiting from the insurance
- C) Fraudulent claims
- D) Double recovery from the same loss

3) The principle of insurable interest is designed to ensure what?

- A) The insured can only insure property or lives that would cause a financial loss if damaged or lost

- B) The insured has a legal relationship with the insurer
- C) The insured pays a premium that accurately reflects the risk
- D) The insured is interested in maintaining the safety of the insured property

4) In the context of insurance, what is 'proximate cause'?

- A) A cause that is legally recognized as the primary reason for the loss
- B) The last cause in a series of events leading to a loss
- C) A cause that has no direct impact on the outcome
- D) The initial incident that sets off a chain reaction leading to a loss

5) Which principle justifies an insurer's pursuit of a third party after a claim has been paid?

- A) Contribution
- B) Indemnity
- C) Subrogation
- D) Insurable interest

6) What is required for an insurance contract to adhere to the principle of utmost good faith?

- A) An application filled out under oath
- B) A physical examination
- C) Full disclosure of material facts by both parties
- D) A background check on the insured

7) How does the principle of indemnity prevent the insured from profiting from a loss?

- A) By requiring a co-pay for all claims
- B) By limiting reimbursement to the loss's actual cash value

- C) By increasing premiums after any claim
- D) By covering only a percentage of the loss

Types of insurers: 6 questions

8) Government insurers are established to provide which of the following?

- A) Insurance for high-risk individuals only
- B) Coverage not typically available from private insurers
- C) Investment opportunities in the stock market
- D) Tax benefits for high-income policyholders

9) Which type of insurer is best known for underwriting through a pool of underwriters who share in profits and losses?

- A) Mutual insurer
- B) Stock insurer
- C) Lloyd's of London
- D) Captive insurer

10) In terms of regulation, how do state insurance departments primarily interact with insurers?

- A) By directly managing the insurers' day-to-day operations
- B) By setting standards for policy forms and rates
- C) By participating in profit sharing
- D) By limiting the types of insurance products they can offer

11) Which type of insurer is directly owned and controlled by its policy-holders, with no external shareholders?

- A) Stock insurer
- B) Mutual insurer

- C) Captive insurer
- D) Lloyd's of London

12) Risk retention groups are formed by whom?

- A) Policyholders in the same industry to insure against common risks
- B) Investors looking for insurance-related investment opportunities
- C) Insurance agents seeking to offer exclusive products
- D) Governments to provide insurance for public sector employees

13) An insurer formed under the laws of the state in which the insurance is sold is called a/an:

- A) Alien insurer
- B) Foreign insurer
- C) Domestic insurer
- D) Offshore insurer

Policy renewals and cancellations: 7 questions

14) What is the effect of a policy reinstatement on a lapse?

- A) It increases the premium automatically
- B) It confirms the policy was never lapsed
- C) It makes the lapse permanent
- D) It nullifies the lapse and reinstates coverage as if the lapse never occurred

15) What typically accompanies a policy cancellation notice from an insurer?

- A) A recommendation for a new insurer
- B) An explanation for the cancellation

- C) A waiver of all future premiums
- D) A notice of premium increase

16) Which statement is true regarding non-renewal notices?

- A) They must be given at least 30 days before the policy end date, although the exact time frame can vary by state
- B) They are not required to be in writing
- C) They can be issued the day before the policy expires
- D) They are optional and at the discretion of the insurer

17) What is usually required for a policy to be reinstated after cancellation?

- A) A new application for insurance must be submitted and approved
- B) The insured must agree to a higher premium
- C) Proof that the risk has decreased significantly
- D) Payment of overdue premiums and possibly a reinstatement fee

18) For which reason can an insurance policy NOT be canceled?

- A) Non-payment of premium
- B) Material misrepresentation on the application
- C) Filing a claim under the policy
- D) A significant increase in the risk insured

19) What does a 'flat cancellation' refer to?

- A) Canceling the policy as of its effective date, resulting in no coverage and a full refund of the premium
- B) Canceling the policy mid-term with no refund of the premium
- C) Increasing the premium rate during the policy term
- D) Reducing coverage amounts without changing the premium

20) Under what condition might a policy be eligible for reinstatement after cancellation due to non-payment of premium?

- · A) The insured provides evidence of insurability
- · B) The insured pays the overdue premium within a grace period
- · C) The insurer fails to provide a written notice of cancellation
- · D) The insured agrees to a shortened coverage term

Property Insurance (Total: 28 Questions)

Dwelling policies: 6 questions

21) The 'Dwelling Under Construction' endorsement in a dwelling policy:

- · A) Provides coverage for tools and building materials on-site
- · B) Is mandatory for all new constructions
- · C) Adjusts the dwelling coverage amount based on the stages of construction
- · D) Excludes coverage for vandalism and malicious mischief

22) How does a 'Broad Theft Coverage' endorsement affect a dwelling policy?

- · A) Extends theft coverage to off-premises locations
- · B) Increases the policy limit for theft claims without additional premium
- · C) Provides theft coverage, which is not included in basic form (DP-1) policies
- · D) Covers theft of building materials before they are installed

23) What is the purpose of the 'Ordinance or Law' coverage endorsement in a dwelling policy?

- A) To cover the cost of legal assistance in case of lawsuits
- B) To pay for increased costs due to the enforcement of building codes during repairs
- C) To insure the property against fines and penalties for code violations
- D) To provide liability coverage when the insured is accused of breaking a law

24) In dwelling policies, 'Named Peril' coverage means:

- A) The policy only covers perils specifically named in the policy documents
- B) The policyholder must name the perils they want to be covered at the time of purchase
- C) All perils are covered except those explicitly named as exclusions
- D) The name of the peril must be disclosed at the time of claim

25) Which type of property would typically NOT be eligible for coverage under a standard dwelling policy?

- A) A single-family home
- B) A duplex where the owner occupies one unit
- C) A seasonal vacation home
- D) A large apartment complex

26) The 'Vandalism and Malicious Mischief' coverage in a dwelling policy:

- A) Is only available as an endorsement to DP-3 policies
- B) Covers acts of vandalism unless the dwelling has been vacant for more than 60 consecutive days
- C) Is automatically included in all dwelling policy forms without exception
- D) Provides unlimited coverage for damage caused by vandalism

Homeowners policies: 8 questions

27) An 'inflation guard' endorsement in a homeowners policy is designed to:

- · A) Protect the insurer against inflation
- · B) Automatically adjust the coverage limit based on inflation rates
- · C) Reduce the premium in times of high inflation
- · D) Increase the deductible during inflationary periods

28) The difference between 'Replacement Cost' and 'Actual Cash Value' in a homeowners policy primarily lies in:

- · A) The amount of deductible applied
- · B) The inclusion of depreciation in the settlement
- · C) The limit of insurance provided
- · D) The type of property covered

29) Which homeowners coverage form is exclusively for tenants or renters?

- · A) HO-2
- · B) HO-3
- · C) HO-4
- · D) HO-6

30) A 'Guaranteed Replacement Cost' endorsement in a homeowners policy means the insurer will:

- · A) Pay up to the coverage limit regardless of the cost to replace the home
- · B) Pay whatever it costs to rebuild the home as it was before the loss, even if it exceeds the policy limit

- C) Guarantee the replacement of lost personal property without depreciation
- D) Only replace the structure with materials of lesser quality to save on costs

31) Personal Property coverage in a homeowners policy typically covers:

- A) Only items within the home
- B) Items owned or used by the insured anywhere in the world
- C) Only items specifically listed and described in the policy
- D) Only high-value items like jewelry and art

32) Which of the following perils is generally covered by a standard homeowners policy?

- A) Earthquake
- B) Flood
- C) Volcanic eruption
- D) Termite damage

33) The 'Duty to Defend' under the Personal Liability portion of a homeowners policy obligates the insurer to:

- A) Pay for damages if the insured is found liable
- B) Defend the insured in court against claims covered by the policy, regardless of the outcome
- C) Only pay for legal defense if the insured is found not guilty
- D) Assist the insured in finding legal representation

34) 'Other Structures' coverage on a homeowners policy typically includes all of the following EXCEPT:

- A) A detached garage

- B) A tool shed
- C) A swimming pool
- D) The main dwelling

Commercial property policies: 8 questions

35) 'Equipment Breakdown Coverage' in a commercial property policy typically includes all EXCEPT:

- A) Mechanical breakdown
- B) Electrical arcing
- C) Wear and tear from normal use
- D) Explosion of steam boilers

36) The 'Businessowners Policy (BOP)' combines which types of coverage?

- A) Property and commercial auto insurance
- B) Liability and workers' compensation
- C) Property and general liability insurance
- D) Commercial auto and liability insurance

37) How does the 'Actual Cash Value (ACV)' settlement option affect a commercial property claim?

- A) It provides new for old replacement without deducting for depreciation
- B) It settles claims based on the replacement cost minus depreciation
- C) It increases the claim payment by accounting for inflation
- D) It covers the full cost of repair regardless of the property's age

38) A 'Commercial Package Policy (CPP)' allows businesses to:

- A) Package multiple types of commercial policies for a discount
- B) Choose only property coverage without liability
- C) Insure commercial vehicles only
- D) Combine personal and commercial insurance needs

39) Which of the following is a characteristic of 'Blanket Insurance' in commercial property policies?

- A) It covers only specific, named perils
- B) It provides a single limit of insurance for multiple properties or types of property
- C) It applies only to blanket liability coverage
- D) It is automatically included in all commercial property policies

40) 'Accounts Receivable Coverage' under a commercial property policy is designed to cover:

- A) The cost to collect unpaid accounts receivable
- B) Losses if business records are destroyed and uncollectible receivables cannot be proven
- C) Interest lost on late payments from customers
- D) Legal fees associated with recovering payments

41) The 'Signs Coverage' endorsement in a commercial property policy specifically insures:

- A) Interior signs that are not attached to the building
- B) Electronic data signs and billboards
- C) Outdoor signs attached to the building
- D) Both A and C

42) 'Utility Services - Direct Damage' coverage in a commercial property policy covers damage resulting from:

- A) Failure of communication services
- B) Interruption of power supply leading to direct physical loss or damage
- C) Billing errors by utility providers
- D) Legal disputes with utility providers

Business interruption: 6 questions

43) Business interruption insurance generally calculates lost income based on:

- A) Future projected profits
- B) Past financial records and trends
- C) The average income of similar businesses in the area
- D) A fixed daily rate determined at the inception of the policy

44) 'Service Interruption' coverage in business interruption insurance protects against losses resulting from:

- A) Disruption of manufacturing processes
- B) Failure of public utilities such as electricity, gas, water, or telecommunications
- C) Interruptions in internet service
- D) Temporary cessation of a service provided by the business

45) In business interruption insurance, 'ordinary payroll' refers to:

- A) Salaries of all employees, regardless of their role
- B) Wages that the policyholder opts to continue paying to employees during the interruption
- C) Only the payroll of the top management and executives
- D) Wages covered by workers' compensation insurance

46) 'Civil Authority' coverage under a business interruption policy applies when access to the insured premises is prevented by:

- A) A general curfew imposed by the government
- B) An official act of a civil authority due to direct physical loss or damage at a nearby location
- C) Road construction or maintenance work by the city
- D) A strike or public demonstration

47) Which statement is true regarding the calculation of a business interruption loss?

- A) Only direct losses are covered, not indirect or consequential losses
- B) The insurer will consider the business's total income without deductions
- C) The calculation is based on the net income that would have been earned if the loss had not occurred
- D) A flat rate is applied based on the industry average

48) The purpose of 'sue and labor' clause in a business interruption policy is to:

- A) Compensate the insured for legal expenses incurred while suing a third party responsible for the loss
- B) Encourage the insured to take reasonable actions to minimize the loss and protect the property
- C) Cover labor disputes that result in an interruption to the business
- D) Reimburse the policyholder for the cost of temporary repairs

Casualty Insurance (Total: 32 Questions)

Auto insurance: 8 questions

49) What action can result in an auto insurance policy being canceled?

- A) Filing a single claim
- B) Non-payment of premiums
- C) Driving more miles than estimated at the start of the policy
- D) Changing the vehicle covered by the policy

50) An auto insurance policy with 'Split Limits' means:

- A) The insurer will only pay claims partially
- B) There are different limits for bodily injury per person, per accident, and for property damage
- C) Coverage is divided between comprehensive and collision
- D) The policy covers multiple vehicles with different levels of coverage

51) The 'Declaration Page' of an auto insurance policy typically includes:

- A) A detailed list of all past claims
- B) The policyholder's driving record
- C) Names of all drivers in the household
- D) Information about the policyholder, vehicle, coverages, and limits

52) 'Non-Owned Auto' coverage in a commercial auto policy is designed for:

- A) Vehicles owned by employees but used for business purposes
- B) Rental vehicles used by the business
- C) Vehicles temporarily substituted for the insured vehicle
- D) A and B

53) In auto insurance, 'Stacking' of uninsured/underinsured motorist

coverage allows:

- A) Combining limits for multiple vehicles on the same policy for a higher total coverage amount
- B) Merging auto and homeowners insurance for comprehensive cover-age
- C) Accumulating coverage limits over time
- D) Doubling the payout for claims involving expensive vehicles

54) The 'Exclusion' section of an auto insurance policy:

- A) Lists the types of vehicles covered
- B) Details the premium calculation method
- C) Specifies what is not covered by the policy
- D) Outlines the policy renewal process

55) 'Towing and Labor' coverage in an auto insurance policy typically includes:

- A) Reimbursement for towing and basic roadside assistance
- B) Compensation for time spent without a vehicle
- C) Labor costs for vehicle repairs after an accident
- D) Towing charges after vehicle theft

56) What factor does NOT affect the cost of auto insurance premiums?

- A) The insured vehicle's safety features
- B) The policyholder's educational level
- C) The policyholder's driving record
- D) The amount of coverage purchased

Workers compensation: 8 questions

57) 'Return to Work' programs under workers' compensation are intended to:

- A) Provide financial incentives for workers to find employment elsewhere
- B) Facilitate the injured worker's transition back to employment, sometimes in a modified or alternative role
- C) Punish employees who are suspected of malingering
- D) Reduce the amount of medical benefits an employee can receive

58) The 'Exclusive Remedy' rule in workers' compensation law:

- A) Allows employees to sue their employers if they accept workers' compensation benefits
- B) Prohibits employees from receiving workers' compensation if they have health insurance
- C) Limits employees to workers' compensation benefits as their sole remedy against their employer for work-related injuries
- D) Requires employees to choose between suing their employer or accepting workers' compensation benefits

59) A workers' compensation policy is primarily required by:

- A) Federal law for all businesses operating within the US
- B) State laws, with requirements varying by state
- C) The Occupational Safety and Health Administration (OSHA) for specific industries
- D) Employer discretion based on the level of risk associated with the job

60) 'Cumulative Injury' claims in workers' compensation refer to injuries

that:

- A) Occur due to a single, catastrophic event
- B) Result from repetitive stress or exposure over time
- C) Are reported by multiple employees within a short timeframe
- D) Accumulate to exceed the policy's deductible

61) For a workers' compensation claim to be valid, the injury must:

- A) Occur during the employee's commute to work
- B) Be reported within 24 hours of the incident
- C) Arise out of and in the course of employment
- D) Result in at least one week of lost work time

62) 'Subrogation' in workers' compensation allows the insurer to:

- A) Reduce benefits if the employee is found partially at fault
- B) Seek reimbursement from third parties responsible for the employee's injury
- C) Deny claims that do not meet certain criteria
- D) Increase premiums after a claim is filed

63) The term 'Statutory Compensation' in workers' compensation refers to:

- A) Benefits that are negotiated between the employer and employee
- B) Payments that are determined by state law
- C) A standardized compensation package offered by all insurance companies
- D) Compensation that exceeds the limits set by state law

64) A 'Monopolistic State Fund' for workers' compensation is:

- A) A private insurance option available in all states
- B) A state-operated fund that is the sole provider of workers' compensation insurance in certain states
- C) An optional fund for employers who wish to self-insure
- D) A federal program that supplements state workers' compensation benefits

Liability insurance: 10 questions

65) In liability insurance, a 'Retroactive Date' in a claims-made policy refers to:

- A) The date before which incidents are not covered, even if the claim is made during the policy period
- B) The expiration date of the policy
- C) The date when the premium rates are recalculated based on claims history
- D) The deadline for filing claims after the policy period ends

66) 'Garage Keepers Liability Insurance' provides coverage for:

- A) Damage to vehicles stored in a commercial garage, not owned by the garage
- B) Personal vehicles of employees stored in the company garage
- C) Theft of tools and equipment from a garage
- D) Liability arising from garage sale activities

67) An 'Aggregate Limit' in a liability policy specifies:

- A) The maximum amount paid for a single claim
- B) The minimum amount the insurer will pay out over the policy period
- C) The total amount the insurer will pay for all claims during the policy period

- D) A fixed amount that must be reached before the insurer begins to pay out

68) Which of the following is NOT typically excluded from a general liability insurance policy?

- A) Intentional acts of harm
- B) Employee injuries covered by workers' compensation
- C) Bodily injury to customers due to a product defect
- D) Contractual liabilities

69) 'Fiduciary Liability Insurance' covers:

- A) Financial losses due to fiduciaries' mismanagement of employee benefit plans
- B) Theft of company funds by fiduciaries
- C) Legal liability for accidents occurring on company property
- D) Mismanagement of company assets not related to employee benefit plans

70) The 'Supplementary Payments' provision in a liability policy typically includes coverage for:

- A) Punitive damages awarded in a lawsuit
- B) Costs above the policy limits, such as certain legal defense costs
- C) Damages for pain and suffering claims
- D) Settlements that exceed the policy's aggregate limit

71) A 'Waiver of Subrogation' endorsement in a liability policy:

- A) Allows the insurer to pursue a third party that caused a loss to the insured
- B) Prevents the insurer from seeking reimbursement from a third party

after paying a claim

- C) Requires the insured to waive their right to sue the insurer
- D) Increases the policy's coverage limits in exchange for an additional premium

72) 'Voluntary Property Damage' coverage in a liability policy:

- A) Covers intentional damage to property owned by the insured
- B) Provides coverage for property damage caused voluntarily by the insured to a third party's property
- C) Insures against property damage claims that are voluntarily submitted by third parties
- D) Covers damage to rental properties

73) In liability insurance, 'Split Limits' refer to:

- A) Dividing the policy limits between property damage and bodily injury coverage
- B) A single limit that is split among all policyholders
- C) Limits that change depending on the time of day the incident occurs
- D) A method of dividing the premium payment into installments

74) What is 'Advertising Injury' coverage in a Commercial General Liability (CGL) policy?

- A) Coverage for injuries sustained during commercial shoots
- B) Protection against claims of slander, libel, or copyright infringement in advertisements
- C) Liability for physical injuries caused by advertising materials
- D) Insurance for the cost of withdrawing offensive advertisements

Umbrella policies: 6 questions

75) Which type of claim is most likely to be covered by an umbrella policy but not by standard auto or homeowners insurance?

- A) A claim for physical damage to the insured's vehicle
- B) A claim for water damage to a home
- C) A libel or slander claim resulting from a blog post
- D) A theft claim for personal property

76) In what circumstance might an umbrella policy deny coverage?

- A) The underlying policy limits have not been exhausted
- B) The claim is for a type of loss not covered by any underlying policy but covered by the umbrella policy
- C) The claim exceeds the limits of the underlying policy by $1,000
- D) The insured has multiple underlying policies

77) The 'self-insured retention' (SIR) in an umbrella policy is:

- A) The amount the policyholder must pay out-of-pocket before the umbrella coverage begins, for claims not covered by any underlying policy
- B) The deductible of the underlying policy
- C) A co-payment required for all claims under the umbrella policy
- D) The total amount the insured must pay annually before the umbrella policy provides coverage

78) Which statement about umbrella policies is TRUE?

- A) They can only be purchased as standalone policies without any underlying coverage
- B) They provide unlimited coverage for all types of liabilities

- C) They typically exclude personal liability coverage
- D) They can cover multiple underlying policies, such as auto and homeowners insurance

79) 'Worldwide Coverage' under an umbrella policy means:

- A) The policy provides coverage anywhere in the world
- B) Coverage is limited to the country where the policy was purchased
- C) International coverage is provided only for business-related travel
- D) Coverage is provided worldwide but only for auto-related liabilities

80) An umbrella policy would most likely provide additional coverage in which of the following situations?

- A) The policyholder's boat is stolen
- B) The policyholder is sued for defamation
- C) The policyholder's home is damaged in a fire
- D) The policyholder incurs medical expenses from a skiing accident

Package Policies (Total: 12 Questions)

Business Owners Policy (BOP): 6 questions

81) A BOP typically offers 'Liability Coverage' for all the following EXCEPT:

- A) Customer injuries at the business premises
- B) Employee discrimination lawsuits
- C) Damage to a customer's property
- D) Product liability claims

82) Which statement about the premium for a BOP is TRUE?

- A) It is based solely on the size of the business premises
- B) It is typically higher than purchasing separate policies for property and liability coverage
- C) It considers factors like business location, type of business, and coverage limits
- D) It is a fixed rate established by the government

83) The 'Electronic Data Processing (EDP)' coverage in a BOP protects against:

- A) Damage to electronic data processing equipment and loss of data
- B) Liabilities arising from the use of electronic data
- C) The cost of upgrading software and hardware
- D) Theft of employees' personal electronic devices

84) What is typically the maximum number of employees a business can have to be eligible for a BOP?

- A) 10
- B) 50
- C) 100
- D) There is no maximum number; eligibility is based on revenue

85) 'Newly Acquired or Constructed Property' coverage in a BOP:

- A) Provides immediate coverage for new properties acquired or constructed, up to a certain limit
- B) Requires a separate policy for each new property
- C) Covers only the construction materials, not the land
- D) Excludes any property not listed at the inception of the policy

86) 'Hired and Non-Owned Auto' coverage in a BOP:

- A) Covers personal vehicles owned by the business owner
- B) Provides liability coverage for vehicles the business hires or that are owned by employees but used for business
- C) Is mandatory for all businesses with a BOP
- D) Covers physical damage to any vehicle the business uses

Commercial package policy: 6 questions

87) 'Commercial Auto' coverage in a CPP includes protection for:

- A) Personal vehicles of the business owner
- B) Vehicles owned, leased, or used by the business
- C) Any vehicle while on the business premises
- D) Damage to products during delivery

88) 'Errors and Omissions' (E&O) insurance is designed to protect against:

- A) Physical injuries occurring on business premises
- B) Damage to the business's owned properties
- C) Mistakes or negligence in professional services provided
- D) Claims related to employment practices

89) Which of the following would typically be excluded from a CPP?

- A) Acts of terrorism
- B) Employee theft
- C) Fire damage to the business premises
- D) Customer injuries on the premises

90) The 'Additional Insured' endorsement in a CPP allows:

- A) Addition of coverage for personal property of employees

- B) Businesses to extend certain coverages to other parties as required by contract
- C) Automatic coverage of new business acquisitions
- D) Increased limits for existing coverages

91) In a CPP, 'Cyber Liability' coverage is important for businesses that:

- A) Operate exclusively offline
- B) Handle sensitive customer data electronically
- C) Do not use computers or the internet
- D) Sell products in physical locations only

92) 'Pollution Liability' coverage in a CPP is specifically designed to address:

- A) Global environmental policies
- B) Liabilities arising from pollution events caused by the insured's operations
- C) Pollution caused by natural disasters
- D) Any legal liabilities related to recycling programs

State-Specific Regulations (Total: 15 Questions)

Licensing requirements: 5 questions

93) Reciprocity between states regarding property and casualty insurance licensing means:

- A) All states have the same licensing requirements
- B) A license obtained in one state is valid in all other states
- C) An agent licensed in one state may qualify for a license in another state without taking that state's exam
- D) Agents must pass a national exam to sell insurance in multiple states

94) How often must a property and casualty insurance license typically be renewed?

- A) Every year
- B) Every two years
- C) Every five years
- D) Licenses do not require renewal

95) Continuing education units (CEUs) required for license renewal for property and casualty agents:

- A) Can be carried over indefinitely from one renewal period to the next
- B) Must be completed in classroom settings only
- C) Are the same across all states
- D) Vary by state and must be completed within the renewal period

96) Which of the following activities generally requires a property and casualty insurance license?

- A) Providing financial advice
- B) Selling, soliciting, or negotiating insurance contracts
- C) Working as a customer service representative in a bank
- D) Offering legal advice on insurance claims

97) A property and casualty insurance agent's license can be revoked or suspended for:

- A) Failing to meet sales quotas
- B) Not completing continuing education requirements
- C) Refusing to sell certain insurance products
- D) Choosing to work for a competitor

State laws governing insurance practices: 6 questions

98) The 'unfair trade practices' act in state insurance law typically prohibits:

- A) Selling insurance from foreign companies
- B) Misrepresentation, false advertising, and defamation by insurers
- C) The sale of life insurance policies
- D) Using the internet for insurance transactions

99) State insurance laws regarding 'rate making' aim to ensure rates are:

- A) The same across all states
- B) Adequate, not excessive, and not unfairly discriminatory
- C) Based solely on the insurer's discretion
- D) Set by the federal government

100) 'Risk-based capital' requirements under state insurance laws are designed to:

- A) Encourage investment in high-risk assets
- B) Ensure insurers have enough capital relative to their risk exposure
- C) Standardize capital requirements regardless of company size or risk
- D) Reduce the amount of capital insurance companies need to hold

101) In terms of insurance, 'prior approval' state laws require:

- A) Insurers to obtain approval from policyholders before increasing rates
- B) State insurance departments to approve rates and forms before they can be used
- C) Federal review of all insurance products before they are marketed
- D) Insurers to approve all claims before they are submitted

102) How do state laws typically address insurance fraud?

- · A) By treating it as a minor administrative issue
- · B) Through specific statutes that define and penalize fraudulent insurance acts
- · C) Ignoring it in favor of federal prosecution
- · D) Allowing insurers to define and handle fraud independently

103) 'Guaranty funds,' as established by state insurance laws, are designed to:

- · A) Guarantee profits for insurance companies
- · B) Protect policyholders if an insurer becomes insolvent
- · C) Fund state insurance department operations
- · D) Ensure that all policies are guaranteed to pay out

Ethical practices and the regulatory environment: 4 questions

104) The regulatory environment in the insurance industry is designed to:

- · A) Eliminate all competition among insurance companies
- · B) Ensure that all insurance policies are identical
- · C) Protect consumers and maintain the integrity of the insurance market
- · D) Increase the tax revenue collected from insurance companies

105) An insurance professional fabricating a client's application details to secure a policy approval is violating which ethical principle?

- · A) Transparency
- · B) Confidentiality
- · C) Honesty

- D) Professionalism

106) What role do continuing education requirements play in promoting ethical practices among insurance professionals?

- A) They ensure that professionals prioritize sales over client needs
- B) They provide updates on regulatory changes and reinforce ethical standards
- C) They are unrelated to ethical practices
- D) They decrease the quality of service provided to clients

107) Misrepresenting the terms of a policy to a policyholder is a breach of:

- A) The policyholder's privacy
- B) The duty of disclosure
- C) The principle of utmost good faith
- D) The agent's right to sell insurance

Insurance Operations (Total: 10 Questions)

Underwriting principles: 4 questions

108) 'Capacity' in underwriting refers to:

- A) The maximum amount of risk the insurer is willing to accept
- B) The insured's ability to pay premiums
- C) The physical space available in an insured building
- D) The legal capacity of the insured to enter into an insurance contract

109) What role does 'reinsurance' play in underwriting?

- A) It allows insurers to underwrite policies without assessing risk

- B) It provides a way for insurers to transfer part of the risk to another insurance company
- C) It eliminates the need for underwriting in large policies
- D) It is a form of insurance purchased by individuals as a supplement to primary insurance

110) The concept of 'retention' in underwriting refers to:

- A) The insurer's decision to retain all premiums without paying claims
- B) The amount of risk an insurer keeps for its own account without passing it to a reinsurer
- C) The practice of retaining policy documents indefinitely
- D) Keeping clients through superior customer service

111) An 'underwriting loss' occurs when:

- A) Premiums collected are less than the insurer's administrative expenses
- B) The insured suffers a loss that is not covered by the policy
- C) Claims paid and expenses exceed premium income
- D) An underwriter incorrectly assesses a risk, resulting in a policy cancellation

Rate making: 3 questions

112) Which of the following best describes 'premium leakage'?

- A) The process of reducing premiums over time to retain policyholders
- B) Loss of premium revenue due to underpricing or inadequate rating
- C) The portion of the premium used to pay agent commissions
- D) Leakage of confidential premium rate information to competitors

113) 'Underwriting profit' in rate making refers to:

- A) The profit made from investing premium payments
- B) The difference between premiums collected and losses paid out
- C) The commission earned by agents for underwriting policies
- D) Profits earned from the sale of additional coverage options

114) How do regulatory bodies influence rate making in the insurance industry?

- A) By requiring all insurers to use the same set of rates
- B) Through reviewing and approving rates to ensure they are not excessive, inadequate, or discriminatory
- C) Dictating the exact rates to be charged for each type of coverage
- D) Allowing insurers complete freedom to set their rates without oversight

Risk management: 3 questions

115) 'Risk reduction' in the context of property and casualty insurance can involve:

- A) Increasing insurance coverage limits
- B) Implementing safety training for employees
- C) Transferring all risks to third parties
- D) Completely avoiding certain types of insurance policies

116) How does 'diversification' function as a risk management strategy?

- A) By spreading investments across various sectors to minimize financial risk
- B) Through purchasing multiple insurance policies for the same risk
- C) By employing a variety of risk management techniques to address different risks
- D) Diversifying does not relate to risk management

117) The concept of 'total cost of risk' (TCOR) in risk management includes:

- A) Only the cost of insurance premiums
- B) Costs related to risk identification, assessment, and control, including financial losses from realized risks
- C) The total amount of risks identified by a company
- D) The cumulative cost of risk management consultants

Miscellaneous Coverages (Total: 3 Questions)

Flood insurance: 1 question

118) Flood insurance policies through the NFIP are available:

- A) Exclusively to homeowners in designated flood plains
- B) Only when purchased in conjunction with a homeowner's insurance policy
- C) To homeowners, renters, and business owners in participating NFIP communities
- D) Without limits on coverage for both residential and commercial properties

Earthquake insurance: 1 question

119) In terms of earthquake insurance, what is 'loss of use' coverage?

- A) Coverage that compensates for the depreciation in property value after an earthquake
- B) Reimbursement for living expenses if the home is uninhabitable due to earthquake damage
- C) Coverage for the loss of personal items used outside the home when the earthquake occurred

- D) Insurance payout for the loss of use of personal electronics and appliances damaged during an earthquake

Crime insurance policies: 1 question

120) How do crime insurance policies differ from property insurance policies?

- A) Crime policies exclusively cover losses from illegal activities, while property policies cover a broad range of perils
- B) Crime policies cover natural disasters, whereas property policies do not
- C) There is no difference; crime insurance is a type of property insurance
- D) Crime policies are for personal protection, and property policies are for businesses

Practice Exam 4 (Total: 120 Questions)

Insurance Basics (Total: 14 Questions)

Principles of insurance: 4 questions

1) Which principle is directly concerned with the distribution of loss among multiple insurers?

- A) Insurable interest
- B) Proximate cause
- C) Contribution
- D) Indemnity

2) Proximate cause in insurance contracts is important because it?

- A) Determines the validity of the policy
- B) Establishes the premium amount
- C) Identifies the primary cause of loss for coverage purposes
- D) Validates the insured's claim to the insurance

3) 'Insurable interest' in the context of property insurance means the policyholder?

- A) Prefers certain types of insurance policies over others

- B) Has a financial stake in the property being insured
- C) Is interested in purchasing additional insurance coverage
- D) Has a legal right to insure any property of choice

4) The principle of 'utmost good faith' obligates which party to disclose all known risks?

- A) The insurer only
- B) The insured only
- C) Both the insurer and the insured
- D) Neither the insurer nor the insured

Types of insurers: 5 questions

5) What characterizes an alien insurance company?

- A) An insurer that offers extraterrestrial insurance products
- B) An insurer incorporated under the laws of another country
- C) An insurer that exclusively provides foreign travel insurance
- D) An insurer formed by non-resident aliens

6) A cooperative insurance company is unique because it:

- A) Only insures agricultural risks
- B) Is owned and operated by its policyholders
- C) Offers insurance exclusively to cooperative members
- D) Provides dividends to stockholders rather than policyholders

7) Which organization operates by allowing individual underwriters to accept risks on behalf of members?

- A) Mutual insurance company
- B) Captive insurance company

- C) Lloyd's of London
- D) Government insurance program

8) Self-insurance is a strategy used by which of the following?

- A) Individuals saving money for potential losses
- B) Large corporations to manage their own risks
- C) Small businesses unable to afford commercial insurance
- D) Insurance agents to cover their professional liabilities

9) Direct writers in the insurance industry refer to:

- A) Authors of insurance textbooks
- B) Insurers that sell policies directly to the public without agents
- C) Policyholders who write their own insurance contracts
- D) Agents who only sell policies from one insurer

Policy renewals and cancellations: 5 questions

10) What is the primary difference between cancellation and non-renewal of an insurance policy?

- A) Cancellation occurs during the policy term, while non-renewal happens at the end of the policy term
- B) Non-renewal requires the insured to pay remaining premiums, whereas cancellation does not
- C) Cancellation is initiated by the insured, whereas non-renewal is initiated by the insurer
- D) There is no difference; both terms mean the same thing

11) Which of the following is NOT a common reason for the cancellation of an insurance policy by the insurer?

- A) An increase in the frequency of natural disasters in the insured's area
- B) The discovery of fraud or material misrepresentation by the insured
- C) The insured's relocation to a state where the insurer is not licensed
- D) Non-payment of premium by the insured

12) How do state laws generally affect insurance policy cancellations and non-renewals?

- A) They provide uniform rules that apply in all states
- B) They specify the conditions under which policies may be canceled or non-renewed
- C) They prohibit insurers from canceling policies under any circumstances
- D) They allow insurers to cancel policies at any time without reason

13) What is the purpose of the notice period before an insurance policy can be canceled by the insurer?

- A) To allow the insurer time to find a replacement policyholder
- B) To give the insured time to address the reasons for cancellation
- C) To ensure the insured has adequate time to find alternative insurance coverage
- D) To provide a cooling-off period for the insurer

14) In the event of a cancellation, what is typically the minimum notice period required by law?

- A) 10 days for non-payment of premium and 30 days for all other reasons
- B) 5 days regardless of the reason
- C) 60 days for any reason
- D) There is no minimum notice period required by law

Property Insurance (Total: 34 Questions)

Dwelling policies: 9 questions

15) Which coverage in a dwelling policy would pay for damage to a detached garage on the insured property?

- A) Personal Property
- B) Other Structures
- C) Dwelling
- D) Loss of Use

16) A 'Water Back-up and Sump Overflow' endorsement in a dwelling policy specifically covers:

- A) Damage caused by floodwaters entering the home
- B) Water damage due to public water mains bursting
- C) Damage from water back-up through sewers or drains or overflow from a sump
- D) Accidental overflow of water from household appliances

17) The 'Actual Cash Value (ACV)' settlement in a dwelling policy means compensation is based on:

- A) The replacement cost minus depreciation
- B) The market value of the property at the time of loss
- C) The initial purchase price of the property
- D) A fixed amount specified in the policy document

18) What does 'open peril' coverage in a DP-3 policy mean?

- A) Only the perils specifically listed in the policy are covered
- B) All perils are covered except those explicitly excluded in the policy

- C) The policy covers any peril that can be reasonably anticipated
- D) The policyholder can open a claim for any reason

19) A dwelling policy with a 'Replacement Cost' endorsement means:

- A) The insurer will pay the cost to replace the damaged property without deduction for depreciation
- B) The insured will receive the cash value of the property at the time of loss
- C) Replacement costs are only covered up to the amount of insurance purchased
- D) The property will be replaced with materials of like kind and quality, but not necessarily the same brand

20) Which statement about 'Loss Settlement' in dwelling policies is correct?

- A) Losses are always settled on a replacement cost basis
- B) Personal property is covered for its actual cash value, unless otherwise specified
- C) Structural damages are compensated based on the property's purchase price
- D) Land value is included in the settlement amount for dwelling losses

21) The 'Earthquake Endorsement' in a dwelling policy:

- A) Covers earthquake damage under all dwelling policy forms as a standard provision
- B) Is available for an additional premium to cover earthquake damage, which is otherwise excluded
- C) Automatically increases the dwelling coverage limit in earthquake-prone areas
- D) Provides coverage for any ground movement, including sinkholes

22) Which of the following would be covered under the 'Internal Explosion' peril in a basic form (DP-1) dwelling policy?

- A) An explosion originating from a natural gas leak inside the home
- B) A blast from a nearby industrial facility
- C) An explosion of an external transformer causing damage to the dwelling
- D) Detonation of explosive materials stored in the dwelling's basement

23) Under a DP-2 (Broad Form) policy, which of the following is true regarding the 'Weight of Ice, Snow, or Sleet' peril?

- A) It covers damage to the dwelling but not to personal property inside
- B) It is excluded from coverage
- C) It only covers the cost to remove ice, snow, or sleet that has caused damage
- D) It includes coverage for both the dwelling and other structures

Homeowners policies: 10 questions

24) Which homeowners policy endorsement would be necessary to fully cover a home-based business?

- A) Scheduled Personal Property Endorsement
- B) Home Business Endorsement
- C) Water Back-up and Sump Overflow Endorsement
- D) Guaranteed Replacement Cost Endorsement

25) Exclusions in homeowners policies typically include all of the following EXCEPT:

- A) Wear and tear
- B) Intentional injury or damage caused by the insured

- C) Nuclear hazard
- D) Theft of personal property

26) What is the primary purpose of requiring a 'deductible' in a home-owners policy?

- A) To decrease the insurer's liability for small claims
- B) To make the policy more affordable for homeowners
- C) To encourage homeowners to prevent losses
- D) To comply with state insurance regulations

27) The 'Aleatory' nature of a homeowners insurance contract means:

- A) The contract is ambiguous and open to interpretation
- B) The value received by each party can be unequal
- C) It only takes effect in certain conditions
- D) It is legally binding only upon the insurer

28) A 'Waiver of Deductible' clause in a homeowners policy would likely apply in cases of:

- A) Small claims that do not exceed the deductible amount
- B) Large losses, where the cost significantly exceeds the deductible
- C) Every claim, regardless of the amount
- D) Claims for personal property only

29) What does the 'Coinsurance Clause' in a homeowners policy encour-age?

- A) Investment in coins and other collectibles
- B) Insuring the home for its full replacement value
- C) Sharing of risk between multiple insurance companies
- D) Periodic review and adjustment of coverage limits

30) The 'Mortgage Clause' in a homeowners policy is designed to protect:

- A) The mortgage lender's interest in the property
- B) The homeowner's equity in the property
- C) The insurer's right to pursue subrogation
- D) The insured's personal property

31) How does an 'Umbrella Policy' supplement a homeowners policy?

- A) By providing additional coverage for the dwelling
- B) By extending liability coverage beyond the limits of the homeowners policy
- C) By covering perils not included in the standard homeowners policy
- D) By reducing the premium of the homeowners policy

32) 'Consequential Loss' coverage in a homeowners policy is designed to cover:

- A) Losses that occur as a direct consequence of a covered peril
- B) The cost to repair or replace damaged property, regardless of its age
- C) Additional living expenses incurred if the home is uninhabitable
- D) The loss of personal property through theft

33) In homeowners insurance, 'Actual Cash Value' settlements are calculated based on:

- A) The cost to replace the property with new property of like kind and quality
- B) The market value of the property at the time of loss
- C) The replacement cost minus depreciation
- D) A predetermined amount agreed upon at the policy inception

Commercial property policies: 10 questions

34) What role does the 'Deductible' play in a commercial property policy?

- A) It represents the maximum amount payable by the insurer
- B) It reduces the premium by transferring some risk back to the policyholder
- C) It is a mandatory fee paid monthly by the policyholder
- D) It increases the policy limits for certain types of claims

35) 'Peak Season Endorsement' in a commercial property policy is used to:

- A) Cover seasonal employees' workers' compensation
- B) Increase coverage limits during seasons when inventory levels are highest
- C) Provide discounts for off-peak seasons
- D) Insure against weather-related damages during peak seasons

36) The 'Fine Arts Coverage' endorsement added to a commercial property policy:

- A) Covers all types of art owned by the business without a valuation
- B) Provides a higher limit of coverage for specified fine art pieces
- C) Automatically appraises art at market value
- D) Excludes coverage for art displayed off-premises

37) In commercial property insurance, 'Valuable Papers and Records Coverage' is intended to:

- A) Cover the cost of replacing documents that cannot be physically replaced
- B) Insure against the loss of digital data only

- C) Provide unlimited coverage for all business documents
- D) Pay the cost to research, replace, or restore lost or damaged valuable papers and records

38) Which of the following best describes 'Terrorism Coverage' under a commercial property policy?

- A) Mandatory coverage for all businesses
- B) Optional coverage that protects against damage due to acts of terrorism
- C) Included only in business interruption insurance
- D) A government-provided insurance program with no private options

39) The 'Electronic Data Processing (EDP) Coverage' in commercial property policies specifically insures:

- A) Any electronic data processing equipment, software, and data
- B) Only the hardware associated with electronic data processing
- C) Losses related to the interruption of electronic data processing
- D) Cyber liability and data breaches

40) What is the 'Debris Removal' coverage in a commercial property policy designed to cover?

- A) Costs to remove debris after a natural disaster, regardless of a claim
- B) Removal of hazardous materials only
- C) Costs to remove debris of covered property after a covered loss
- D) Cleaning services for the property regardless of debris

41) 'Pollutant Clean Up and Removal' coverage in a commercial property policy:

- A) Provides comprehensive coverage for any type of pollution event

- B) Is typically limited to a specified amount per policy period for cleanup costs due to a covered loss
- C) Covers fines and penalties associated with pollution
- D) Insures against all environmental liabilities

42) How does 'Inflation Guard' coverage benefit a commercial property policyholder?

- A) It ensures that property values are automatically adjusted to keep up with inflation
- B) It reduces the premium as the property value increases
- C) It provides additional coverage for inflation-related expenses
- D) It locks in the property value at the time of purchase

43) The 'Glass Coverage Form' under a commercial property policy:

- A) Excludes coverage for glass breakage under all circumstances
- B) Provides coverage for glass breakage, including windows and doors
- C) Covers only stained glass installations
- D) Is an optional endorsement for high-risk locations

Business interruption: 5 questions

44) What does the 'coinsurance' clause in a business interruption policy encourage policyholders to do?

- A) Insure their business for a percentage of its actual value to save on premiums
- B) Purchase additional insurance policies to cover gaps
- C) Accurately declare their business income to ensure adequate coverage
- D) Share the risk with another insurer

45) 'Named Perils' coverage in a business interruption policy:

- A) Covers all possible causes of business interruption
- B) Only covers perils that are specifically named in the policy
- C) Includes coverage for unnamed but common risks
- D) Is an all-risk coverage that includes every conceivable peril

46) Business interruption insurance is usually effective:

- A) Immediately upon the purchase of the policy
- B) After a specified waiting period from the date of the direct physical loss
- C) Only during business hours
- D) When a civil authority issues an evacuation order

47) The 'Payroll Coverage Extension' in a business interruption policy:

- A) Excludes payroll expenses from the calculation of business interruption losses
- B) Provides coverage for payroll expenses for a specified period to retain employees
- C) Covers only the payroll of executive staff
- D) Automatically includes all payroll expenses without limits

48) Which of the following would NOT trigger business interruption coverage?

- A) A mandatory evacuation due to a nearby wildfire
- B) A voluntary closure for remodeling the business premises
- C) A cyber-attack that halts operations
- D) A supply chain disruption due to a covered peril

Casualty Insurance (Total: 30 Questions)

Auto insurance: 7 questions

49) 'Single Limit' liability coverage in an auto insurance policy:

- A) Applies the same maximum amount per accident for both bodily injury and property damage
- B) Limits coverage to a single claim per policy period
- C) Offers unlimited coverage for bodily injury to a single person
- D) Provides separate limits for each person injured in an accident

50) 'SR-22' insurance is:

- A) A special policy for sports and luxury cars
- B) A form required for drivers with a suspended license to prove financial responsibility
- C) An optional endorsement for high-risk drivers
- D) A discounted policy for safe drivers

51) The 'Part D - Coverage for Damage to Your Auto' in a personal auto policy includes:

- A) Liability coverage
- B) Comprehensive and collision coverage
- C) Medical payments coverage
- D) Uninsured motorist coverage

52) An auto insurance policy's 'Territory' provision specifies:

- A) The geographical area in which the policy provides coverage
- B) Locations where parking the insured vehicle is permitted
- C) The designated driving area for the primary policyholder

· D) Areas excluded from coverage due to high risk

53) What is the primary function of 'No-Fault' auto insurance?

· A) To eliminate the need for liability insurance
· B) To provide immediate medical payments without determining fault
· C) To increase the speed of vehicle repairs by not assigning blame
· D) To prevent lawsuits for minor accidents

54) 'Agreed Value' coverage in an auto insurance policy is most commonly used for:

· A) Vehicles with rapidly depreciating values
· B) High-value or classic cars where the value is agreed upon at the policy inception
· C) Leased vehicles
· D) Commercial fleets

55) 'Diminution in Value' claims in auto insurance refer to:

· A) The decreased value of a vehicle after it has been repaired following an accident
· B) The value of a vehicle after a total loss claim
· C) The difference in value between new and used parts for repairs
· D) A reduction in premium after a vehicle depreciates

Workers compensation: 8 questions

56) Which factor is commonly used to determine workers' compensation premiums?

· A) The age of the employees
· B) The number of employees who smoke

- C) The company's industry classification and experience modification factor
- D) The geographical location of the company's headquarters

57) 'Self-Insurance' for workers' compensation means:

- A) The employer sets aside funds to directly pay for workers' compensation claims
- B) Employees must use their personal insurance for work-related injuries
- C) The employer is exempt from providing workers' compensation
- D) The employer purchases insurance from a private company but handles claims internally

58) What is an 'Independent Medical Examination' (IME) used for in workers' compensation?

- A) To provide a second opinion on the treatment plan proposed by the employee's doctor
- B) To assess the extent of the employee's work-related injury or illness
- C) To determine if an employee is fit to return to work
- D) B and C

59) 'Notice of Injury' in workers' compensation is:

- A) A formal accusation against the employer for unsafe working conditions
- B) The document an employee files to report a work-related injury or illness
- C) A notification from the insurer regarding a change in policy terms
- D) An announcement to employees about a workplace hazard

60) The 'Pay-As-You-Go' option in workers' compensation insurance

allows employers to:

- A) Delay premium payments until the end of the policy term
- B) Pay premiums based on actual, rather than estimated, payroll figures
- C) Opt out of coverage for certain employees
- D) Pay for insurance only in months when there are active employees

61) Under workers' compensation, a 'Permanent Total Disability' (PTD) benefit is paid when:

- A) The employee can no longer work in their previous profession, but can work in another field
- B) The employee is expected to recover fully but will be out of work for an extended period
- C) The employee is unable to return to any type of gainful employment
- D) The disability lasts more than one year but is not considered permanent

62) Which of the following best describes the 'First Report of Injury' in workers' compensation?

- A) A preliminary medical report from the first doctor who examines the employee
- B) An internal company report detailing how the injury occurred
- C) The initial claim form that must be filed with the state workers' compensation board or insurance carrier
- D) A report filed by a witness to the injury

63) 'Scheduled Injuries' in workers' compensation refer to:

- A) Injuries that occur on a predictable basis due to the nature of the job
- B) Specific types of injuries that have predetermined benefit amounts or durations

- C) Injuries that must be reported within a scheduled timeframe
- D) Injuries that are planned for statistical purposes

Liability insurance: 10 questions

64) 'Employment Practices Liability Insurance' (EPLI) covers the business against claims from employees alleging:

- A) Physical injuries sustained in the workplace
- B) Damage to employee personal property
- C) Workplace discrimination, harassment, wrongful termination, etc.
- D) Financial losses due to poor management decisions

65) Which coverage is specifically designed to protect professionals against liability arising from their professional services?

- A) Commercial Property Insurance
- B) General Liability Insurance
- C) Professional Liability Insurance
- D) Product Liability Insurance

66) 'Pollution Liability Insurance' provides coverage for:

- A) Cleanup costs and third-party claims due to environmental pollution caused by the insured
- B) Natural disasters that result in pollution
- C) Pollution caused intentionally by the insured
- D) Pollution emanating from neighboring properties

67) A 'Business Owners Policy' (BOP) combines which two types of coverage?

- A) Professional Liability and Product Liability

- B) General Liability and Property Insurance
- C) Auto Liability and Workers' Compensation
- D) Directors and Officers Liability and Employment Practices Liability

68) 'Cyber Liability Insurance' is designed to cover:

- A) Physical damage to computers and servers
- B) Liability for data breaches, cyber-attacks, and information security
- C) The cost of recovering lost data without third-party claims
- D) Cyber extortion demands

69) What is the 'Duty to Indemnify' in a liability insurance policy?

- A) The insurer's obligation to defend the insured in court
- B) The insured's duty to reimburse the insurer for settlements
- C) The insurer's obligation to pay for damages or settlements up to the policy limit
- D) The insured's responsibility to prevent further damages after a claim

70) 'Liquor Liability Insurance' is essential for businesses that:

- A) Serve non-alcoholic beverages
- B) Manufacture, sell, or serve alcoholic beverages
- C) Host occasional company events where alcohol is served
- D) Provide catering services without including alcohol

71) Which scenario is an example of a 'Third-Party Over Action' claim in liability insurance?

- A) An employee sues their employer for injuries sustained on the job
- B) A customer sues a business for a defective product
- C) An injured worker's spouse sues the employer for loss of consortium
- D) An employee's injury claim leads to a lawsuit against a third party,

who then seeks indemnification from the employer

72) 'Products-Completed Operations Hazard' in a CGL policy covers:

- A) Liability arising from products manufactured, sold, or distributed by the insured
- B) Operations that are in progress
- C) The cost of completing operations that were interrupted
- D) Damage to the insured's completed work by their products

73) In liability insurance, 'Per Occurrence Limit' refers to:

- A) The maximum amount the insurer will pay for all claims during the policy period
- B) The total amount the insurer will reimburse for claims, regardless of the number
- C) The maximum amount the insurer will pay for a single claim
- D) The fixed amount paid for every claim submitted

Umbrella policies: 5 questions

74) What is the importance of maintaining underlying policy limits in relation to an umbrella policy?

- A) Lower underlying limits can reduce the premium of the umbrella policy
- B) Insufficient underlying limits can result in a gap in coverage before the umbrella policy applies
- C) Higher underlying limits can eliminate the need for an umbrella policy
- D) Underlying limits determine the total coverage amount of the umbrella policy

75) Which of the following scenarios would typically be excluded from coverage under an umbrella policy?

- A) An accident involving a recreational vehicle owned by the policy-holder
- B) A lawsuit alleging discrimination by the policyholder
- C) Damages resulting from the policyholder's participation in a riot
- D) Legal fees associated with a lawsuit for breach of contract by the policyholder

76) The cost of an umbrella policy is generally influenced by:

- A) The policyholder's educational background
- B) The number of residences the policyholder owns
- C) The policyholder's driving record and number of vehicles
- D) The policyholder's employment history

77) How do insurance companies typically handle claims that involve both an underlying policy and an umbrella policy?

- A) The underlying policy must pay its limits before the umbrella policy contributes to a covered loss
- B) The umbrella policy pays first, and any excess is covered by the underlying policy
- C) Claims are split evenly between the underlying and umbrella policies
- D) The umbrella policy covers the deductible of the underlying policy

78) Which of the following best illustrates the concept of 'drop-down' coverage' in an umbrella policy?

- A) The umbrella policy increases its coverage limit to match that of the underlying policy
- B) The umbrella policy provides primary coverage when underlying

limits are exhausted
- C) The umbrella policy's coverage drops down to fill in gaps not covered by underlying policies
- D) Coverage limits drop as the insured ages

Package Policies (Total: 16 Questions)

Business Owners Policy (BOP): 8 questions

79) How does a BOP differ from a 'Commercial Package Policy' (CPP)?

- A) A BOP is for large corporations, while a CPP is for small businesses
- B) A BOP offers broader coverage in a single package, while a CPP allows for more customization of coverages
- C) A BOP is more expensive than a CPP
- D) A CPP includes health insurance, while a BOP does not

80) The 'Premises and Operations' coverage within a BOP liability insurance covers:

- A) Operations conducted away from the business premises
- B) Only the operations that occur within the owned premises
- C) Both the conditions at the business premises and operations conducted by the business
- D) The maintenance of the premises and equipment

81) 'Spoilage Coverage' under a BOP is important for businesses that:

- A) Deal with perishable goods
- B) Require refrigeration for their products
- C) Operate in the technology sector
- D) A and B

82) 'Employee Dishonesty Coverage' included in a BOP protects against:

- A) Accidental injuries to employees
- B) Theft or fraud committed by employees
- C) Dishonest acts by customers
- D) Liability claims made by employees

83) Which coverage extension is typically NOT available under a BOP?

- A) Outdoor property
- B) Professional liability
- C) Accounts receivable
- D) Valuable papers and records

84) The 'Protective Safeguards' endorsement in a BOP requires the insured to:

- A) Maintain specific safety and security measures as a condition of coverage
- B) Install protective devices on all company vehicles
- C) Guard against employee theft and fraud
- D) Protect all digital data with encryption

85) What is the 'Automatic Increase in Insurance' endorsement in a BOP?

- A) Automatically increases coverage limits annually based on inflation
- B) Increases the premium automatically every year
- C) Automatically adds new locations to the policy
- D) Provides automatic coverage increases for seasonal inventory

86) Under a BOP, 'Ordinance or Law Coverage' provides protection for:

- A) Fines and penalties due to violating laws or ordinances

- B) The increased cost of construction to meet current building codes after a covered loss
- C) Legal defense costs for ordinance violations
- D) Compliance with federal regulations

Commercial package policy: 8 questions

87) 'Directors and Officers' (D&O) liability insurance within a CPP is intended to protect:

- A) The personal assets of corporate directors and officers against claims related to their managerial decisions
- B) The company's assets from mismanagement by directors and officers
- C) All employees equally, regardless of position
- D) The company against claims made by directors and officers

88) Which is an essential feature of the 'Business Income' coverage in a CPP?

- A) It covers projected income increases indefinitely
- B) Compensation for lost net income and continuing expenses during restoration after a covered loss
- C) It provides a fixed daily income regardless of actual losses
- D) Coverage for income lost due to competition

89) 'Umbrella Liability' insurance as part of a CPP:

- A) Extends coverage limits beyond what is offered in the primary liability policies included in the CPP
- B) Provides primary liability coverage, replacing the need for any other liability insurance
- C) Covers personal liabilities not related to the business

- D) Is only available to businesses in certain industries

90) Which of the following best describes 'Builders Risk' insurance in a CPP?

- A) It covers the risk of building new structures only
- B) Insurance for contractors against claims made by clients
- C) Covers buildings under construction, including materials and equipment on site
- D) Provides liability coverage for builders and developers

91) A 'Business Owners Policy' (BOP) differs from a CPP in that:

- A) A BOP offers more extensive coverage options than a CPP
- B) A CPP is customizable, while a BOP offers standard packages
- C) CPPs are intended for larger businesses, while BOPs are not available to them
- D) BOPs require additional liability coverage to be purchased separately

92) The advantage of including 'Employment Practices Liability Insurance' (EPLI) in a CPP is to protect against claims from:

- A) Physical injuries on the job
- B) Damage to customer property
- C) Employment-related issues such as discrimination or wrongful termination
- D) Professional errors or omissions

93) 'Liquor Liability' coverage within a CPP is crucial for businesses that:

- A) Manufacture alcoholic beverages
- B) Serve or sell alcohol as part of their operations
- C) Host company events where alcohol is served

- D) B and C

94) 'Non-Owned and Hired Auto Liability' coverage in a CPP is important for businesses that:

- A) Own a large fleet of vehicles
- B) Occasionally rent vehicles for business use or have employees who use their personal vehicles for business tasks
- C) Operate in the transportation sector
- D) Provide company vehicles to all employees for personal use

State-Specific Regulations (Total: 14 Questions)

Licensing requirements: 4 questions

95) In most states, an individual selling property and casualty insurance must:

- A) Be at least 25 years old
- B) Have a minimum of 5 years of experience in the insurance industry
- C) Hold a valid driver's license
- D) Pass a licensing exam and fulfill education requirements

96) Which of the following is NOT a typical section on a property and casualty insurance license exam?

- A) Insurance policy analysis
- B) State laws and regulations
- C) Personal interview techniques
- D) Insurance terms and concepts

97) An individual applying for a property and casualty insurance license typically needs to:

- A) Submit fingerprints for a background check
- B) Provide proof of residency in the state for at least two years
- C) Show evidence of a minimum annual income
- D) Have a recommendation from a state senator or representative

98) Ethics training as part of continuing education for property and casualty insurance agents is important because:

- A) It is a requirement for higher-level certifications
- B) It ensures agents understand their legal responsibilities to their clients
- C) Ethics training is optional but recommended
- D) It qualifies agents for international insurance sales

State laws governing insurance practices: 5 questions

99) State insurance laws governing 'market conduct' focus on:

- A) The international conduct of insurance companies
- B) How insurers and agents market and sell insurance products
- C) The stock market investments of insurance companies
- D) Regulating the number of insurance products in the market

100) The 'file and use' regulation in some states allows insurers to:

- A) Use new rates and forms immediately after filing them with the state insurance department, without prior approval
- B) File claims on behalf of policyholders without their consent
- C) Use any underwriting criteria they choose, without state oversight
- D) File for exemptions from state insurance laws

101) Under state insurance laws, 'producer compensation disclosure' requirements are intended to:

- A) Disclose the salaries of insurance company executives to policyholders
- B) Inform customers about how agents and brokers are compensated for selling policies
- C) Require agents to disclose their personal financial information
- D) Limit the amount of compensation an agent can receive

102) The 'surplus lines' regulation under state laws permits:

- A) The sale of excess insurance coverage beyond what is available in the admitted market
- B) Insurers to maintain surplus reserves for emergencies
- C) Policyholders to purchase additional coverage directly from the state
- D) States to sell leftover insurance policies at a discount

103) In state insurance law, the 'use it or lose it' policy refers to:

- A) The expiration of insurance policies if not claimed within a year
- B) Prohibiting insurers from canceling or non-renewing policies solely because a policyholder filed a claim
- C) The practice of revoking licenses if insurance agents do not sell enough policies
- D) Mandatory policy cancellation if the insured moves out of state

Ethical practices and the regulatory environment: 5 questions

104) Which practice is essential for maintaining ethical standards in the regulatory environment of insurance?

- A) Avoiding disclosure of all fees and commissions
- B) Recommending only those products that offer the highest commission
- C) Transparent communication with clients regarding policy terms and

costs
- D) Sharing client information with third parties without consent

105) How does the regulatory environment support ethical practices in handling claims?

- A) By allowing insurers to use their discretion in all claim settlements
- B) Through strict guidelines that ensure fair and timely processing of claims
- C) By mandating automatic approval of all claims
- D) Through regulations that prioritize insurer profitability

106) 'Twisting' in the insurance industry refers to:

- A) Changing policy details at renewal without informing the policy-holder
- B) The practice of persuading a policyholder to cancel an existing policy unnecessarily for the benefit of the agent
- C) Adjusting the terms of a policy to better protect the client
- D) The ethical obligation to provide clients with a variety of insurance options

107) The principle of 'utmost good faith' in insurance obligates all parties to:

- A) Share all known risks and relevant information honestly
- B) Keep the insurance premiums at the lowest possible level
- C) Guarantee the profitability of insurance contracts
- D) Ensure that all insurance sales result in a commission

108) What is the impact of non-compliance with state insurance regulations on an insurance professional?

- A) It enhances the professional's reputation in the industry
- B) Mandatory promotion within the company
- C) Possible fines, license suspension, or revocation
- D) Increased commissions and bonuses

Insurance Operations (Total: 8 Questions)

Underwriting principles: 3 questions

109) 'Automated underwriting systems' are used in the insurance industry to:

- A) Replace human underwriters entirely
- B) Streamline the underwriting process by using algorithms to assess risks
- C) Automatically approve all applications received by the insurer
- D) Predict future losses based on past claims data

110) In underwriting, 'loadings' refer to:

- A) Discounts applied to premiums for low-risk applicants
- B) Additional charges applied to the premium to cover increased risk or administrative costs
- C) The maximum amount of insurance coverage available
- D) Fees charged for policy amendments

111) Which statement best describes 'conditional coverage' in underwriting?

- A) Coverage that applies only in certain conditions, such as specific weather events
- B) Temporary coverage provided between the application submission and the formal policy issuance

- C) A condition that must be met for the underwriting process to begin
- D) Insurance that is conditional on the completion of a home inspection

Rate making: 3 questions

112) 'Territorial rating' in insurance rate making is based on:

- A) The territory or geographic area where the insured risk is located, due to differences in risk exposure
- B) The size of the territory an insurance agent covers
- C) The international territories where the policy is effective
- D) The territory of the home office of the insurance company

113) The 'combined ratio' in rate making measures:

- A) The combination of premiums collected from all lines of insurance
- B) The financial strength of the insurance company
- C) The ratio of losses and expenses to earned premiums
- D) The ratio of combined life and property insurance policies sold

114) Which method of rate making involves adjusting the base premium up or down based on individual loss history?

- A) Manual rating
- B) Experience rating
- C) Schedule rating
- D) Judgment rating

Risk management: 2 questions

115) 'Risk concentration' refers to:

- A) Focusing on the most significant risk a company faces

- B) The accumulation of risk in a particular geographic area or asset
- C) The practice of concentrating all risk management efforts on pre-ventable risks
- D) Centralizing the risk management function within an organization

116) In the risk management process, 'exposure analysis' is used to:

- A) Determine the premium rates for different exposures
- B) Identify and quantify the potential impact of risks on an organization
- C) Analyze the exposure of the company to media scrutiny
- D) Calculate the exposure of employees to workplace hazards

Miscellaneous Coverages (Total: 4 Questions)

Flood insurance: 1 question

117) The NFIP defines a flood as:

- A) Overflow of inland or tidal waters, unusual and rapid accumulation or runoff of surface waters, or mudslides
- B) Water damage caused by a broken appliance within the home
- C) Leaks in the roof during a rainstorm
- D) Isolated pooling of water in a basement

Earthquake insurance: 1 question

118) How does the location of a property influence the cost of earthquake insurance?

- A) Properties located closer to fault lines generally have lower premi-ums due to increased risk
- B) Location has no impact on the cost; premiums are standardized nationwide

- C) Premiums are higher for properties located in areas with higher seismic activity due to the increased risk of damage
- D) Urban properties always have higher premiums than rural properties, regardless of seismic risk

Crime insurance policies: 2 questions

119) Which of the following scenarios would likely be covered by a 'Forgery or Alteration' coverage in a crime insurance policy?

- A) A flood damaging important company documents
- B) An employee altering checks to embezzle funds from the company
- C) A customer slipping and falling in the company premises
- D) External hacking into the company's computer system

120) 'Computer Fraud Coverage' under a crime insurance policy protects against losses from:

- A) Physical damage to computers and servers
- B) Theft of company data by employees
- C) Unauthorized electronic funds transfer due to hacking
- D) Viruses and malware that slow down system operations

Practice Exam 5 (Total: 121 Questions)

Insurance Basics (Total: 18 Questions)

Principles of insurance: 6 questions

1) Why is the principle of indemnity foundational to insurance contracts?

- A) It establishes a profit margin for insurers
- B) It ensures fair competition among insurers
- C) It prevents the insured from profiting from their loss
- D) It allows for unlimited coverage amounts

2) What does the principle of subrogation accomplish for the insurance industry?

- A) It reduces overall risk
- B) It encourages risk-taking
- C) It prevents the insured from claiming the same loss twice
- D) It allows insurers to recover funds from third parties responsible for losses

3) Which principle supports the idea that insurance should restore the insured to their financial position before the loss?

- A) Contribution
- B) Indemnity
- C) Insurable interest
- D) Utmost good faith

4) In insurance terminology, 'risk pooling' refers to what?

- A) The accumulation of premiums in a common fund
- B) The combination of various types of risks into one policy
- C) Spreading the financial risk of losses across many policyholders
- D) The practice of insurers sharing risk with reinsurance companies

5) The principle of contribution applies when?

- A) An insured has multiple policies covering the same peril
- B) A policyholder defaults on premium payments
- C) An insurer needs to increase premium rates
- D) The policyholder has no insurable interest in the insured property

6) Which of the following best exemplifies the principle of utmost good faith in action?

- A) An insurer investigates a claim before paying
- B) A policyholder accurately reports their medical history on an insurance application
- C) A claimant refuses to provide proof of loss
- D) An insurer uses complex language in the policy documents

Types of insurers: 6 questions

7) Which of the following insurers operates similarly to mutual insurers but focuses on life insurance for military members and their families?

- A) Fraternal benefit societies
- B) Military insurers
- C) Veterans' insurance companies
- D) Service insurers

8) An insurance company that sells policies in states other than where it was incorporated is known as a/an:

- A) Alien insurer
- B) Domestic insurer
- C) Foreign insurer
- D) International insurer

9) The main difference between a 'foreign' and an 'alien' insurer is based on:

- A) The size of the company
- B) The location of incorporation relative to the market it serves
- C) The types of insurance policies offered
- D) The financial stability of the company

10) Excess and surplus lines insurers are important because they:

- A) Only insure governmental entities
- B) Offer standard insurance products at lower rates
- C) Provide coverage for risks that standard insurers decline
- D) Operate exclusively in the reinsurance market

11) 'Direct writers' and 'independent agents' are terms used to describe different:

- A) Methods of underwriting insurance policies
- B) Types of insurance policies

- C) Channels for selling insurance products
- D) Regulatory approaches to insurance

12) A key feature of a reciprocal insurance exchange is that it:

- A) Functions without any formal structure
- B) Is managed by an attorney-in-fact
- C) Offers insurance without premiums
- D) Operates for profit, distributing dividends to shareholders

Policy renewals and cancellations: 6 questions

13) Which of the following best describes an automatic renewal clause in an insurance policy?

- A) The policy will automatically cancel unless the insured notifies the insurer
- B) The policy will automatically renew at the end of its term unless the insured or insurer decides otherwise
- C) The policy terms and premiums automatically change at renewal
- D) The policy coverage amounts decrease automatically at renewal

14) What does 'conditional renewal' of a policy imply?

- A) The policy will renew only if certain conditions are met, such as a change in premium or coverage terms
- B) The policy will renew under the same conditions as the original policy
- C) The policy renewal is dependent on the insurer's financial condition
- D) The policy will not renew under any circumstances

15) A cancellation fee is charged by the insurer to cover what?

- A) The cost of processing the cancellation

- B) The administrative costs associated with finding a new policyholder
- C) The loss of premium income for the remainder of the policy term
- D) The expenses incurred from underwriting the now-canceled policy

16) What is typically required by insurers before reinstating a canceled policy due to non-payment?

- A) A detailed explanation of why the payment was missed
- B) A signed affidavit promising no future payments will be missed
- C) Payment of past due premiums and possibly a reinstatement fee
- D) A new policy application and underwriting process

17) What might an insured expect to receive if their policy is canceled for reasons other than non-payment?

- A) A prorated refund of the unused premium
- B) An automatic offer of a new policy with higher premiums
- C) A list of recommended insurers
- D) Compensation for any claims that would have been filed during the remainder of the policy term

18) Which action is NOT a right of the insured upon receiving a cancellation notice?

- A) Requesting a detailed explanation for the cancellation
- B) Demanding immediate reinstatement without addressing the reasons for cancellation
- C) Seeking coverage from another insurer
- D) Contesting the cancellation if it's believed to be unjustified

Property Insurance (Total: 26 Questions)

Dwelling policies: 6 questions

19) Under a DP-2 (Broad Form) policy, which of the following is true regarding the 'Weight of Ice, Snow, or Sleet' peril?

- A) It covers damage to the dwelling but not to personal property inside
- B) It is excluded from coverage
- C) It only covers the cost to remove ice, snow, or sleet that has caused damage
- D) It includes coverage for both the dwelling and other structures

20) What is the 'Liberalization Clause' in dwelling policies?

- A) A provision that allows the insured to adjust coverage limits without penalty
- B) A clause that automatically applies any favorable changes in policy terms to existing policies
- C) A provision that liberalizes the requirements for proving a loss
- D) A clause allowing for the temporary suspension of coverage

21) Which coverage in a dwelling policy applies to medical expenses of guests accidentally injured on your property?

- A) Medical Payments to Others
- B) Personal Liability
- C) Dwelling
- D) Additional Living Expenses

22) How does the 'Inflation Guard Endorsement' affect a dwelling policy?

- A) It decreases the amount of insurance annually to match depreciation
- B) It automatically increases the dwelling coverage amount periodically to keep up with inflation

- C) It adjusts premiums based on the current rate of inflation without changing coverage amounts
- D) It provides additional coverage for inflation-related expenses

23) A 'Scheduled Personal Property Endorsement' in a dwelling policy is used to:

- A) List specific items of personal property for coverage above the standard policy limits
- B) Schedule times when personal property is covered
- C) Decrease premiums by scheduling coverage for when the property is most at risk
- D) Exclude certain personal property items from coverage

24) The 'Non-Occupancy Clause' in a dwelling policy refers to:

- A) A provision that excludes coverage if the dwelling is not occupied for a certain period
- B) A clause that provides coverage for dwellings under construction
- C) A provision allowing for short-term rental of the dwelling
- D) An exclusion for liability claims when the dwelling is not occupied by the owner

25) What is the effect of a 'Mortgagee Clause' in a dwelling policy?

- A) It provides the mortgagee (lender) with certain rights and protections under the policy
- B) It obligates the mortgagee to pay the insurance premiums
- C) It increases the coverage limits to satisfy the mortgagee's requirements
- D) It excludes the mortgagee from any claim settlements

Homeowners policies: 8 questions

26) Which of the following would likely NOT be covered by the Personal Liability section of a homeowners policy?

- A) Injury to a guest who slips on your icy sidewalk
- B) Your dog biting a neighbor on your property
- C) Damages awarded for slander or libel
- D) Accidental damage to your own property

27) An 'Accidental Discharge or Overflow of Water' endorsement to a homeowners policy covers:

- A) Flood damage from external sources
- B) Water damage from a public water main break
- C) Accidental overflow of water from plumbing, heating, or air conditioning systems
- D) Intentional acts that result in water damage

28) 'Landlord's Furnishings' coverage in a homeowners policy is intended to cover:

- A) Personal property owned by tenants
- B) Appliances and furniture provided by the landlord for the tenant's use
- C) Structural improvements made by the tenant
- D) Outdoor furniture not stored within the rented dwelling

29) Which statement about 'Named Peril' coverage in homeowners policies is TRUE?

- A) It covers all perils without exception
- B) It covers only those perils specifically named in the policy

- C) It is the only coverage option available in all homeowners policies
- D) It applies only to the dwelling and not to personal property

30) The 'Extended Replacement Cost' endorsement on a homeowners policy:

- A) Provides a fixed amount for replacing the home, regardless of the actual cost
- B) Pays up to a certain percentage over the insured amount to rebuild the home
- C) Guarantees replacement of the home at current market prices
- D) Covers the cost to replace the home with materials of lesser quality

31) What is typically required for 'Personal Property Replacement Cost' coverage in a homeowners policy?

- A) An appraisal of all personal property items
- B) A separate endorsement and additional premium
- C) Itemized receipts for all personal property
- D) A minimum property value

32) The 'All Risk' coverage in homeowners policies is another term for:

- A) Named perils coverage
- B) Open perils coverage
- C) Standard coverage
- D) Basic coverage

33) 'Special Personal Property Coverage' in a homeowners policy enhances protection by:

- A) Covering personal property on an open perils basis, except for specific exclusions

- B) Increasing the coverage limit for high-value items without additional premium
- C) Extending coverage to pets and animals owned by the insured
- D) Providing liability coverage for incidents occurring off the property

Commercial property policies: 7 questions

34) A 'Time Element Coverage' in commercial property insurance refers to:

- A) Coverage that is only valid during business hours
- B) Protection against losses due to the passage of time, such as business income and extra expense coverage
- C) The period it takes for a claim to be settled
- D) The timeframe during which coverage is effective

35) 'Newly Acquired or Constructed Property' coverage in a commercial property policy:

- A) Automatically covers new properties acquired or constructed for a limited time
- B) Requires immediate notification and premium adjustment to cover new properties
- C) Only covers newly constructed properties, not acquisitions
- D) Provides indefinite coverage for all new properties without need for notification

36) Which statement is true regarding the 'Standard Mortgage Clause' in a commercial property policy?

- A) It protects the mortgage lender's interests in the insured property
- B) It requires the mortgage lender to pay the insurance premiums
- C) It excludes the mortgage lender from any claim payments

- D) It provides coverage for the mortgage payment in case of the business's income loss

37) 'Outdoor Property Coverage' endorsement in a commercial property policy typically includes:

- A) Landscaping, signs, fences, and satellite dishes
- B) Parking lots and paved surfaces
- C) Vehicles and mobile equipment stored outdoors
- D) Air conditioning units and external building surfaces

38) The 'Selling Price Clause' in a commercial property policy is beneficial for businesses that:

- A) Sell products at variable prices
- B) Want to insure their inventory at the selling price rather than the cost price
- C) Require coverage for the cost price of all inventory
- D) Operate exclusively online without physical inventory

39) 'Ordinance or Law Increased Cost of Construction' coverage in a commercial property policy:

- A) Covers the additional costs to comply with current building codes after a covered loss
- B) Is automatically included in all commercial property policies
- C) Only applies to buildings over 50 years old
- D) Provides coverage for the demolition of undamaged parts of the building

40) The 'Electronic Data Processing (EDP) Coverage' in commercial property policies specifically insures:

- A) Any electronic data processing equipment, software, and data
- B) Only the hardware associated with electronic data processing
- C) Losses related to the interruption of electronic data processing
- D) Cyber liability and data breaches

Business interruption: 5 questions

41) 'Leader Property' coverage in a business interruption policy covers losses resulting from damage to:

- A) The insured's primary competitor
- B) A nearby property that attracts customers to the insured's business
- C) The insured's most valuable property
- D) Properties owned by leaders in the industry

42) The inclusion of 'fungus, wet rot, dry rot, and bacteria' coverage in a business interruption policy would:

- A) Cover losses due to spoilage of perishable goods
- B) Provide specific coverage for damage caused by these perils, typically excluded
- C) Extend the indemnity period for losses caused by these risks
- D) Increase the premium due to the high risk associated with these perils

43) How does the 'Monthly Limit of Indemnity' option affect a business interruption policy?

- A) It limits the amount the insurer will pay out for any single month's loss
- B) It defines the maximum duration the policy will cover business interruption losses
- C) It increases the total amount of coverage available over the policy

period
- D) It specifies the minimum amount payable for any loss

44) 'Contingent Business Interruption' coverage is particularly important for businesses that:

- A) Operate on a seasonal basis
- B) Rely heavily on online sales
- C) Depend on a few key suppliers or customers for their operations
- D) Have a high turnover of employees

45) The 'Extended Business Income' coverage in a business interruption policy:

- A) Compensates for income lost before the physical damage occurred
- B) Covers additional expenses not covered under the basic policy
- C) Provides income coverage after the business has resumed operations, for a specified period
- D) Extends coverage indefinitely until the business fully recovers

Casualty Insurance (Total: 32 Questions)

Auto insurance: 8 questions

46) In auto insurance, the 'Right to Appraisal' clause allows:

- A) The insurer to determine the value of damages without input from the policyholder
- B) The policyholder and insurer to engage independent appraisers to resolve disputes over the value of a claim
- C) The policyholder to demand a higher payout than offered
- D) Automatic arbitration in the event of a claim dispute

47) Which of the following typically qualifies for a 'Good Driver Discount' in auto insurance?

- · A) Drivers who have used their insurance frequently
- · B) Drivers with at least one at-fault accident in the past three years
- · C) Drivers without any moving violations or accidents for a specified period
- · D) New drivers with less than a year of driving experience

48) 'Comprehensive' coverage for commercial auto insurance:

- · A) Covers only collisions with other vehicles
- · B) Includes liability coverage for the business
- · C) Protects against theft, vandalism, and other non-collision damage
- · D) Is mandatory for all commercial vehicles

49) The primary difference between 'Personal' and 'Commercial' auto insurance is:

- · A) The type of vehicles covered
- · B) The liability limits available
- · C) The intended use of the insured vehicle
- · D) The geographic coverage area

50) In auto insurance, 'Permissive Use' refers to:

- · A) Allowing anyone to drive the insured vehicle with the owner's permission
- · B) The insurer's permission to drive in restricted areas
- · C) Permitting the insured vehicle to be used for commercial purposes
- · D) Granting permission to tow trailers or other vehicles

51) What does the 'Loss Payee' clause in an auto insurance policy specify?

- A) The method by which losses will be paid out
- B) The party to be compensated first in the event of a loss, typically a lienholder or lessor
- C) The maximum amount the insurer will pay for a loss
- D) The deductible amount the policyholder must pay

52) 'Custom Parts and Equipment (CPE)' coverage in an auto policy is intended for:

- A) Stock parts only, as custom parts are excluded
- B) Aftermarket modifications and customizations not originally installed by the manufacturer
- C) Repairs using only new OEM (Original Equipment Manufacturer) parts
- D) Personal belongings within the vehicle

53) A 'Named Driver Exclusion' in an auto insurance policy:

- A) Excludes specific drivers from coverage under the policy
- B) Names drivers who are covered, excluding all others
- C) Applies only to drivers not named in the policy, but who have permission to drive
- D) Is a clause naming the primary driver of the insured vehicle

Workers compensation: 8 questions

54) The 'Dual Capacity' doctrine in workers' compensation law allows:

- A) Employees to collect benefits from both workers' compensation and personal injury lawsuits under certain conditions
- B) Employers to act as both the insurer and the employer
- C) Workers to be classified as both employees and independent contractors

- D) Employers to receive compensation for injuries sustained by employees

55) In workers' compensation, 'Repetitive Stress Injuries' (RSIs) are:

- A) Covered only if they result from a single, identifiable incident
- B) Considered to be pre-existing conditions and not covered
- C) Covered as they are injuries that occur over time due to repetitive motions or strain
- D) Excluded unless they can be directly linked to a workplace accident

56) 'Death Benefits' provided by workers' compensation insurance to dependents of a deceased worker typically include:

- A) A lump-sum payment only
- B) Reimbursement for funeral expenses and ongoing support payments
- C) Compensation for the worker's pain and suffering prior to death
- D) A scholarship fund for the worker's children

57) What is the significance of the 'Maximum Medical Improvement' (MMI) in workers' compensation?

- A) It marks the point when an employee is considered fully recovered and can return to work without restrictions
- B) It indicates the highest level of recovery the injured worker is expected to achieve, which may involve permanent disability
- C) It is the deadline for filing a claim for compensation
- D) It signifies the maximum amount of medical benefits an employee can receive

58) The concept of 'Constructive Notice' in workers' compensation implies that:

- A) Employers are presumed to know of any hazards that could lead to injuries
- B) Employees must construct a written notice of injury
- C) Notice of injury must be given in a constructive, rather than critical, manner
- D) Employers must post notice of workers' compensation rights in a conspicuous place

59) Which is NOT a typical exclusion from workers' compensation coverage?

- A) Injuries sustained while the employee was committing a crime
- B) Injuries that occur during company-sponsored recreational activities
- C) Illnesses unrelated to the workplace
- D) Injuries resulting from natural disasters while at work

60) 'Alternative Dispute Resolution' (ADR) mechanisms in workers' compensation are used to:

- A) Determine the amount of compensation without going to court
- B) Resolve disputes between insurance companies over who is liable
- C) Provide an alternative to receiving workers' compensation benefits
- D) Settle disagreements between employees over workplace injuries

61) The 'Waiting Period' in workers' compensation refers to the time:

- A) Before an injured worker can return to work
- B) An employer has to contest a claim
- C) Before benefits start, typically a few days after an injury
- D) An employee must wait before filing a lawsuit against the employer

Liability insurance: 10 questions

62) 'Motor Truck Cargo Liability Insurance' covers:

- · A) Damage to the truck in an accident
- · B) Liability for goods damaged or lost while in transit
- · C) Personal injuries sustained by the truck driver
- · D) Theft of the cargo truck

63) What is 'Contingent Liability' coverage?

- · A) Coverage for liabilities that may occur, depending on the outcome of an uncertain event
- · B) Insurance for liabilities that are not directly caused by the insured
- · C) Liability coverage that is secondary to another policy
- · D) Coverage for liabilities assumed under contract

64) 'Hired and Non-Owned Auto Liability Insurance' is particularly important for businesses that:

- · A) Own and operate a large fleet of vehicles
- · B) Lease all their vehicles for business use
- · C) Do not own vehicles but occasionally rent or use employees' vehicles for business purposes
- · D) Specialize in auto repair and servicing

65) The 'Care, Custody, or Control' exclusion in a liability policy applies to:

- · A) Property owned by the insured
- · B) Property in the insured's care, custody, or control
- · C) Injuries to the insured's employees
- · D) Damage to public property

66) 'Excess Liability Insurance' differs from an 'Umbrella Policy' in that it:

- A) Only provides additional limits over specified underlying policies without broader coverage
- B) Offers broader coverage terms and can provide primary coverage where underlying policies do not exist
- C) Covers personal liabilities not included in home or auto policies
- D) Is automatically included with every commercial policy

67) Which of the following best describes 'Premises Liability'?

- A) Liability for injuries that occur off the premises during business operations
- B) Liability for injuries and damages that occur on the insured's premises
- C) The insured's liability for products manufactured or sold
- D) Liability for damages caused by the insured's completed operations

68) 'Legal Defense Costs' in a liability policy:

- A) Are included within the policy limits and reduce the amount available for settlement
- B) Are covered in addition to the policy limits
- C) Must be paid out of pocket by the insured
- D) Are only covered if the insured is found liable

69) A 'Named Insured Endorsement' in a liability policy:

- A) Changes the name of the insured on the policy
- B) Adds a person or entity to the policy as an insured
- C) Specifies only certain individuals as insured
- D) Limits coverage to named perils

70) 'Stop Gap' coverage in a workers' compensation and employers liability policy is intended to:

- A) Fill the gaps in coverage for employees not covered by standard workers' compensation laws
- B) Provide temporary coverage until a new policy takes effect
- C) Cover the employer's liability in monopolistic states where workers' compensation does not include employer liability
- D) Stop the policy from covering certain types of claims

71) In liability insurance, the 'Cross-Liability' provision:

- A) Allows for coverage disputes between insurers to be resolved
- B) Treats each insured as a separate entity for the purpose of insurance coverage
- C) Prevents one insured from suing another under the same policy
- D) Requires all parties to share equally in the liability

Umbrella policies: 6 questions

72) An individual with which of the following characteristics is MOST likely to benefit from an umbrella policy?

- A) Someone with minimal personal assets
- B) A person who does not own a car or home
- C) An individual with significant assets and potential exposure to large liability claims
- D) A person with a history of filing frequent small insurance claims

73) 'Excess Liability Insurance' differs from an 'Umbrella Policy' primarily in that:

- A) It only provides additional limits over an existing liability policy

without broader coverages
- B) It includes coverage for claims not covered by underlying policies
- C) It is cheaper and more accessible for individuals without major assets
- D) It covers all types of liability without any underlying policy requirements

74) Which activity would MOST likely necessitate additional coverage under an umbrella policy?

- A) Regularly participating in community service
- B) Employing domestic staff at home
- C) Volunteering at local non-profit organizations
- D) Engaging in high-risk sports as a hobby

75) What typically triggers the coverage under an umbrella policy?

- A) A claim that is specifically excluded under an underlying policy
- B) Any claim, regardless of other insurance coverage
- C) The exhaustion of underlying policy limits for a covered claim
- D) A claim filed directly with the umbrella insurer without involving underlying policies

76) An umbrella policy's coverage for 'Uninsured/Underinsured Motorist' (UM/UIM):

- A) Is automatically included in all umbrella policies
- B) Must be specifically added as an endorsement in most cases
- C) Covers the policyholder for all auto-related incidents, regardless of fault
- D) Is not necessary if the policyholder has health insurance

77) Which statement is true regarding the purchase of an umbrella policy?

- A) It is only available to individuals with a high net worth
- B) It requires the purchase of maximum limits on all underlying policies
- C) It is typically available as an add-on to a homeowners policy without additional requirements
- D) It can be purchased independently of other personal liability policies

Package Policies (Total: 14 Questions)

Business Owners Policy (BOP): 7 questions

78) A BOP generally offers which of the following advantages over separate policies?

- A) Higher coverage limits
- B) Broader exclusions
- C) Cost savings and simplicity
- D) More extensive international coverage

79) Which of the following businesses would typically NOT qualify for a BOP?

- A) A small accounting firm
- B) A home-based crafts seller
- C) A large manufacturing plant
- D) A downtown café

80) The 'Money and Securities' coverage in a BOP protects against:

- A) Loss of income due to business interruption
- B) Theft, destruction, or disappearance of money and securities either on-premises or in transit
- C) Changes in currency value affecting the business
- D) Investment losses

81) 'Equipment Breakdown' coverage in a BOP:

- A) Covers mechanical failures of the business owner's personal vehicles
- B) Insures against breakdowns of office equipment like computers and printers
- C) Applies only to manufacturing equipment
- D) Covers loss due to the breakdown of machinery and equipment necessary for business operations

82) Which scenario would be covered under the liability portion of a BOP?

- A) An employee is injured on the job
- B) A customer slips and falls in the store
- C) The business owner crashes a company car
- D) A fire damages the business premises

83) The 'Personal and Advertising Injury' coverage under a BOP protects against claims of:

- A) Physical injury to customers or employees
- B) Injury arising from slander, libel, and violation of privacy rights
- C) Injuries sustained during company-sponsored events
- D) False advertising practices

84) In a BOP, the 'Business Income' coverage is designed to:

- A) Compensate the business for lost revenue during temporary shutdowns due to covered property damage
- B) Cover the lost income of the business owner personally
- C) Provide a steady income to employees during business closures
- D) Replace lost income due to poor sales or market conditions

Commercial package policy: 7 questions

85) The 'Waiver of Subrogation' endorsement in a CPP:

- · A) Allows the insurer to pursue a third party responsible for a loss
- · B) Prevents the insurer from seeking recovery from a third party after paying a loss
- · C) Waives all coverage under the policy
- · D) Requires the insured to waive their right to sue the insurer

86) Which coverage is NOT standard in a CPP but can be added as an endorsement?

- · A) Commercial Property
- · B) General Liability
- · C) Professional Liability
- · D) Business Interruption

87) 'Ordinance or Law' coverage in a CPP addresses costs related to:

- · A) Legal defense fees in lawsuits against the business
- · B) Updating a damaged building to current building codes during repairs
- · C) Fines and penalties for code violations discovered after a loss
- · D) Compliance with federal employment laws

88) The 'Named Peril' option in a CPP specifies that coverage is provided:

- · A) For all perils except those specifically named in the policy
- · B) Only for perils specifically named in the policy
- · C) For an unlimited number of perils without exclusions
- · D) For any peril as long as it is named at the time of the claim

89) A 'Monoline Policy' differs from a CPP in that it:

- A) Offers bundled coverage options for businesses
- B) Provides coverage for a single line of insurance only
- C) Is available exclusively to mono-line businesses
- D) Cannot be combined with other insurance policies

90) In a CPP, the 'Coinsurance Clause' typically requires that:

- A) The business co-pays a percentage of all claims with the insurer
- B) The property is insured for a certain percentage of its value to avoid a penalty in the event of a partial loss
- C) The insurer and insured share responsibilities for coinvesting in property upgrades
- D) Coverage is split evenly among all insured parties

91) Which of the following best describes the 'Aggregate Limit' in a CPP?

- A) The maximum amount the insurer will pay for a single claim
- B) The total amount the insurer will pay for all claims during the policy period
- C) A predetermined limit for each type of coverage within the policy
- D) The limit the business must pay out-of-pocket before the insurer pays a claim

State-Specific Regulations (Total: 16 Questions)

Licensing requirements: 5 questions

92) Temporary licenses for property and casualty insurance agents:

- A) Are issued for agents to sell insurance without passing the licensing exam
- B) Allow individuals to sell insurance while completing pre-licensing education

- C) Are given to agents relocating from another state
- D) Can be granted under special circumstances, such as when an agent is undergoing a lengthy licensing process

93) Non-resident licensing for property and casualty insurance agents allows:

- A) Agents to bypass continuing education requirements in their home state
- B) Agents to sell insurance in a state where they do not reside, often with reciprocity agreements
- C) Unlimited sales across state lines without additional licensing
- D) Agents to sell insurance only online in non-resident states

94) The application fee for a property and casualty insurance license:

- A) Is a one-time fee that covers all future renewals
- B) Varies significantly from state to state
- C) Is standardized across all states
- D) Includes the cost of the licensing exam

95) What impact does a felony conviction have on obtaining a property and casualty insurance license?

- A) It has no impact as long as the conviction is not related to insurance fraud
- B) It automatically disqualifies the applicant in all states
- C) It may disqualify the applicant, depending on the nature of the felony and state laws
- D) Applicants with felony convictions are required to work under supervision for a probationary period

96) The 'look-back' period for criminal convictions when applying for a

property and casualty insurance license:

- A) Does not exist; all convictions must be reported regardless of when they occurred
- B) Is typically 5-10 years, depending on state regulations
- C) Varies, but most states do not consider convictions older than 20 years
- D) Is determined by the severity of the crime

State laws governing insurance practices: 6 questions

97) How do state laws typically regulate 'captive insurance' companies?

- A) By prohibiting their formation
- B) Allowing businesses to form their own insurance companies for self-insurance, with specific regulations and requirements
- C) Treating them the same as large, commercial insurers
- D) Requiring them to offer policies to the general public

98) State insurance departments often provide which of the following services to consumers?

- A) Investment advice for purchasing insurance company stocks
- B) Mediation and arbitration for disputes between insurers and policy-holders
- C) Direct sales of insurance policies
- D) Compensation for uninsured losses

99) What is the typical state requirement for 'insurance company re-serves'?

- A) Reserves must be invested in the stock market
- B) Insurers are required to keep a certain percentage of premiums to

cover future claims
- C) There are no specific reserve requirements at the state level
- D) Reserves must equal the total value of all policies issued

100) 'Binding authority' for agents under state insurance laws allows them to:

- A) Bind coverage on behalf of the insurer, within certain limits
- B) Legally bind policyholders to renew policies
- C) Set binding arbitration as the sole dispute resolution method
- D) Determine binding premium rates without insurer approval

101) In the context of state insurance laws, 'rebating' is:

- A) Offering a premium discount as an incentive for prompt payment
- B) The return of a portion of the agent's commission to the policyholder as an inducement to purchase
- C) A common practice allowed in all states
- D) A type of risk-sharing among insurers

102) State insurance regulations regarding 'data security' typically require insurers to:

- A) Store all customer data on state-maintained servers
- B) Implement measures to protect sensitive policyholder information from breaches
- C) Share data freely among insurers for underwriting purposes
- D) Collect only the minimum necessary personal information

Ethical practices and the regulatory environment: 5 questions

103) Ethical marketing practices in insurance require:

- A) Promising more than what the policy delivers to secure sales
- B) Full disclosure of policy benefits, limitations, and costs
- C) The use of technical jargon to impress potential clients
- D) Avoiding the discussion of policy exclusions and limitations

104) In the regulatory environment, the purpose of 'anti-rebating' laws is to:

- A) Ensure that all clients receive the same level of service
- B) Prohibit the practice of offering inducements to buy insurance that are not outlined in the policy
- C) Allow agents to offer personal gifts to clients for purchasing policies
- D) Encourage competition based on the quality of service and coverage

105) The ethical handling of premium payments involves:

- A) Using premiums collected from clients for personal or operational expenses
- B) Promptly forwarding premiums to the insurer or designated third party
- C) Holding onto premiums until a claim is filed
- D) Investing client premiums in high-risk stocks for potential returns

106) A conflict of interest in the insurance industry arises when:

- A) An agent acts in the best interest of the client
- B) An insurance professional has personal interests that could influence their professional duties
- C) Professionals strictly adhere to ethical guidelines

- D) Agents provide unbiased advice to all clients

107) The principle of 'indemnity' in insurance ethics is designed to:

- A) Allow clients to profit from insurance claims
- B) Ensure that clients are restored to their financial position prior to a loss, no more and no less
- C) Encourage inflated insurance claims for mutual benefit
- D) Limit the insurer's liability to a fixed amount regardless of the loss

Insurance Operations (Total: 10 Questions)

Underwriting principles: 4 questions

108) 'Underwriting profit' is achieved when:

- A) The insurer's investment income exceeds its underwriting losses
- B) Premiums collected exceed the costs of claims and underwriting expenses
- C) The policyholder profits from their insurance policy
- D) Reinsurance costs are lower than expected

109) The 'Law of Large Numbers' is important in underwriting because it:

- A) Guarantees that every large policy will be profitable
- B) Allows underwriters to predict loss occurrences more accurately with larger pools of similar risks
- C) States that larger insurance companies are more successful
- D) Ensures that policies with large coverage limits are underwritten more strictly

110) 'Insurable Interest' must be established in the underwriting process

to:

- A) Determine the premium payment schedule
- B) Ensure that the policyholder stands to suffer a financial loss from the insured event
- C) Identify potential beneficiaries of the policy
- D) Calculate the amount of coverage needed

111) How do underwriters use 'loss history' during the underwriting process?

- A) To predict the exact date of future losses
- B) As a guide to assess the likelihood and potential cost of future claims based on past claims
- C) To increase premiums for all policyholders annually
- D) To exclude coverage for any previously claimed losses

Rate making: 3 questions

112) 'Judgment rating' in rate making is typically used when:

- A) There is insufficient historical data to use other rating methods
- B) The insured insists on a personalized premium rate
- C) The policy covers a common, well-understood risk
- D) Automated systems calculate the premiums

113) The purpose of 'loading' in the premium calculation is to:

- A) Increase the premium for high-risk policyholders only
- B) Account for the insurer's operational costs and profit margin
- C) Load additional coverages onto a basic policy without increasing the premium
- D) Reflect the load of claims expected during the policy period

114) In rate making, the term 'actuarial fairness' refers to:

- A) The fairness in salaries between actuaries and underwriters
- B) Setting premiums that are proportional to the risk and expected losses
- C) Ensuring all policyholders pay the same premium
- D) The equitable distribution of profits from investments

Risk management: 3 questions

115) Which of the following best exemplifies 'risk mitigation' in property and casualty insurance?

- A) Purchasing the maximum possible insurance coverage for all risks
- B) Implementing a business continuity plan to maintain operations after a loss
- C) Avoiding any business activities that carry a risk of liability
- D) Investing exclusively in low-risk financial instruments

116) The 'risk management policy statement' of a company typically includes:

- A) A detailed list of all insurance policies held by the company
- B) The company's objectives and guidelines for managing risk
- C) The financial limits assigned to each type of risk
- D) A declaration of the company's insurance broker

117) 'Contingent risk' in the context of risk management refers to:

- A) Risks that are dependent on or contingent upon certain events
- B) The risk that contingency plans fail
- C) Risks that cannot be insured against
- D) The likelihood of an insurer becoming insolvent

Miscellaneous Coverages (Total: 4 Questions)

Flood insurance: 2 questions

118) What is a 'Preferred Risk Policy' (PRP) in the context of flood insurance?

- A) A policy offered to properties that have never been flooded
- B) Flood insurance offered at a reduced rate to properties in low to moderate-risk areas
- C) A policy for high-value homes only
- D) A policy available exclusively to commercial properties

119) How often can flood insurance policies be renewed through the NFIP?

- A) Annually, with the option to purchase multi-year policies at a discount
- B) Every five years, coinciding with FEMA's flood zone reevaluations
- C) Bi-annually, with mandatory inspections
- D) Annually, with no guarantee of renewal if the property's risk level changes

Earthquake insurance: 1 question

120) What is typically excluded from standard earthquake insurance policies?

- A) Damage to the exterior of the building, including windows and siding
- B) Fire damage resulting from an earthquake
- C) Damage to vehicles, even if they are on the property
- D) Land subsidence or sinkholes even if caused by an earthquake

Crime insurance policies: 1 question

121) In the context of crime insurance, what does 'Social Engineering Fraud Coverage' typically insure against?

- · A) Losses incurred due to employees using social media during work hours
- · B) The manipulation of employees by third parties to transfer money or property based on fraudulent instructions
- · C) The costs associated with improving company culture and employee relations
- · D) Expenses for training employees on social interaction skills

VII

Part VI: Full Length Practice Exam Answer Key

Practice Exam 1 (Total: 124 Questions) - Answers & Explanations

Insurance Basics (Total: 18 Questions)

Principles of insurance: 6 questions

1) What is the principle of indemnity in insurance?

Correct Answer is C - The principle of indemnity ensures that insurance policies compensate for losses up to the insured's economic loss but do not allow the insured to profit from the insurance claim. This principle maintains fairness and prevents moral hazard.

2) Which principle describes the sharing of loss by all members of a group?

Correct Answer is C - Risk pooling describes the process of spreading financial risk among all members of a group, thereby reducing the burden on any single member in the event of a loss.

3) The principle of utmost good faith requires which of the following?

Correct Answer is B - The principle of utmost good faith, or uberrima fides, requires both the insurer and the insured to enter into the insurance contract in good faith, fully disclosing all relevant facts that could influence the decision to enter into the contract.

4) What does the principle of subrogation enable an insurer to do?

Correct Answer is C - The principle of subrogation allows an insurer to pursue a third party that caused a loss to the insured, in order to recover the amount of the claim paid to the insured for the loss.

5) Which principle prevents the insured from profiting from insurance?

Correct Answer is B - The principle of indemnity prevents the insured from profiting from insurance by ensuring compensation only up to the actual amount of loss.

6) Insurable interest must exist at which time?

Correct Answer is C - Insurable interest must exist at both the time of the contract's inception and at the time of the loss to validate the insurance claim and contract.

Types of insurers: 4 questions

7) Which type of insurer is owned by its policyholders?

Correct Answer is B - A mutual insurer is owned by its policyholders, who may receive dividends or reductions in premiums as a return of surplus.

8) What is a stock insurance company?

Correct Answer is B - A stock insurance company is owned by shareholders who invest capital to establish the company and share in its profits through dividends.

9) Which insurer operates on a non-profit basis by returning surplus funds to its policyholders?

Correct Answer is B - Mutual insurers operate on a non-profit basis by returning surplus funds to its policyholders in the form of dividends or reduced future premiums.

10) A captive insurance company is primarily established for what purpose?

Correct Answer is B - A captive insurance company is established primarily to insure the risks of its parent company, providing a form of self-insurance.

Policy renewals and cancellations: 8 questions

11) What is a policy renewal?

Correct Answer is B - A policy renewal involves continuing an existing insurance policy term without changes, extending the coverage period.

12) Which of the following reasons might an insurer cancel an insurance policy?

Correct Answer is C - Non-payment of premium is a common reason an insurer might cancel an insurance policy, as it constitutes a breach of the policy terms.

13) What is the grace period in an insurance policy?

Correct Answer is C - The grace period in an insurance policy is a specified period after a missed payment during which the policy remains in force, allowing the insured extra time to pay the premium without losing coverage

14) Under what circumstance can a short-rate cancellation occur?

Correct Answer is B - A short-rate cancellation occurs when the insured decides to cancel the policy before its expiration date, often incurring a penalty for early cancellation.

15) Which term describes the automatic renewal of a policy for a new term?

Correct Answer is D - An evergreen policy describes the automatic renewal of a policy for a new term, ensuring continuous coverage without the need for the insured to take action.

16) What must an insurer provide to an insured if they decide not to renew a policy?

Correct Answer is B - If an insurer decides not to renew a policy, they must provide the insured with written notice of non-renewal within a specified time frame before the policy expires to allow the insured time to seek alternative coverage.

17) In the context of insurance, what does 'pro-rata cancellation' mean?

Correct Answer is A - Pro-rata cancellation means the insurer cancels the policy and returns the unused premium to the insured on a proportional basis, reflecting the unused portion of the coverage period.

18) What is the primary reason an insurer might non-renew a policy?

Correct Answer is B - The primary reason an insurer might non-renew a policy is if the risk profile of the insured has significantly changed, making the policy riskier than the insurer is willing to cover.

Property Insurance (Total: 32 Questions)

Dwelling policies: 8 questions

19) What is a dwelling policy primarily used to insure?

Correct Answer is C - A dwelling policy is primarily used to insure residential properties not typically covered by standard homeowners policies, such as rental properties or homes that do not meet certain underwriting criteria.

20) Which of the following is NOT covered under a basic dwelling policy?

Correct Answer is B - Theft is not covered under a basic dwelling policy, which typically provides coverage for specific perils like fire, lightning, and internal explosion but not for theft.

21) Dwelling Policy Program offers how many coverage forms?

Correct Answer is C - The Dwelling Policy Program offers three coverage forms: DP-1 (Basic Form), DP-2 (Broad Form), and DP-3 (Special Form), allowing policyholders to choose the level of coverage that best suits their needs.

22) What does DP-1, or Basic Form Dwelling Policy, typically cover?

Correct Answer is A - DP-1, or Basic Form Dwelling Policy, typically covers fire, lightning, and internal explosion only. It is the most basic level of coverage, offering protection against a limited number of perils.

23) Which Dwelling Policy form provides the broadest coverage?

Correct Answer is C - DP-3 provides the broadest coverage as it is an open peril (or all risk) form, meaning it covers all perils except those specifically excluded in the policy documents.

24) In dwelling policies, 'Other Structures' coverage is:

Correct Answer is A - 'Other Structures' coverage is automatically included at 10% of the dwelling coverage amount in dwelling policies, providing additional protection for structures not attached to the main dwelling.

25) What is the primary difference between DP-2 and DP-3 coverage forms?

Correct Answer is A - The primary difference between DP-2 and DP-3 coverage forms is that DP-2 covers named perils, while DP-3 offers open perils coverage, meaning DP-3 provides a broader range of protection.

26) Which peril is typically covered by a DP-2 (Broad Form) dwelling policy but NOT by a DP-1 (Basic Form)?

Correct Answer is D - Falling objects are typically covered by a DP-2 (Broad Form) dwelling policy but are not covered by a DP-1 (Basic Form), which offers more limited coverage.

Homeowners policies: 10 questions

27) Which of the following is NOT a type of coverage typically provided by a homeowners policy?

```
Correct Answer is C - Automobile coverage is not typically
provided by a homeowners policy, as these policies focus on
residential property and liability protection, not vehicle
insurance.
```

28) What does Coverage A in a standard homeowners policy insure?

```
Correct Answer is A - Coverage A in a standard homeowners policy
insures the main dwelling on the property, providing protection
against various perils to the structure itself.
```

29) Personal Liability coverage in a homeowners policy protects the insured against claims for:

```
Correct Answer is C - Personal Liability coverage in a
homeowners policy protects the insured against claims for both
bodily injury to others and property damage caused by the
insured, offering broad liability protection.
```

30) Which homeowners policy form is specifically designed for renters?

```
Correct Answer is B - HO-4 policy form is specifically designed
for renters, providing coverage for personal property and
liability but not for the dwelling itself.
```

31) The 'open perils' coverage in a homeowners policy means the policy

covers:

Correct Answer is B - 'Open perils' coverage means the policy covers all perils except those specifically excluded, offering comprehensive protection against a wide range of risks.

32) Which of the following is typically excluded from a standard home-owners policy?

Correct Answer is C - Earth movement, including earthquakes and landslides, is typically excluded from standard homeowners policies due to the high risk and potential for significant damage.

33) What is the purpose of 'Medical Payments to Others' coverage in a homeowners policy?

Correct Answer is B - 'Medical Payments to Others' coverage is designed to pay for medical expenses of guests injured on the property, regardless of fault, ensuring prompt medical attention without legal disputes.

34) HO-6 insurance policies are designed specifically for:

Correct Answer is B - HO-6 insurance policies are designed specifically for condominium owners, covering personal property and parts of the unit not covered by the condo association's policy.

35) In a homeowners policy, 'Other Structures' coverage (Coverage B) typically covers:

Correct Answer is C - 'Other Structures' coverage (Coverage B)
typically covers structures on the property not attached to the
dwelling, such as a detached garage, providing protection for a
range of auxiliary structures.

36) Which coverage in a homeowners policy would cover the insured in case of a lawsuit for accidentally injuring someone off their property?

Correct Answer is D - Personal Liability coverage in a
homeowners policy would cover the insured in case of a lawsuit
for accidentally injuring someone off their property, offering
liability protection beyond the home premises.

Commercial property policies: 8 questions

37) What is the primary purpose of commercial property insurance?

Correct Answer is C - The primary purpose of commercial property
insurance is to insure the business's physical assets against
loss or damage, protecting the company's tangible property.

38) Which of the following is typically NOT covered under a standard commercial property policy?

Correct Answer is B - Customer data is typically not covered
under a standard commercial property policy, as these policies
focus on physical assets rather than intangible assets like data.

39) The 'Building and Personal Property Coverage Form' in a commercial

property policy covers:

Correct Answer is D - The 'Building and Personal Property Coverage Form' in a commercial property policy covers both the building and permanently installed fixtures, as well as business personal property on premises, offering comprehensive protection for physical assets.

40) What does 'Coinsurance' in a commercial property policy require?

Correct Answer is A - 'Coinsurance' in a commercial property policy requires the policyholder to share in the risk by insuring the property to a specified percentage of its value, encouraging adequate insurance coverage to avoid penalties in the event of a partial loss.

41) 'Business Income Coverage' in a commercial property policy is designed to:

Correct Answer is A - Business Income Coverage is designed to replace lost income during a period of restoration following a covered loss. This ensures that a business can maintain its financial stability and continue operations after a disaster.

42) Which of the following would be covered under 'Extra Expense Coverage' in a commercial property policy?

Correct Answer is B - Extra Expense Coverage covers expenses to relocate temporarily following a covered loss. This enables businesses to continue operations while their primary location is being repaired or rebuilt.

43) The 'Cause of Loss - Basic Form' in a commercial property policy

typically includes coverage for:

Correct Answer is B - The 'Cause of Loss - Basic Form' in a commercial property policy typically includes coverage for basic perils such as fire, lightning, and explosion, offering foundational protection for businesses.

44) What is the purpose of the 'Builders Risk Coverage Form' in commercial property insurance?

Correct Answer is B - The 'Builders Risk Coverage Form' in commercial property insurance is designed to insure buildings under construction against specified perils, protecting the investment in the property during the construction phase.

Business interruption: 6 questions

45) What is the primary purpose of business interruption insurance?

Correct Answer is B - The primary purpose of business interruption insurance is to compensate for lost income during a period of restoration after a covered loss, helping businesses cover ongoing expenses and lost profits.

46) Business interruption insurance typically covers income lost due to:

Correct Answer is B - Business interruption insurance typically covers income lost due to a natural disaster that damages the insured property, providing financial support to help businesses recover from significant disruptions.

47) Which of the following is typically required for a business interruption

claim to be valid?

Correct Answer is A - For a business interruption claim to be valid, the interruption must result from a direct physical loss or damage to the property. This criterion ensures that the policy responds to tangible disruptions to business operations.

48) What does the 'period of restoration' refer to in a business interruption policy?

Correct Answer is C - The 'period of restoration' refers to the time from the occurrence of the damage until the property should be repaired, rebuilt, or replaced. It defines the timeframe during which business interruption coverage is applicable.

49) 'Extra Expense' coverage in a business interruption policy is designed to:

Correct Answer is A - 'Extra Expense' coverage in a business interruption policy is designed to compensate for expenses beyond normal operating expenses that a business incurs to continue operation during restoration, such as temporary relocation costs.

50) Which factor is NOT considered when calculating the amount of business interruption coverage needed?

Correct Answer is D - When calculating the amount of business interruption coverage needed, the physical size of the business premises is not considered. Factors like historical profit margins, the cost of moving to a temporary location, and projected revenue growth are relevant to determining coverage amounts.

Casualty Insurance (Total: 34 Questions)

Auto insurance: 8 questions

51) What does Liability coverage in an auto insurance policy provide?

Correct Answer is B - Liability coverage in an auto insurance policy provides coverage for injuries or damages the policyholder causes to others, ensuring financial protection against claims resulting from the policyholder's actions.

52) Under an auto insurance policy, what is 'Medical Payments' coverage designed to do?

Correct Answer is A - 'Medical Payments' coverage is designed to pay for the medical expenses of the policyholder and passengers regardless of fault, offering prompt payment for medical treatments following an accident.

53) What does Comprehensive coverage in an auto insurance policy typically include?

Correct Answer is C - Comprehensive coverage in an auto insurance policy typically includes damage to the vehicle from non-collision incidents, such as theft, vandalism, or environmental damage.

54) 'Collision' coverage in an auto insurance policy specifically covers:

Correct Answer is A - 'Collision' coverage specifically covers damage to your vehicle when it hits, or is hit by, another vehicle or object, providing financial protection for repairs or replacement.

55) What is the primary purpose of 'Uninsured Motorist' coverage?

Correct Answer is B - 'Uninsured Motorist' coverage protects against damage from drivers without sufficient insurance coverage, offering compensation for injuries or damages incurred in accidents with underinsured or uninsured drivers.

56) Which type of coverage would pay for damage to your car from a hail storm?

Correct Answer is B - Comprehensive coverage would pay for damage to your car from a hail storm, as it covers a wide range of non-collision damages to the vehicle.

57) In auto insurance, 'Personal Injury Protection' (PIP) coverage is:

Correct Answer is D - 'Personal Injury Protection' (PIP) coverage is designed to cover medical expenses and lost wages, regardless of fault, offering broad protection for personal injuries in auto accidents.

58) What does the 'Property Damage Liability' portion of an auto insurance policy cover?

Correct Answer is B - The 'Property Damage Liability' portion of an auto insurance policy covers damage you cause to someone else's property with your vehicle, ensuring financial responsibility for the damage inflicted.

Workers compensation: 8 questions

59) What is the primary purpose of workers' compensation insurance?

```
Correct Answer is B - The primary purpose of workers'
compensation insurance is to provide benefits to employees for
injuries or illnesses related to work, ensuring medical care and
financial support during recovery.
```

60) Which of the following is typically covered under workers' compensation insurance?

```
Correct Answer is C - Occupational diseases contracted as a
result of the work environment are typically covered under
workers' compensation insurance, recognizing the risks
associated with certain workplaces and occupations.
```

61) What is the 'exclusive remedy' provision in workers' compensation law?

```
Correct Answer is B - The 'exclusive remedy' provision in
workers' compensation law states that workers' compensation
benefits are the sole remedy for employees injured on the job,
barring most lawsuits against employers. This legal framework is
designed to protect both employees and employers by ensuring
workers receive guaranteed compensation for work-related
injuries while limiting the liability exposure of employers.
```

62) How are workers' compensation premiums typically calculated for an employer?

Correct Answer is C - Workers' compensation premiums are typically calculated based on the company's past claims history and payroll amount. This method helps insurers assess the risk level of the business and the potential cost of claims, with higher payrolls and more extensive claims histories generally resulting in higher premiums.

63) What does 'Temporary Total Disability' (TTD) benefits in workers' compensation provide?

Correct Answer is B - 'Temporary Total Disability' (TTD) benefits provide compensation for the time an employee is completely unable to work on a temporary basis. This ensures that workers are financially supported during periods when their injuries prevent them from performing their job duties.

64) Under workers' compensation, the 'Waiting Period' refers to:

Correct Answer is B - Under workers' compensation, the 'Waiting Period' refers to the duration an injured worker must wait after an injury before benefits begin. This period is typically a few days and is meant to differentiate between minor injuries and those serious enough to warrant ongoing compensation.

65) 'Permanent Partial Disability' (PPD) benefits are intended for employees who:

Correct Answer is A - 'Permanent Partial Disability' (PPD) benefits are intended for employees who can return to work but with permanent restrictions due to their injury. These benefits compensate for the worker's reduced earning capacity caused by the lasting effects of their injury.

66) Which of the following injuries would typically NOT be covered by workers' compensation?

Correct Answer is B - A car accident occurring while commuting from home to the workplace is typically not covered by workers' compensation. This is because injuries sustained during commuting are generally considered outside the scope of employment, unless the transportation is provided by the employer or the employee is engaged in a work-related task during the commute.

Liability insurance: 12 questions

67) What is the primary purpose of liability insurance?

Correct Answer is B - The primary purpose of liability insurance is to protect the insured against claims for bodily injury or property damage to others. This type of insurance is crucial for covering the costs associated with legal claims or judgments that may arise from accidents or negligence.

68) 'Bodily Injury Liability' coverage in an auto insurance policy covers:

Correct Answer is C - 'Bodily Injury Liability' coverage in an auto insurance policy covers injuries the policyholder causes to someone else. This is a key component of liability insurance, helping to ensure that victims of automobile accidents receive compensation for their injuries.

69) Which of the following is typically covered by a 'General Liability Insurance' policy?

Correct Answer is C - A 'General Liability Insurance' policy typically covers claims of false advertising. This coverage protects businesses against claims alleging that misleading advertising practices caused harm to a consumer or competitor.

70) 'Property Damage Liability' coverage is intended to:

Correct Answer is B - 'Property Damage Liability' coverage is intended to cover damage policyholders cause to someone else's property. This aspect of liability insurance is essential for compensating others when the policyholder is at fault for causing property damage.

71) What does 'Personal and Advertising Injury' coverage in a General Liability policy include?

Correct Answer is B - 'Personal and Advertising Injury' coverage in a General Liability policy includes damage to the insured's reputation due to slander or libel. This coverage is crucial for protecting businesses against claims that their actions or advertisements harmed someone's reputation.

72) The 'Medical Payments' coverage in a General Liability policy:

Correct Answer is B - The 'Medical Payments' coverage in a General Liability policy pays for medical expenses of third parties injured on the insured's property, regardless of fault. This coverage facilitates prompt medical treatment for injuries occurring on the insured's premises.

73) What is a 'Combined Single Limit' (CSL) in liability insurance?

Correct Answer is A - A 'Combined Single Limit' (CSL) in liability insurance is a limit that combines property damage and bodily injury payments into one total available limit. This simplifies the payout process by providing a single maximum payment amount for all damages arising from a single incident.

74) An 'Umbrella Policy' in liability insurance:

Correct Answer is B - An 'Umbrella Policy' in liability insurance extends the limits of underlying liability policies. This type of policy provides additional coverage beyond what is offered by primary policies, covering claims that exceed the primary policy's limits.

75) 'Employers Liability Insurance' is part of which policy?

Correct Answer is A - 'Employers Liability Insurance' is part of the Workers' Compensation policy. This coverage is designed to protect employers against lawsuits arising from work-related injuries or diseases that are not covered under the workers' compensation statutes.

76) Which of the following best describes 'Products Liability' insurance?

Correct Answer is D - 'Products Liability' insurance covers damage caused by products sold or manufactured by the insured and insures against injuries sustained by the use of a product. This coverage is essential for businesses involved in the production or sale of goods, providing protection against claims related to product defects or harm.

77) 'Cyber Liability Insurance' primarily covers:

Correct Answer is B - 'Cyber Liability Insurance' primarily covers liability for data breaches and loss of digital information. This insurance is crucial for protecting businesses against the financial and reputational costs associated with cyber incidents and data security breaches.

78) In liability insurance, 'Duty to Defend' refers to:

Correct Answer is B - In liability insurance, the 'Duty to Defend' refers to the insurer's obligation to provide legal defense for the insured against covered claims. This ensures that the insured receives legal representation in the event of a lawsuit, with the costs typically covered by the insurance policy.

Umbrella policies: 6 questions

79) What is the primary purpose of an umbrella policy?

Correct Answer is B - The primary purpose of an umbrella policy is to extend liability coverage beyond the limits of an underlying policy. This provides an additional layer of protection for the insured against potentially catastrophic liability claims.

80) An umbrella policy typically provides coverage for:

Correct Answer is C - An umbrella policy typically provides coverage for both personal and business liabilities, depending

on the policy. This broad coverage is designed to offer an extra
layer of protection over and above the insured's existing
liability policies.

81) Which of the following is NOT typically covered by an umbrella policy?

Correct Answer is D - Professional services liability is not
typically covered by an umbrella policy. Umbrella policies
extend liability coverage beyond existing limits for bodily
injury, property damage, and personal injury, but professional
liability often requires a separate policy.

82) How does an umbrella policy work in conjunction with underlying policies?

Correct Answer is D - An umbrella policy provides additional
coverage after the limits of the underlying policy are reached.
It acts as a secondary layer of protection once the primary
insurance policy's limits have been exhausted.

83) What is typically required to purchase an umbrella policy?

Correct Answer is A - To purchase an umbrella policy, a minimum
amount of liability coverage on underlying policies is typically
required. This ensures that there is a basic level of coverage
before the umbrella policy provides additional protection.

84) Which scenario would likely trigger coverage under an umbrella policy?

Correct Answer is A - A covered loss under a homeowner's policy that exceeds its liability limits would likely trigger coverage under an umbrella policy. Umbrella policies are designed to offer additional coverage in situations where primary policy limits are exceeded.

Package Policies (Total: 14 Questions)

Business Owners Policy (BOP): 7 questions

85) What is a Business Owners Policy (BOP)?

Correct Answer is B - A Business Owners Policy (BOP) is a packaged policy combining property and liability insurance for small businesses. It is designed to provide a broad range of coverage in a single policy for small and medium-sized businesses.

86) Which type of business is typically eligible for a BOP?

Correct Answer is B - Small to medium-sized retail stores are typically eligible for a BOP. These policies are tailored to meet the needs of smaller businesses by offering comprehensive coverage in a single package.

87) What does the property insurance portion of a BOP cover?

Correct Answer is C - The property insurance portion of a BOP covers damage to the business premises and its contents. This includes protection against a variety of risks to the physical assets of a business.

88) BOP liability coverage protects a business against claims involving:

Correct Answer is C - BOP liability coverage protects a business against claims involving bodily injury or property damage caused to others. This includes liability for customer injuries that occur within the business premises.

89) Which of the following is NOT typically covered by a BOP?

Correct Answer is B - Professional liability claims are not typically covered by a BOP. Professional liability, or errors and omissions insurance, usually requires a separate policy.

90) Business Interruption Insurance included in a BOP covers:

Correct Answer is B - Business Interruption Insurance included in a BOP covers losses resulting from the business having to temporarily close or relocate due to covered property damage. This helps a business recover from the financial impact of being unable to operate as usual.

91) What additional coverage can often be added to a BOP?

Correct Answer is C - Data breach/cyber liability insurance can often be added to a BOP. This coverage is increasingly important for businesses as it protects against losses resulting from data breaches or other cyber events.

Commercial package policy: 7 questions

92) What is a Commercial Package Policy (CPP)?

Correct Answer is B - A Commercial Package Policy (CPP) is a
bundled insurance policy that combines various commercial
coverages for businesses. It allows businesses to customize
their insurance package to fit their specific needs.

93) Which of the following coverages can typically be included in a CPP?

Correct Answer is C - Commercial property insurance can
typically be included in a CPP. CPPs are designed to offer a
customizable package of coverages, including commercial
property, to protect against various business risks.

94) The primary advantage of a CPP over purchasing separate policies is:

Correct Answer is C - The primary advantage of a CPP over
purchasing separate policies is the flexibility and potential
cost savings from bundling coverages. CPPs allow businesses to
tailor their coverage in a cost-effective manner.

95) Which statement is true regarding the customization of a CPP?

Correct Answer is B - Businesses can choose specific coverages
to meet their unique needs in a CPP. This customization is a key
feature of CPPs, allowing businesses to select the coverages
that best match their risk profiles.

96) 'Business Interruption' coverage in a CPP is designed to:

Correct Answer is B - 'Business Interruption' coverage in a CPP
is designed to compensate for lost income when business
operations are disrupted due to a covered cause of loss. This
coverage helps businesses maintain financial stability during
periods of involuntary closure or reduced operation.

**97) 'Commercial General Liability' (CGL) insurance within a CPP protects
a business against claims of:**

Correct Answer is A - 'Commercial General Liability' (CGL)
insurance within a CPP protects a business against claims of
property damage caused by the company's operations. CGL coverage
is crucial for protecting businesses against liability for
damages their operations may cause to others.

98) What does 'Commercial Property' insurance cover in a CPP?

Correct Answer is C - 'Commercial Property' insurance in a CPP
covers damage to the business premises and its contents due to
covered perils. This includes protection for the physical assets
of a business, such as the building and the contents inside.

State-Specific Regulations (Total: 10 Questions)

Licensing requirements: 3 questions

**99) What is the primary purpose of licensing requirements for property
and casualty insurance agents?**

```
Correct Answer is B - The primary purpose of licensing
requirements for property and casualty insurance agents is to
ensure agents have the necessary knowledge and skills to serve
the public effectively. Licensing ensures that agents are
qualified to advise on and sell insurance products responsibly.
```

100) Which entity typically regulates the licensing of property and casualty insurance agents?

```
Correct Answer is C - State insurance departments or commissions
typically regulate the licensing of property and casualty
insurance agents. These state entities establish the
requirements and standards for licensing to ensure agents are
properly qualified.
```

101) Pre-licensing education for property and casualty insurance agents usually includes:

```
Correct Answer is C - Pre-licensing education for property and
casualty insurance agents usually includes education on
state-specific insurance laws, policies, and ethics. This
foundational knowledge ensures agents understand the legal and
ethical framework within which they must operate.
```

State laws governing insurance practices: 4 questions

102) What entity typically enforces state laws governing insurance practices?

Correct Answer is C - State Insurance Departments or Commissions typically enforce state laws governing insurance practices. These entities regulate the insurance industry at the state level, ensuring compliance with laws and regulations designed to protect consumers.

103) Which of the following is a primary focus of state laws governing insurance practices?

Correct Answer is B - A primary focus of state laws governing insurance practices is regulating insurance rates and policy forms. This ensures that insurance products are fairly priced and offer clear, understandable coverage to consumers.

104) State laws governing insurance practices typically require insurers to:

Correct Answer is B - State laws governing insurance practices typically require insurers to submit rates and forms for approval before use. This regulatory oversight helps ensure that rates are fair and that policy forms meet state standards for coverage and consumer protection.

105) The purpose of 'solvency regulations' under state insurance laws is to:

Correct Answer is A - The purpose of solvency regulations under state insurance laws is to ensure that insurance companies maintain sufficient reserves to cover future claims. This financial stability requirement protects policyholders by ensuring insurers can fulfill their obligations.

Ethical practices and the regulatory environment: 3 questions

106) What is the primary purpose of ethical practices in the insurance industry?

Correct Answer is C - The primary purpose of ethical practices in the insurance industry is to foster trust and fairness between insurers, agents, and policyholders. Ethical behavior is essential for maintaining confidence in the insurance process and ensuring equitable treatment for all parties.

107) Which entity is primarily responsible for regulating the insurance industry and ensuring ethical practices?

Correct Answer is B - State Insurance Departments or Commissions are primarily responsible for regulating the insurance industry and ensuring ethical practices. These state-level entities oversee the conduct of insurers and agents within their jurisdictions.

108) Confidentiality in handling client information is a key ethical practice because it:

Correct Answer is B - Confidentiality in handling client information is a key ethical practice because it protects the personal and financial information of policyholders. This respect for privacy is fundamental to maintaining trust and integrity in the insurance relationship.

Insurance Operations (Total: 10 Questions)

Underwriting principles: 4 questions

109) What is the primary purpose of underwriting in the insurance industry?

Correct Answer is B - The primary purpose of underwriting in the insurance industry is to determine the risk of insuring a potential client and set appropriate premiums. Underwriting assesses the likelihood of a claim and calculates premiums that reflect the risk level.

110) Which factor is NOT typically considered during the underwriting process for property and casualty insurance?

Correct Answer is D - The insured's educational background is not typically considered during the underwriting process for property and casualty insurance. Underwriting focuses on factors directly related to the risk of loss, such as claim history, property condition, and credit score.

111) 'Risk Classification' in underwriting refers to:

Correct Answer is C - 'Risk Classification' in underwriting refers to the process of assigning potential insureds into groups based on perceived risk levels. This classification helps insurers accurately price policies according to the likelihood and potential cost of claims.

112) How does 'moral hazard' influence the underwriting process?

Correct Answer is B - 'Moral hazard' influences the underwriting process as it is a factor that increases the likelihood of a loss due to the insured's behavior or character. Recognizing moral hazard helps insurers mitigate risks associated with insuring individuals who may take greater risks because they are insured.

Rate making: 3 questions

113) What is the primary goal of rate making in insurance?

Correct Answer is B - The primary goal of rate making in insurance is to set premiums that are fair, adequate, and not unfairly discriminatory. Rate making aims to balance the insurer's need to be financially viable with the policyholder's need for affordable, equitable coverage.

114) Which factor is NOT typically considered in the rate-making process for property and casualty insurance?

Correct Answer is A - The insured's age and gender are not typically considered in the rate-making process for property and casualty insurance, which focuses on the risk associated with the insured property or liability exposure rather than personal characteristics of the insured.

115) 'Experience rating' in the context of rate making refers to:

Correct Answer is A - 'Experience rating' in the context of rate making refers to the use of historical data from the insured's own experience to determine premiums. This method tailors premium rates to the insured's specific loss history, reflecting their individual risk level.

Risk management: 3 questions

116) What is the primary goal of risk management in the context of property and casualty insurance?

```
Correct Answer is C - The primary goal of risk management in the
context of property and casualty insurance is to identify and
mitigate potential losses through various strategies. Effective
risk management helps protect against financial loss by
minimizing the impact of risks.
```

117) Which of the following best describes 'risk avoidance' in risk management?

```
Correct Answer is B - 'Risk avoidance' in risk management
involves choosing not to engage in activities that carry a risk
of loss. This strategy eliminates exposure to certain risks by
avoiding activities or situations that could lead to a loss.
```

118) 'Risk transfer' is a strategy that typically involves:

```
Correct Answer is C - 'Risk transfer' is a strategy that
typically involves purchasing insurance to shift financial
responsibility of losses to the insurer. This allows businesses
or individuals to manage financial risks by transferring the
cost of potential losses to an insurance company.
```

Miscellaneous Coverages (Total: 6 Questions)

Flood insurance: 2 questions

119) What entity is primarily responsible for underwriting flood insurance policies in the United States?

```
Correct Answer is B - The National Flood Insurance Program
(NFIP) is primarily responsible for underwriting flood insurance
policies in the United States. The NFIP provides flood insurance
to property owners, renters, and businesses in participating
communities.
```

120) Which of the following properties would typically be eligible for flood insurance under the NFIP?

```
Correct Answer is C - Commercial properties in a high-risk flood
zone would typically be eligible for flood insurance under the
NFIP, as long as they are located in communities that
participate in the program.
```

Earthquake insurance: 2 questions

121) What does earthquake insurance typically cover?

```
Correct Answer is B - Earthquake insurance typically covers
structural damage and personal property inside the building but
not land movement. This coverage is designed to provide
financial protection against the physical damage to property
caused by an earthquake.
```

122) Which of the following is a common feature of earthquake insurance policies?

Correct Answer is C - A common feature of earthquake insurance policies is high deductibles as a percentage of the property's replacement value. This reflects the potentially high cost of earthquake damage and the risk management approach of sharing some of the loss cost with the policyholder.

Crime insurance policies: 2 questions

123) What is the primary purpose of crime insurance policies?

Correct Answer is B - The primary purpose of crime insurance policies is to provide coverage for businesses against losses due to criminal activities. This includes protection against theft, fraud, and other crimes that result in financial loss to the business.

124) Which of the following is typically covered under a commercial crime insurance policy?

Correct Answer is B - Employee theft of company assets is typically covered under a commercial crime insurance policy. This coverage protects businesses from financial losses resulting from dishonest acts committed by employees.

Practice Exam 2 (Total: 120 Questions) - Answers & Explanations

Insurance Basics (Total: 16 Questions)

Principles of insurance: 5 questions

1) What is proximate cause in insurance?

Correct Answer is D - Proximate cause is the event directly
leading to a loss without the intervention of any other event.
It establishes a clear, unbroken chain of events that resulted
in the loss.

2) Which principle allows insurers to divide their liability with other insurers?

Correct Answer is B - The principle that allows insurers to
divide their liability with other insurers is Contribution. This
principle ensures that when multiple policies cover a loss, each
pays its fair share.

3) What best defines the principle of contribution?

Correct Answer is B - The principle of contribution means insurers must contribute to losses according to their liability. It's used when more than one insurance policy covers a claim.

4) How does the principle of indemnity affect the insurance payout?

Correct Answer is B - The principle of indemnity affects the insurance payout by limiting it to the actual value of the loss. This ensures that policyholders are compensated for their loss without profiting from it.

5) Which of the following best describes 'risk pooling'?

Correct Answer is C - 'Risk pooling' is defined as distributing losses among a large group of people. This spreads the financial burden of losses, making insurance possible.

Types of insurers: 5 questions

6) Which of the following is known for its syndicates that insure unique and specialized risks?

Correct Answer is C - Lloyd's of London is known for its syndicates that insure unique and specialized risks. It's a marketplace where members join together to insure those risks.

7) What type of insurer is typically formed under the laws of countries outside the United States to provide tax advantages and regulatory ease?

Correct Answer is C - An insurer typically formed under the laws of countries outside the United States to provide tax advantages and regulatory ease is known as an Alien insurer.

8) Which of the following best describes a reinsurance company?

Correct Answer is B - A reinsurance company provides insurance to insurance companies. This helps insurers manage their risk exposure by spreading the risk of large claims.

9) A fraternal benefit society primarily provides insurance to who?

Correct Answer is C - A fraternal benefit society primarily provides insurance to members based on religious, social, or fraternal ties. These organizations offer insurance as part of their membership benefits.

10) What distinguishes a mutual insurance company from a stock insurance company?

Correct Answer is B - What distinguishes a mutual insurance company from a stock insurance company is that stock insurance companies do not return profits to their policyholders, whereas mutual insurance companies may return surplus income to their policyholders in the form of dividends or reduced future premiums.

Policy renewals and cancellations: 6 questions

11) Which of the following best defines a cancellation provision in an insurance policy?

Correct Answer is B - A cancellation provision in an insurance policy is a statement specifying the insurer's right to terminate the policy before its expiration date under certain conditions.

12) How does the 'notice of cancellation' benefit the insured?

Correct Answer is C - The 'notice of cancellation' benefits the insured by giving them time to find alternative coverage before the policy is terminated. This notice period helps ensure that the insured does not become unintentionally uninsured.

13) What action can an insured take if they disagree with a cancellation decision?

Correct Answer is B - If they disagree with a cancellation decision, an insured can seek arbitration to reverse the decision. Arbitration is a form of dispute resolution that can be less formal than going to court.

14) A policy that is set to expire without being renewed is subject to what?

Correct Answer is B - A policy that is set to expire without being renewed is subject to lapse. A lapse results in the termination of coverage due to non-renewal.

15) Which of the following is true about a policy lapse?

Correct Answer is C - A policy lapse happens when the policy is not renewed or the premium is not paid. This leads to a cessation of coverage.

16) When can an insurer legally cancel an auto insurance policy?

Correct Answer is B - An insurer can legally cancel an auto insurance policy only after providing notice within a specified period as required by state law. This ensures that policyholders are treated fairly and given adequate warning.

Property Insurance (Total: 30 Questions)

Dwelling policies: 7 questions

17) Personal Property coverage in a dwelling policy is:

Correct Answer is C - Personal Property coverage in a dwelling policy is optional and requires an additional premium. It is not automatically included and must be specifically added to the policy.

18) What does the 'Fair Rental Value' coverage in a dwelling policy provide?

Correct Answer is B - The 'Fair Rental Value' coverage in a dwelling policy provides reimbursement for lost rental income if a covered peril makes the rental portion of the dwelling uninhabitable. This helps landlords maintain their income stream during repairs.

19) Which of the following is typically excluded from all dwelling policy forms?

Correct Answer is C - Earth movement is typically excluded from all dwelling policy forms. Coverage for losses caused by earth movement, such as earthquakes and landslides, usually requires separate insurance.

20) The 'automatic increase in insurance' endorsement in a dwelling policy is designed to:

Correct Answer is A - The 'automatic increase in insurance' endorsement in a dwelling policy is designed to automatically increase the policy limits annually in line with inflation. This helps ensure that the coverage amount keeps pace with the increasing cost of repairing or replacing the insured property.

21) Under a dwelling policy, the coverage for 'Additional Living Expense' is:

Correct Answer is C - The coverage for 'Additional Living Expense' is only included in DP-3 policy forms. This coverage helps pay for extra costs incurred if the insured property becomes uninhabitable due to a covered loss.

22) A DP-3 policy form is sometimes referred to as:

Correct Answer is C - A DP-3 policy form is sometimes referred to as Special Form. It offers the broadest coverage among dwelling policy forms, including open perils coverage for the dwelling.

23) Which of the following would NOT be covered under the 'Personal

Liability Supplement' in a dwelling policy?

Correct Answer is C - Damages due to intentional acts of violence by the insured would not be covered under the 'Personal Liability Supplement' in a dwelling policy. Liability coverage typically excludes intentional acts.

Homeowners policies: 9 questions

24) Which coverage in a homeowners policy would cover the insured in case of a lawsuit for accidentally injuring someone off their property?

Correct Answer is D - Personal Liability coverage in a homeowners policy would cover the insured in case of a lawsuit for accidentally injuring someone off their property. This coverage extends to bodily injury and property damage caused by the insured or their family members.

25) What does the 'Loss of Use' coverage in a homeowners policy provide?

Correct Answer is B - The 'Loss of Use' coverage in a homeowners policy provides reimbursement for living expenses if the home is uninhabitable due to a covered loss. This can include costs for hotel stays, meals, and other additional living expenses.

26) HO-3 homeowners policies provide broad coverage for the dwelling and personal property against:

Correct Answer is C - HO-3 homeowners policies provide broad coverage for the dwelling against all perils except those specifically excluded and named perils for personal property. It is one of the most common types of homeowners policies.

27) Which type of homeowners policy is often purchased for older homes where replacement costs far exceed the market value?

Correct Answer is D - An HO-8 policy type is often purchased for older homes where the replacement costs far exceed the market value. This policy form is designed to provide adequate coverage for older homes with unique valuation challenges.

28) The 'Replacement Cost' coverage in a homeowners policy means the insurer will:

Correct Answer is B - The 'Replacement Cost' coverage in a homeowners policy means the insurer will pay to repair or replace the damaged property without deduction for depreciation. This ensures that policyholders can fully restore or replace their property after a covered loss.

29) A homeowners policy with 'Actual Cash Value (ACV)' settlement will compensate losses based on:

Correct Answer is C - A homeowners policy with 'Actual Cash Value (ACV)' settlement will compensate losses based on the replacement cost minus depreciation. This reflects the current value of an item, considering wear and tear.

30) Which coverage component of a homeowners policy covers injuries to a guest in your home, regardless of fault?

Correct Answer is C - Medical Payments to Others coverage component of a homeowners policy covers injuries to a guest in your home, regardless of fault. It is designed to pay for immediate medical expenses, providing a quick response to accidents.

31) Water damage from a sewer backup is typically:

```
Correct Answer is B - Water damage from a sewer backup is
typically excluded from standard homeowners policies but can be
covered with an endorsement. Adding this coverage helps protect
against specific risks not included in the base policy.
```

32) 'Scheduled Personal Property Endorsement' on a homeowners policy is used to: A)

```
Correct Answer is A - 'Scheduled Personal Property Endorsement'
on a homeowners policy is used to increase coverage limits on
specific high-value items. This ensures that items like jewelry,
art, and collectibles are adequately covered beyond standard
policy limits.
```

Commercial property policies: 9 questions

33) In commercial property insurance, the 'Agreed Value' option means:

```
Correct Answer is A - In commercial property insurance, the
'Agreed Value' option means the insurer and insured agree on the
value of the property at policy inception, suspending the
coinsurance clause. This agreement helps avoid underinsurance
penalties in the event of a claim.
```

34) Which condition must be met for 'Replacement Cost' coverage to apply in a commercial property policy?

```
Correct Answer is B - For 'Replacement Cost' coverage to apply
in a commercial property policy, the damaged property must be
```

repaired or replaced before payment is made. This encourages property owners to promptly restore their property to its pre-loss condition.

35) 'Inland Marine Insurance' under a commercial property policy is designed to cover:

Correct Answer is B - 'Inland Marine Insurance' under a commercial property policy is designed to cover property in transit over land. This includes coverage for items being shipped, mobile equipment, and property frequently moved from one location to another.

36) What is a 'Bailee's Customer Policy' in commercial property insurance?

Correct Answer is B - A 'Bailee's Customer Policy' in commercial property insurance covers customers that leave property in the care of the business. It protects against loss or damage to customer property while it is under the business's custody.

37) 'Ordinance or Law Coverage' in a commercial property policy covers:

Correct Answer is B - 'Ordinance or Law Coverage' in a commercial property policy covers increased costs due to enforcing building codes after a covered loss. This addresses the additional expenses involved in bringing a damaged property up to current building standards.

38) The 'Spoilage Coverage' endorsement in a commercial property policy is intended to protect against loss of:

Correct Answer is B - The 'Spoilage Coverage' endorsement in a commercial property policy is intended to protect against the loss of perishable goods due to power outages or equipment breakdown. It's crucial for businesses that rely on refrigeration or controlled environments for their inventory.

39) Which of the following best describes 'Vacancy Permit Coverage' in commercial property insurance?

Correct Answer is A - 'Vacancy Permit Coverage' in commercial property insurance allows for temporary vacancy of the property without loss of coverage. This endorsement is important for properties that may undergo periods of vacancy but still require protection.

40) A 'Condominium Commercial Unit-Owners' Coverage Form' is designed specifically for:

Correct Answer is C - A 'Condominium Commercial Unit-Owners' Coverage Form' is designed specifically for owners of commercial condominium units. It provides property and liability coverage tailored to the needs of commercial condo unit owners.

41) What does the 'Leasehold Interest Coverage' protect in commercial property insurance?

Correct Answer is B - The 'Leasehold Interest Coverage' protects the value of the lease in case the leased premises become unusable due to a covered loss. It compensates the lessee for any financial loss associated with the leasehold value.

Business interruption: 5 questions

42) How is the indemnity period in a business interruption policy defined?

Correct Answer is A - The indemnity period in a business
interruption policy is defined as the maximum time that the
insurer will make payments for a covered loss. It determines the
length of time compensation is provided for business
interruption losses.

43) What is typically excluded from business interruption insurance coverage?

Correct Answer is D - Losses from pandemics or infectious
diseases, unless specifically included, are typically excluded
from business interruption insurance coverage. These exclusions
require businesses to seek specific endorsements or policies for
coverage against such events.

44) 'Contingent Business Interruption' insurance covers losses resulting from:

Correct Answer is B - 'Contingent Business Interruption'
insurance covers losses resulting from damage to a supplier's or
customer's premises that directly affects the insured's
business. It addresses the financial impact of disruptions in
the supply chain or customer base.

45) The 'extended period of indemnity' option in a business interruption policy:

Correct Answer is C - The 'extended period of indemnity' option in a business interruption policy extends coverage beyond the period of restoration for a specified duration. This helps businesses recover financially even after repairs are completed and operations resume.

46) Which of the following best describes 'gross earnings' under a business interruption policy?

Correct Answer is D - 'Gross earnings' under a business interruption policy refer to the sum of net profit and fixed costs. This figure is used to calculate the amount of income loss covered by the policy.

Casualty Insurance (Total: 35 Questions)

Auto insurance: 9 questions

47) How does 'Actual Cash Value' (ACV) affect a claim under an auto insurance policy?

Correct Answer is C - 'Actual Cash Value' (ACV) affects a claim under an auto insurance policy by representing the insurer's valuation of the vehicle at the time of the loss, considering depreciation. It determines the payout amount based on the current market value of the vehicle, less any depreciation.

48) What is typically NOT covered under a standard auto liability insurance policy?

Correct Answer is C - Damage to the policyholder's own vehicle is typically not covered under a standard auto liability insurance policy. Liability coverage is designed to pay for bodily injury and property damage to others for which the policyholder is responsible.

49) 'Gap Insurance' in auto policies is designed to:

Correct Answer is B - 'Gap Insurance' in auto policies is designed to pay the difference between the vehicle's actual cash value and what is still owed on the loan or lease. It addresses the financial gap when the loan balance exceeds the vehicle's depreciated value.

50) Which scenario would likely be covered under 'Comprehensive' but not 'Collision' coverage?

Correct Answer is C - A tree falling on your car during a storm would likely be covered under 'Comprehensive' but not 'Collision' coverage. Comprehensive coverage applies to non-collision incidents, while Collision coverage addresses damage from vehicle collisions.

51) 'Deductibles' in auto insurance policies are:

Correct Answer is B - 'Deductibles' in auto insurance policies are a fixed amount the policyholder must pay before insurance coverage begins. This out-of-pocket cost applies to covered losses and helps manage the overall cost of insurance.

52) Which of the following would typically be excluded from coverage under an auto insurance policy?

Correct Answer is A - Mechanical breakdown is typically excluded from coverage under an auto insurance policy. Auto insurance generally covers losses due to accidents, theft, and other specified perils, not mechanical failures.

53) 'Rental Reimbursement' coverage in auto insurance policies:

Correct Answer is C - 'Rental Reimbursement' coverage in auto insurance policies covers the cost of renting a car if your vehicle is stolen. This coverage is optional and helps mitigate the inconvenience of not having a personal vehicle due to theft.

54) What determines the premium for an auto insurance policy?

Correct Answer is B - The premium for an auto insurance policy is determined by the policyholder's driving history, age, type of vehicle, and coverage selected. These factors collectively assess the risk and cost associated with insuring the driver.

55) 'Underinsured Motorist' coverage is intended to:

Correct Answer is B - 'Underinsured Motorist' coverage is intended to provide protection when the at-fault driver's insurance is insufficient. It covers the gap between the other driver's coverage limits and the actual cost of the damages or injuries.

Workers compensation: 9 questions

56) The 'Second Injury Fund' under workers' compensation is designed to:

Correct Answer is B - The 'Second Injury Fund' under workers' compensation is designed to encourage the hiring of previously injured workers by limiting employer liability for subsequent injuries. It promotes the employment of workers with pre-existing conditions or injuries.

57) 'Experience Modification Rate' (EMR) affects an employer's workers' compensation premium by:

Correct Answer is B - 'Experience Modification Rate' (EMR) affects an employer's workers' compensation premium by adjusting rates based on the company's claim history relative to others in the industry. A better-than-average claim history can lead to lower premiums.

58) In workers' compensation, 'Vocational Rehabilitation' benefits are provided to:

Correct Answer is C - In workers' compensation, 'Vocational Rehabilitation' benefits are provided to assist employees in finding new employment if they cannot return to their previous job due to injury. These benefits support the injured worker's transition to suitable employment.

59) Which statement about workers' compensation insurance is FALSE?

Correct Answer is A - The statement that workers' compensation insurance provides coverage for intentional injuries inflicted by the employer is FALSE. Workers' compensation covers work-related injuries and illnesses that are accidental, not intentional acts by the employer.

60) 'Death Benefits' in a workers' compensation policy are designed to:

Correct Answer is D - 'Death Benefits' in a workers' compensation policy are designed to compensate the deceased worker's family for future earnings lost and cover the funeral and burial expenses of the deceased worker. These benefits support the family financially in the aftermath of a work-related death.

61) Which type of workers' compensation benefit is designed to cover medical and rehabilitation costs?

Correct Answer is B - Medical benefits in workers' compensation are designed to cover medical and rehabilitation costs. This ensures that injured workers receive necessary medical care without incurring personal expenses.

62) The principle of 'no-fault' in workers' compensation means:

Correct Answer is C - The principle of 'no-fault' in workers' compensation means benefits are paid regardless of who is at fault for the injury. This simplifies the process, allowing for quicker assistance to the injured worker without determining fault.

63) 'Employers Liability Insurance', often part of workers' compensation

policies, covers:

Correct Answer is C - 'Employers Liability Insurance', often part of workers' compensation policies, covers the employer against lawsuits for work-related injuries not covered under workers' compensation. This provides additional legal protection beyond the standard workers' compensation benefits.

64) What is the role of a 'Workers' Compensation Board' or 'Commission'?

Correct Answer is C - The role of a 'Workers' Compensation Board' or 'Commission' is to adjudicate disputes over benefits and eligibility. They serve as the governing body to resolve conflicts between employees and employers or insurers regarding workers' compensation claims.

Liability insurance: 11 questions

65) What is 'Directors and Officers (D&O)' liability insurance designed to protect?

Correct Answer is A - 'Directors and Officers (D&O)' liability insurance is designed to protect the personal assets of corporate directors and officers in the event of legal action against them for corporate activities. It safeguards individuals against financial losses from lawsuits related to their roles within the organization.

66) 'Professional Liability Insurance' is also known as:

Correct Answer is B - 'Professional Liability Insurance' is also known as Errors and Omissions Insurance. This coverage protects professionals against claims of negligence, errors, or omissions in the services they provide.

67) Which scenario would NOT typically be covered under a standard Commercial General Liability (CGL) policy?

Correct Answer is B - An employee's personal property being stolen from their office would NOT typically be covered under a standard Commercial General Liability (CGL) policy. CGL policies cover third-party bodily injury and property damage, not personal property of employees.

68) 'Host Liquor Liability' insurance is designed to cover:

Correct Answer is B - 'Host Liquor Liability' insurance is designed to cover individuals hosting parties where alcohol is served. It provides protection against liability arising from alcohol-related incidents without the sale of alcohol being involved.

69) The 'Pollution Exclusion' in a liability insurance policy:

Correct Answer is B - The 'Pollution Exclusion' in a liability insurance policy excludes coverage for pollution, unless coverage is specifically added by endorsement. This exclusion addresses liabilities arising from the release of pollutants.

70) Which type of liability insurance would cover a business against claims of discrimination or wrongful termination?

Correct Answer is C - Employment Practices Liability Insurance
(EPLI) would cover a business against claims of discrimination
or wrongful termination. EPLI protects employers from lawsuits
alleging various employment-related issues.

71) 'Completed Operations Coverage' in a CGL policy is intended to:

Correct Answer is B - 'Completed Operations Coverage' in a CGL
policy is intended to insure the business against liabilities
arising from completed work or services. This protects
businesses from claims related to the work after it has been
finished.

72) 'Liquor Liability Insurance' is most important for businesses that:

Correct Answer is B - 'Liquor Liability Insurance' is most
important for businesses that serve or sell alcohol. It covers
the business against claims resulting from the sale or service
of alcoholic beverages.

73) What distinguishes 'Claims-Made' from 'Occurrence' policies in liability insurance?

Correct Answer is C - 'Claims-Made' policies differ from
'Occurrence' policies based on the time period in which a claim
must be made or occur for coverage to apply. 'Claims-Made'
policies cover claims made during the policy period, while
'Occurrence' policies cover incidents that occur during the
policy period, regardless of when the claim is made.

74) 'Non-Owned Auto Liability Insurance' is particularly important for businesses that:

Correct Answer is B - 'Non-Owned Auto Liability Insurance' is particularly important for businesses that do not own vehicles but have employees who use their personal vehicles for business purposes. It provides liability coverage for accidents involving the personal vehicles of employees while used for business activities.

75) 'Tenant's Legal Liability' coverage is designed to protect against claims arising from:

Correct Answer is A - 'Tenant's Legal Liability' coverage is designed to protect against claims arising from damage to rented premises caused by the tenant's negligence. It addresses liabilities tenants may face for damage to the property they lease.

Umbrella policies: 6 questions

76) 'Personal Injury' coverage in an umbrella policy includes protection against:

Correct Answer is B - 'Personal Injury' coverage in an umbrella policy includes protection against claims of slander, libel, and invasion of privacy. This extends liability coverage beyond physical injuries to include certain non-physical claims.

77) Umbrella policies typically include coverage for:

Correct Answer is C - Umbrella policies typically include certain legal defense costs outside the limits of the policy.

This can provide additional financial protection for legal expenses incurred in defending against covered claims.

78) Which of the following best describes the coverage provided by an umbrella policy?

Correct Answer is C - The coverage provided by an umbrella policy is broad coverage for various liabilities not specifically excluded. It supplements existing policies by covering additional risks and higher limits.

79) An umbrella policy may provide coverage for claims that are:

Correct Answer is A - An umbrella policy may provide coverage for claims that are not covered by any underlying policies due to exclusions. This extends protection beyond the scope of primary insurance policies.

80) The limits of an umbrella policy typically:

Correct Answer is C - The limits of an umbrella policy are typically higher than the limits of the underlying policies. This provides an additional layer of protection once the limits of the primary coverage are exhausted.

81) What factor is NOT typically used to determine the premium of an umbrella policy?

Correct Answer is B - The insured's credit score is not typically used to determine the premium of an umbrella policy. Premiums are generally based on the limits of the policy, the coverage limits of underlying policies, and the number and type

of vehicles owned by the insured, among other factors related to
liability risk, but not the credit score.

Package Policies (Total: 15 Questions)

Business Owners Policy (BOP): 8 questions

82) The liability insurance included in a BOP typically covers:

Correct Answer is C - The liability insurance included in a
Business Owners Policy (BOP) typically covers third-party claims
of bodily injury and property damage. This coverage is essential
for protecting businesses against common risks and financial
losses due to lawsuits.

83) A BOP may exclude coverage for:

Correct Answer is B - A BOP may exclude coverage for flood or
earthquake damage. These perils often require separate policies
or endorsements due to the higher risk and potential cost
associated with covering such events.

84) Which feature is a common benefit of purchasing a BOP?

Correct Answer is A - A common benefit of purchasing a Business
Owners Policy (BOP) is simplified policy management with
combined coverage. BOPs bundle various types of insurance
coverages, making it easier for small and medium-sized
businesses to manage their insurance needs.

85) How does 'Coinsurance' work within the context of a BOP?

Correct Answer is B - Coinsurance within the context of a BOP requires the business to insure the property to a specified percentage of its value. This clause encourages businesses to insure their property adequately and helps prevent underinsurance.

86) The 'Named Perils' coverage in a BOP specifies that:

Correct Answer is A - The 'Named Perils' coverage in a BOP specifies that only perils named in the policy are covered. This contrasts with 'all-risk' policies, which cover all perils except those explicitly excluded.

87) What type of business property is typically excluded from a BOP?

Correct Answer is C - Outdoor signs not attached to the building are typically excluded from a BOP. Coverage for such property often requires additional endorsements or separate policies.

88) In a BOP, the 'Deductible' refers to:

Correct Answer is C - In a BOP, the 'Deductible' refers to the amount the business pays before the insurance coverage begins. It's an out-of-pocket cost to the business for each claim before insurance benefits are paid.

89) 'Business Income Insurance' within a BOP is designed to:

Correct Answer is B - 'Business Income Insurance' within a BOP is designed to cover ongoing expenses and lost income during temporary closure due to a covered loss. This helps businesses maintain financial stability during periods when they cannot operate normally.

Commercial package policy: 7 questions

90) In a CPP, 'Crime Coverage' protects against losses from:

Correct Answer is B - In a Commercial Package Policy (CPP), 'Crime Coverage' protects against losses from employee dishonesty and theft. This coverage is crucial for businesses to safeguard against internal risks of financial loss.

91) Which coverage is NOT typically available in a CPP?

Correct Answer is C - Personal life insurance for the business owner is NOT typically available in a Commercial Package Policy (CPP). CPPs focus on commercial risks and coverages relevant to business operations, not personal life insurance.

92) 'Equipment Breakdown' coverage in a CPP would cover:

Correct Answer is D - 'Equipment Breakdown' coverage in a CPP would cover the cost of renting temporary equipment while repairs are made and losses from business interruption due to equipment breakdown, addressing both direct and indirect financial impacts of equipment failures.

93) The 'Declarations Page' of a CPP includes all of the following EXCEPT:

Correct Answer is D - The 'Declarations Page' of a CPP includes the insured's name and address, the policy period, but not the personal credit score of the business owner. Credit scores are not relevant to the coverage details listed on the declarations page.

94) How does 'Inland Marine' insurance within a CPP differ from 'Commercial Property' insurance?

Correct Answer is A - 'Inland Marine' insurance within a CPP differs from 'Commercial Property' insurance by covering goods in transit over land, as well as certain moveable property. It's designed for property that moves or is transportable, offering broader coverage than stationary commercial property insurance.

95) A CPP 'Conditions' section would typically outline:

Correct Answer is B - The 'Conditions' section in a CPP would typically outline the responsibilities of the insured and insurer in the event of a loss. This section sets the rules for how claims are handled and what is expected from both parties.

96) Which type of business would MOST benefit from including 'Liquor Liability' in their CPP?

Correct Answer is C - A restaurant that serves alcohol would MOST benefit from including 'Liquor Liability' in their Commercial Package Policy. This coverage is vital for businesses that serve alcohol to protect against liability arising from alcohol-related incidents.

State-Specific Regulations (Total: 12 Questions)

Licensing requirements: 4 questions

97) The property and casualty insurance license exam typically tests on:

```
Correct Answer is B - The property and casualty insurance
license exam typically tests on insurance laws, principles,
coverages, and state-specific regulations. It assesses the
candidate's knowledge necessary for professional practice in the
insurance industry.
```

98) Continuing education for licensed property and casualty insurance agents is required to:

```
Correct Answer is C - Continuing education for licensed property
and casualty insurance agents is required to keep agents
up-to-date with changes in laws and industry practices. This
ensures agents remain knowledgeable and compliant with current
standards.
```

99) Which of the following might disqualify someone from obtaining a property and casualty insurance license?

```
Correct Answer is C - Past criminal convictions, particularly
involving fraud or dishonesty, might disqualify someone from
obtaining a property and casualty insurance license. Integrity
and trustworthiness are crucial in the insurance industry due to
the nature of the work.
```

100) The process of obtaining a property and casualty insurance license generally includes:

Correct Answer is C - The process of obtaining a property and casualty insurance license generally includes passing a written examination and a background check. These steps ensure candidates have the necessary knowledge and meet ethical standards for the profession.

State laws governing insurance practices: 5 questions

101) State laws governing insurance practices often include provisions for:

Correct Answer is B - State laws governing insurance practices often include provisions for consumer protection and the handling of claims and complaints. These provisions aim to ensure fair treatment of policyholders and establish standards for the timely and fair handling of insurance matters.

102) Which is an example of a state-specific regulation that may affect insurance practices?

Correct Answer is B - An example of a state-specific regulation that may affect insurance practices is mandates for minimum levels of property and casualty insurance coverage. These requirements can vary significantly from one state to another, reflecting local priorities and risk assessments.

103) How do state laws typically regulate the use of credit information in underwriting insurance policies?

Correct Answer is C - State laws typically regulate the use of credit information in underwriting insurance policies by setting guidelines on how credit information can be used and ensuring consumer rights are protected. These laws aim to balance the insurers' needs for risk assessment with the protection of individual privacy and fairness.

104) State regulations regarding insurance rebates and inducements generally:

Correct Answer is B - State regulations regarding insurance rebates and inducements generally prohibit the offering of rebates and inducements to avoid unfair discrimination. These laws ensure that all policyholders are treated equitably and that insurance rates are based on risk rather than competitive incentives.

105) What role do state laws play in regulating insurance agent licensing and conduct?

Correct Answer is A - State laws play a crucial role in regulating insurance agent licensing and conduct by defining ethical standards and educational requirements for licensure. This ensures that agents are qualified to advise consumers on insurance matters and adhere to professional and ethical standards.

Ethical practices and the regulatory environment: 3 questions

106) An insurance agent recommending coverage options that are not in the best interest of the client, but generate higher commissions, is an example of:

Correct Answer is C - An insurance agent recommending coverage options that are not in the best interest of the client, but generate higher commissions, is an example of a conflict of interest. Such behavior prioritizes the agent's financial gain over the client's needs, which is unethical and potentially harmful to the client.

107) In the context of ethical practices, 'fiduciary responsibility' refers to:

Correct Answer is B - In the context of ethical practices, 'fiduciary responsibility' refers to the duty to act in the best interest of the client. This principle obligates insurance professionals to prioritize their clients' needs and interests in their professional actions and recommendations.

108) Which of the following actions is considered unethical in the insurance industry?

Correct Answer is A - Using confidential client information for personal gain is considered unethical in the insurance industry. Confidentiality is fundamental to the trust between insurers and their clients, and exploiting this information undermines that trust and violates privacy norms.

Insurance Operations (Total: 9 Questions)

Underwriting principles: 3 questions

109) In underwriting, the term 'adverse selection' refers to:

Correct Answer is B - In underwriting, the term 'adverse selection' refers to the tendency of higher-risk individuals to seek or maintain insurance coverage more often than lower-risk individuals. This phenomenon can lead to imbalances in the insurance pool and increased costs for insurers.

110) 'Exposure' in the context of underwriting principles means:

Correct Answer is B - 'Exposure' in the context of underwriting principles means the potential frequency and severity of loss associated with a particular risk. It assesses how likely a risk is to occur and the possible magnitude of that risk, which is crucial for accurate risk assessment and premium setting.

111) Which is an example of a 'physical hazard' in property insurance underwriting?

Correct Answer is A - An example of a 'physical hazard' in property insurance underwriting is a wood-burning stove in a home. Physical hazards are tangible conditions that increase the likelihood or potential severity of a loss.

Rate making: 3 questions

112) How does 'loss frequency' impact rate making for property and casualty insurance?

Correct Answer is C - Higher loss frequency can lead to higher premiums for the insured. Insurers use loss frequency as an indicator of risk, and more frequent claims are typically associated with higher risk and therefore higher premiums.

113) 'Class rating' is a rate-making technique that:

Correct Answer is B - 'Class rating' is a rate-making technique that groups policyholders with similar risk characteristics and assigns rates based on the group's overall loss experience. This approach allows insurers to apply rates that reflect the collective experience of similar risks.

114) In rate making, 'catastrophe modeling' is used to:

Correct Answer is B - In rate making, 'catastrophe modeling' is used to estimate the potential losses from catastrophic events for setting premiums. This involves using statistical models to predict the impact of disasters on insurance losses, helping insurers prepare for and price coverage for such events.

Risk management: 3 questions

115) In risk management, 'risk retention' refers to:

Correct Answer is B - In risk management, 'risk retention' refers to accepting the financial consequences of risk internally. This means that an entity decides to bear the cost of certain risks itself rather than transferring them to an insurer.

116) What role does 'risk assessment' play in the risk management process?

Correct Answer is B - 'Risk assessment' plays a crucial role in the risk management process by identifying and evaluating potential risks to prioritize management efforts. It involves analyzing the nature and extent of risks facing an organization to inform effective risk mitigation strategies.

117) Which of the following is NOT a common risk management technique?

Correct Answer is B - 'Risk speculation' is not a common risk management technique. Risk management typically involves identifying, assessing, and taking steps to minimize or mitigate risks, rather than speculating on them.

Miscellaneous Coverages (Total: 3 Questions)

Flood insurance: 1 question

118) What does the flood insurance policy cover in terms of property damage?

Correct Answer is B - The flood insurance policy covers both the building's structure and its contents, though contents coverage is optional. This provides comprehensive protection against flood damage, allowing policyholders to choose the level of coverage that best meets their needs.

Earthquake insurance: 1 question

119) Why might homeowners in low-risk areas still consider purchasing earthquake insurance?

Correct Answer is A - Homeowners in low-risk areas might still consider purchasing earthquake insurance because earthquakes are unpredictable and can cause significant damage even in areas not known for seismic activity. This precautionary measure provides financial protection against the potential for unexpected and devastating losses.

Crime insurance policies: 1 question

120) 'Fidelity Bonds' provided as part of crime insurance policies protect against losses from:

Correct Answer is A - 'Fidelity Bonds' provided as part of crime insurance policies protect against losses from employee dishonesty and fraudulent acts. This coverage safeguards businesses against financial losses resulting from the fraudulent actions of their employees.

Practice Exam 3 (Total: 120 Questions) - Answers & Explanations

Insurance Basics (Total: 20 Questions)

Principles of insurance: 7 questions

1) Utmost good faith is a mutual obligation requiring which of the following from the insured?

```
Correct Answer is A - Utmost good faith is a mutual obligation
requiring the disclosure of all relevant facts from the insured.
This ensures that both the insurer and the insured are fully
informed about the risks being insured.
```

2) What role does the principle of subrogation play in preventing?

```
Correct Answer is D - The principle of subrogation plays a role
in preventing double recovery from the same loss by allowing
insurers to pursue third parties responsible for causing a loss
after compensating the insured.
```

3) The principle of insurable interest is designed to ensure what?

Correct Answer is A - The principle of insurable interest is designed to ensure that the insured can only insure property or lives that would cause a financial loss if damaged or lost. This principle establishes a legitimate interest in the insured risk.

4) In the context of insurance, what is 'proximate cause'?

Correct Answer is A - In the context of insurance, 'proximate cause' is a cause that is legally recognized as the primary reason for the loss. It determines the cause most closely linked to the loss in a direct and uninterrupted chain.

5) Which principle justifies an insurer's pursuit of a third party after a claim has been paid?

Correct Answer is C - Subrogation justifies an insurer's pursuit of a third party after a claim has been paid, allowing the insurer to recover the amount paid to the insured from the party responsible for the loss.

6) What is required for an insurance contract to adhere to the principle of utmost good faith?

Correct Answer is C - For an insurance contract to adhere to the principle of utmost good faith, full disclosure of material facts by both parties is required. This ensures that both the insurer and insured enter the contract with a complete understanding of the risks involved.

7) How does the principle of indemnity prevent the insured from profiting from a loss?

Correct Answer is B - The principle of indemnity prevents the insured from profiting from a loss by limiting reimbursement to the loss's actual cash value. This ensures that compensation reflects the true value of the loss without leading to a financial gain for the insured.

Types of insurers: 6 questions

8) Government insurers are established to provide which of the following?

Correct Answer is B - Government insurers are established to provide coverage not typically available from private insurers. This includes insurance for high-risk individuals or properties and coverage for risks that the private market is unwilling or unable to insure.

9) Which type of insurer is best known for underwriting through a pool of underwriters who share in profits and losses?

Correct Answer is C - Lloyd's of London is best known for underwriting through a pool of underwriters who share in profits and losses. It is a marketplace where members join together to insure diverse and complex risks.

10) In terms of regulation, how do state insurance departments primarily interact with insurers?

Correct Answer is B - In terms of regulation, state insurance departments primarily interact with insurers by setting standards for policy forms and rates. They ensure that insurance products are fair, reasonable, and meet state regulatory requirements.

11) Which type of insurer is directly owned and controlled by its policy-holders, with no external shareholders?

Correct Answer is B - A mutual insurer is directly owned and controlled by its policyholders, with no external shareholders. Profits are either reinvested for future growth or returned to policyholders in the form of dividends or reduced premiums.

12) Risk retention groups are formed by whom?

Correct Answer is A - Risk retention groups are formed by policyholders in the same industry to insure against common risks. This allows members to pool their risks and potentially achieve lower insurance costs and tailored coverage.

13) An insurer formed under the laws of the state in which the insurance is sold is called a/an:

Correct Answer is C - An insurer formed under the laws of the state in which the insurance is sold is called a domestic insurer. This designation is based on the legal jurisdiction where the insurer is incorporated and operates.

Policy renewals and cancellations: 7 questions

14) What is the effect of a policy reinstatement on a lapse?

Correct Answer is D - The effect of a policy reinstatement on a
lapse is that it nullifies the lapse and reinstates coverage as
if the lapse never occurred. Reinstatement restores the policy
to its original state before the lapse.

15) What typically accompanies a policy cancellation notice from an insurer?

Correct Answer is B - A policy cancellation notice from an
insurer typically accompanies an explanation for the
cancellation. This provides the insured with the reason(s) why
the insurer has decided to terminate the policy.

16) Which statement is true regarding non-renewal notices?

Correct Answer is A - Non-renewal notices must be given at least
30 days before the policy end date, although the exact time
frame can vary by state. This requirement ensures that
policyholders are adequately informed in advance of non-renewal.

17) What is usually required for a policy to be reinstated after cancellation?

Correct Answer is D - For a policy to be reinstated after
cancellation, payment of overdue premiums and possibly a
reinstatement fee is usually required. This allows the policy to
become active again after being canceled for non-payment.

18) For which reason can an insurance policy NOT be canceled?

Correct Answer is C - An insurance policy cannot be canceled for
filing a claim under the policy. Canceling a policy for this

reason would undermine the very purpose of insurance.

19) What does a 'flat cancellation' refer to?

Correct Answer is A - A 'flat cancellation' refers to canceling the policy as of its effective date, resulting in no coverage and a full refund of the premium. This is as if the policy had never been in effect.

20) Under what condition might a policy be eligible for reinstatement after cancellation due to non-payment of premium?

Correct Answer is B - A policy might be eligible for reinstatement after cancellation due to non-payment of premium if the insured pays the overdue premium within a grace period. This allows the policy to be reactivated under the original terms.

Property Insurance (Total: 28 Questions)

Dwelling policies: 6 questions

21) The 'Dwelling Under Construction' endorsement in a dwelling policy:

Correct Answer is C - The 'Dwelling Under Construction' endorsement in a dwelling policy adjusts the dwelling coverage amount based on the stages of construction. It reflects the increasing value of the property as construction progresses.

22) How does a 'Broad Theft Coverage' endorsement affect a dwelling policy?

Correct Answer is C - A 'Broad Theft Coverage' endorsement affects a dwelling policy by providing theft coverage, which is not included in basic form (DP-1) policies. It extends the policy to cover theft, a peril not covered under the most basic form.

23) What is the purpose of the 'Ordinance or Law' coverage endorsement in a dwelling policy?

Correct Answer is B - The purpose of the 'Ordinance or Law' coverage endorsement in a dwelling policy is to pay for increased costs due to the enforcement of building codes during repairs. This coverage is important when local building ordinances increase the cost of rebuilding or repairing a damaged property to current standards.

24) In dwelling policies, 'Named Peril' coverage means:

Correct Answer is A - In dwelling policies, 'Named Peril' coverage means the policy only covers perils specifically named in the policy documents. This contrasts with all-risk policies that cover all perils except those explicitly excluded.

25) Which type of property would typically NOT be eligible for coverage under a standard dwelling policy?

Correct Answer is D - A large apartment complex would typically NOT be eligible for coverage under a standard dwelling policy. Dwelling policies are generally intended for single-family homes, duplexes, and sometimes seasonal or vacation homes, not large multi-unit buildings.

26) The 'Vandalism and Malicious Mischief' coverage in a dwelling policy:

```
Correct Answer is B - The 'Vandalism and Malicious Mischief'
coverage in a dwelling policy covers acts of vandalism unless
the dwelling has been vacant for more than 60 consecutive days.
This provision is common to prevent claims on properties that
are not actively maintained.
```

Homeowners policies: 8 questions

27) An 'inflation guard' endorsement in a homeowners policy is designed to:

```
Correct Answer is B - An 'inflation guard' endorsement in a
homeowners policy is designed to automatically adjust the
coverage limit based on inflation rates. This helps ensure that
the coverage amount remains adequate over time despite inflation.
```

28) The difference between 'Replacement Cost' and 'Actual Cash Value' in a homeowners policy primarily lies in:

```
Correct Answer is B - The difference between 'Replacement Cost'
and 'Actual Cash Value' in a homeowners policy primarily lies in
the inclusion of depreciation in the settlement. Actual Cash
Value takes depreciation into account, whereas Replacement Cost
does not.
```

29) Which homeowners coverage form is exclusively for tenants or renters?

```
Correct Answer is C - HO-4 coverage form is exclusively for
tenants or renters. It provides personal property and liability
coverage suitable for individuals renting or leasing their
living space.
```

30) A 'Guaranteed Replacement Cost' endorsement in a homeowners policy means the insurer will:

```
Correct Answer is B - A 'Guaranteed Replacement Cost'
endorsement in a homeowners policy means the insurer will pay
whatever it costs to rebuild the home as it was before the loss,
even if it exceeds the policy limit. This provides the most
comprehensive protection against underinsurance.
```

31) Personal Property coverage in a homeowners policy typically covers:

```
Correct Answer is B - Personal Property coverage in a homeowners
policy typically covers items owned or used by the insured
anywhere in the world. This global coverage extends protection
beyond the home.
```

32) Which of the following perils is generally covered by a standard homeowners policy?

```
Correct Answer is C - Volcanic eruption is generally covered by
a standard homeowners policy. Unlike earthquakes and floods,
which typically require separate policies, volcanic eruptions
are often included as covered perils.
```

33) The 'Duty to Defend' under the Personal Liability portion of a homeowners policy obligates the insurer to:

```
Correct Answer is B - The 'Duty to Defend' under the Personal
Liability portion of a homeowners policy obligates the insurer
to defend the insured in court against claims covered by the
policy, regardless of the outcome. This is a key protection
provided by liability insurance.
```

34) 'Other Structures' coverage on a homeowners policy typically includes all of the following EXCEPT:

```
Correct Answer is D - 'Other Structures' coverage on a
homeowners policy typically includes detached garages, tool
sheds, and swimming pools, but EXCLUDES the main dwelling. The
main dwelling is covered under a separate portion of the policy.
```

Commercial property policies: 8 questions

35) 'Equipment Breakdown Coverage' in a commercial property policy typically includes all EXCEPT:

```
Correct Answer is C - 'Equipment Breakdown Coverage' in a
commercial property policy typically includes mechanical
breakdown, electrical arcing, and explosion of steam boilers,
but EXCLUDES wear and tear from normal use. Normal wear and tear
is not considered a sudden and accidental event.
```

36) The 'Businessowners Policy (BOP)' combines which types of coverage?

```
Correct Answer is C - The 'Businessowners Policy (BOP)' combines
property and general liability insurance. This packaged policy
```

is designed to meet the basic needs of small and medium-sized businesses.

37) How does the 'Actual Cash Value (ACV)' settlement option affect a commercial property claim?

Correct Answer is B - The 'Actual Cash Value (ACV)' settlement option affects a commercial property claim by settling claims based on the replacement cost minus depreciation. This takes into account the depreciated value of the property at the time of the loss.

38) A 'Commercial Package Policy (CPP)' allows businesses to:

Correct Answer is A - A 'Commercial Package Policy (CPP)' allows businesses to package multiple types of commercial policies for a discount. This flexibility lets businesses tailor their insurance coverage to their specific needs.

39) Which of the following is a characteristic of 'Blanket Insurance' in commercial property policies?

Correct Answer is B - 'Blanket Insurance' in commercial property policies provides a single limit of insurance for multiple properties or types of property. This approach simplifies coverage for businesses with multiple locations or varied property types.

40) 'Accounts Receivable Coverage' under a commercial property policy is designed to cover:

Correct Answer is B - 'Accounts Receivable Coverage' under a commercial property policy is designed to cover losses if business records are destroyed and uncollectible receivables cannot be proven. This financial protection helps businesses recover from the loss of important financial records.

41) The 'Signs Coverage' endorsement in a commercial property policy specifically insures:

Correct Answer is C - The 'Signs Coverage' endorsement in a commercial property policy specifically insures outdoor signs attached to the building. This endorsement provides targeted coverage for signs, which are often excluded or limited under standard commercial property policies.

42) 'Utility Services - Direct Damage' coverage in a commercial property policy covers damage resulting from:

Correct Answer is B - 'Utility Services - Direct Damage' coverage in a commercial property policy covers damage resulting from the interruption of power supply leading to direct physical loss or damage. This coverage helps businesses manage the risk of utility service interruptions that can cause significant damage to property and disrupt operations.

Business interruption: 6 questions

43) Business interruption insurance generally calculates lost income based on:

Correct Answer is B - Business interruption insurance generally calculates lost income based on past financial records and trends. This method provides a basis for estimating the income that the business would have earned had the interruption not occurred, taking into account seasonal variations and growth trends.

44) 'Service Interruption' coverage in business interruption insurance protects against losses resulting from:

Correct Answer is B - 'Service Interruption' coverage in business interruption insurance protects against losses resulting from the failure of public utilities such as electricity, gas, water, or telecommunications. This coverage is crucial for businesses that depend heavily on these services for their operations.

45) In business interruption insurance, 'ordinary payroll' refers to:

Correct Answer is B - In business interruption insurance, 'ordinary payroll' refers to wages that the policyholder opts to continue paying to employees during the interruption. This coverage decision allows businesses to maintain their workforce during a temporary closure.

46) 'Civil Authority' coverage under a business interruption policy applies when access to the insured premises is prevented by:

Correct Answer is B - 'Civil Authority' coverage under a business interruption policy applies when access to the insured premises is prevented by an official act of a civil authority due to direct physical loss or damage at a nearby location. This coverage addresses the business income losses resulting from such government-imposed restrictions.

47) Which statement is true regarding the calculation of a business interruption loss?

Correct Answer is C - The calculation of a business interruption loss is based on the net income that would have been earned if the loss had not occurred. This approach considers both the revenue the business would have generated and the ongoing operating expenses, providing a fair measure of the income loss.

48) The purpose of 'sue and labor' clause in a business interruption policy is to:

Correct Answer is B - The purpose of the 'sue and labor' clause in a business interruption policy is to encourage the insured to take reasonable actions to minimize the loss and protect the property. This clause acknowledges the insured's efforts to mitigate damages and may cover some of the expenses associated with these actions.

Casualty Insurance (Total: 32 Questions)

Auto insurance: 8 questions

49) What action can result in an auto insurance policy being canceled?

Correct Answer is B - Non-payment of premiums can result in an auto insurance policy being canceled. This is a common reason for cancellation, as it reflects the policyholder's failure to meet the contractual agreement of paying premiums for continued coverage.

50) An auto insurance policy with 'Split Limits' means:

Correct Answer is B - An auto insurance policy with 'Split Limits' means there are different limits for bodily injury per person, per accident, and for property damage. This provides flexibility in coverage limits for different aspects of liability insurance.

51) The 'Declaration Page' of an auto insurance policy typically includes:

Correct Answer is D - The 'Declaration Page' of an auto insurance policy typically includes information about the policyholder, vehicle, coverages, and limits. This page serves as a summary of the policy's key information, making it easy for policyholders to understand their coverage.

52) 'Non-Owned Auto' coverage in a commercial auto policy is designed for:

Correct Answer is D - 'Non-Owned Auto' coverage in a commercial auto policy is designed for vehicles owned by employees but used for business purposes and rental vehicles used by the business. This coverage extends the business's auto liability insurance to vehicles that the business does not own, providing protection in the course of business use.

53) In auto insurance, 'Stacking' of uninsured/underinsured motorist coverage allows:

Correct Answer is A - In auto insurance, 'Stacking' of uninsured/underinsured motorist coverage allows combining limits for multiple vehicles on the same policy for a higher total coverage amount. This can provide additional protection in case of an accident with an uninsured or underinsured driver.

54) The 'Exclusion' section of an auto insurance policy:

Correct Answer is C - The 'Exclusion' section of an auto insurance policy specifies what is not covered by the policy. This section is crucial for understanding the policy's limitations and ensures policyholders are aware of the coverage boundaries.

55) 'Towing and Labor' coverage in an auto insurance policy typically includes:

Correct Answer is A - 'Towing and Labor' coverage in an auto insurance policy typically includes reimbursement for towing and basic roadside assistance. This coverage provides financial protection for services to assist with vehicle breakdowns.

56) What factor does NOT affect the cost of auto insurance premiums?

Correct Answer is B - The policyholder's educational level does not affect the cost of auto insurance premiums. Factors influencing premiums include the vehicle's safety features, the policyholder's driving record, and the amount of coverage purchased, among others.

Workers compensation: 8 questions

57) 'Return to Work' programs under workers' compensation are intended to:

Correct Answer is B - 'Return to Work' programs under workers' compensation are intended to facilitate the injured worker's transition back to employment, sometimes in a modified or alternative role. These programs aim to reintegrate injured employees into the workforce in a capacity that accommodates their recovery.

58) The 'Exclusive Remedy' rule in workers' compensation law:

Correct Answer is C - The 'Exclusive Remedy' rule in workers' compensation law limits employees to workers' compensation benefits as their sole remedy against their employer for work-related injuries. This legal framework provides a trade-off: employees receive guaranteed compensation for injuries, while employers are protected from lawsuits.

59) A workers' compensation policy is primarily required by:

Correct Answer is B - A workers' compensation policy is primarily required by state laws, with requirements varying by state. Each state has its own regulations and mandates regarding workers' compensation coverage for businesses operating within its jurisdiction.

60) 'Cumulative Injury' claims in workers' compensation refer to injuries that:

Correct Answer is B - 'Cumulative Injury' claims in workers' compensation refer to injuries that result from repetitive stress or exposure over time. These injuries develop gradually and are associated with the nature of the work performed, rather than a single incident.

61) For a workers' compensation claim to be valid, the injury must:

Correct Answer is C - For a workers' compensation claim to be valid, the injury must arise out of and in the course of employment. This ensures that the injury is directly related to the job duties or occurred while performing work-related tasks.

62) 'Subrogation' in workers' compensation allows the insurer to:

Correct Answer is B - 'Subrogation' in workers' compensation allows the insurer to seek reimbursement from third parties responsible for the employee's injury. This process helps recover costs for claims that were caused by the actions of someone other than the employer or employee.

63) The term 'Statutory Compensation' in workers' compensation refers to:

Correct Answer is B - The term 'Statutory Compensation' in workers' compensation refers to payments that are determined by state law. These laws set the benefits levels and conditions under which they are paid, ensuring a standardized approach across different cases.

64) A 'Monopolistic State Fund' for workers' compensation is:

Correct Answer is B - A 'Monopolistic State Fund' for workers' compensation is a state-operated fund that is the sole provider of workers' compensation insurance in certain states. Employers in these states must obtain their workers' compensation coverage exclusively from the state fund.

Liability insurance: 10 questions

65) In liability insurance, a 'Retroactive Date' in a claims-made policy refers to:

Correct Answer is A - In liability insurance, a 'Retroactive Date' in a claims-made policy refers to the date before which incidents are not covered, even if the claim is made during the policy period. This date limits the insurer's exposure to claims arising from incidents that occurred before the policy was effective.

66) 'Garage Keepers Liability Insurance' provides coverage for:

Correct Answer is A - 'Garage Keepers Liability Insurance' provides coverage for damage to vehicles stored in a commercial garage, not owned by the garage. This is important for businesses that hold customer vehicles, protecting them against potential damages while in their care.

67) An 'Aggregate Limit' in a liability policy specifies:

Correct Answer is C - An 'Aggregate Limit' in a liability policy specifies the total amount the insurer will pay for all claims

during the policy period. This cap sets the maximum financial
responsibility of the insurer for the policy term.

68) Which of the following is NOT typically excluded from a general liability insurance policy?

Correct Answer is C - Bodily injury to customers due to a
product defect is NOT typically excluded from a general
liability insurance policy. General liability policies often
cover such claims, whereas intentional acts of harm, employee
injuries covered by workers' compensation, and contractual
liabilities are commonly excluded.

69) 'Fiduciary Liability Insurance' covers:

Correct Answer is A - 'Fiduciary Liability Insurance' covers
financial losses due to fiduciaries' mismanagement of employee
benefit plans. This insurance is crucial for those who manage
such plans, protecting them against claims of mismanagement and
the financial consequences thereof.

70) The 'Supplementary Payments' provision in a liability policy typically includes coverage for:

Correct Answer is B - The 'Supplementary Payments' provision in
a liability policy typically includes coverage for costs above
the policy limits, such as certain legal defense costs. This can
include attorney fees, court costs, and other expenses
associated with defending a claim.

71) A 'Waiver of Subrogation' endorsement in a liability policy:

Correct Answer is B - A 'Waiver of Subrogation' endorsement in a liability policy prevents the insurer from seeking reimbursement from a third party after paying a claim. This waiver is often used in contracts where parties agree to limit their right to recover damages from one another.

72) 'Voluntary Property Damage' coverage in a liability policy:

Correct Answer is B - 'Voluntary Property Damage' coverage in a liability policy provides coverage for property damage caused voluntarily by the insured to a third party's property. This coverage is particularly relevant in situations where the insured damages someone else's property in the course of their business activities.

73) In liability insurance, 'Split Limits' refer to:

Correct Answer is A - In liability insurance, 'Split Limits' refer to dividing the policy limits between property damage and bodily injury coverage. This allows for separate coverage limits for different types of damages within the same policy.

74) What is 'Advertising Injury' coverage in a Commercial General Liability (CGL) policy?

Correct Answer is B - 'Advertising Injury' coverage in a Commercial General Liability (CGL) policy provides protection against claims of slander, libel, or copyright infringement in advertisements. This coverage is essential for businesses engaged in advertising activities, offering protection against certain legal liabilities.

Umbrella policies: 6 questions

75) Which type of claim is most likely to be covered by an umbrella policy but not by standard auto or homeowners insurance?

Correct Answer is C - A libel or slander claim resulting from a blog post is most likely to be covered by an umbrella policy but not by standard auto or homeowners insurance. Umbrella policies provide broader liability coverage, including for personal injury claims like libel or slander.

76) In what circumstance might an umbrella policy deny coverage?

Correct Answer is A - An umbrella policy might deny coverage if the underlying policy limits have not been exhausted. Umbrella policies typically require that the primary insurance limits are used up before they step in to provide additional coverage.

77) The 'self-insured retention' (SIR) in an umbrella policy is:

Correct Answer is A - The 'self-insured retention' (SIR) in an umbrella policy is the amount the policyholder must pay out-of-pocket before the umbrella coverage begins, for claims not covered by any underlying policy. This acts similarly to a deductible for claims that fall under the umbrella but not under any primary policy.

78) Which statement about umbrella policies is TRUE?

Correct Answer is D - A true statement about umbrella policies is that they can cover multiple underlying policies, such as auto and homeowners insurance. Umbrella policies provide an extra layer of protection above the limits of the underlying policies.

79) 'Worldwide Coverage' under an umbrella policy means:

Correct Answer is A - 'Worldwide Coverage' under an umbrella
policy means the policy provides coverage anywhere in the world.
This global coverage is a key feature of umbrella policies,
offering protection for the insured against liabilities,
regardless of where they occur.

80) An umbrella policy would most likely provide additional coverage in which of the following situations?

Correct Answer is B - An umbrella policy would most likely
provide additional coverage in the situation where the
policyholder is sued for defamation. Umbrella policies offer
broader coverage for various liability claims, including
defamation, which may not be covered under standard policies.

Package Policies (Total: 12 Questions)

Business Owners Policy (BOP): 6 questions

81) A BOP typically offers 'Liability Coverage' for all the following EXCEPT:

Correct Answer is B - A BOP typically offers 'Liability
Coverage' for customer injuries at the business premises, damage
to a customer's property, and product liability claims, but
EXCEPT for employee discrimination lawsuits, which are generally
covered under employment practices liability insurance, not

included in a standard BOP.

82) Which statement about the premium for a BOP is TRUE?

Correct Answer is C - The premium for a BOP considers factors
like business location, type of business, and coverage limits.
This comprehensive approach allows insurers to assess the risk
associated with insuring the business accurately.

83) The 'Electronic Data Processing (EDP)' coverage in a BOP protects against:

Correct Answer is A - The 'Electronic Data Processing (EDP)'
coverage in a BOP protects against damage to electronic data
processing equipment and loss of data. This coverage is
essential for businesses reliant on computers and electronic
data for their operations.

84) What is typically the maximum number of employees a business can have to be eligible for a BOP?

Correct Answer is C - Typically, the maximum number of employees
a business can have to be eligible for a BOP is around 100,
although this can vary by insurer and the type of business.
Eligibility is not solely based on revenue but often considers
the business's size and nature.

85) 'Newly Acquired or Constructed Property' coverage in a BOP:

Correct Answer is A - 'Newly Acquired or Constructed Property'
coverage in a BOP provides immediate coverage for new properties

acquired or constructed, up to a certain limit. This ensures that expansions or additions are automatically covered without the need for immediate policy adjustments.

86) 'Hired and Non-Owned Auto' coverage in a BOP:

Correct Answer is B - 'Hired and Non-Owned Auto' coverage in a BOP provides liability coverage for vehicles the business hires or that are owned by employees but used for business. This covers a gap that typical commercial auto policies might not cover, especially for businesses that do not own their vehicles.

Commercial package policy: 6 questions

87) 'Commercial Auto' coverage in a CPP includes protection for:

Correct Answer is B - 'Commercial Auto' coverage in a CPP includes protection for vehicles owned, leased, or used by the business. This encompasses a wide range of vehicles used for business purposes, offering comprehensive coverage.

88) 'Errors and Omissions' (E&O) insurance is designed to protect against:

Correct Answer is C - 'Errors and Omissions' (E&O) insurance is designed to protect against mistakes or negligence in professional services provided. This coverage is crucial for professionals whose services could harm clients due to errors or oversights.

89) Which of the following would typically be excluded from a CPP?

Correct Answer is A - Acts of terrorism are typically excluded from a CPP. This is because the potential losses from such acts can be extremely high and unpredictable, often requiring specialized insurance coverage.

90) The 'Additional Insured' endorsement in a CPP allows:

Correct Answer is B - The 'Additional Insured' endorsement in a CPP allows businesses to extend certain coverages to other parties as required by contract. This is common in situations where a business needs to provide proof of insurance to another party, such as a landlord or client.

91) In a CPP, 'Cyber Liability' coverage is important for businesses that:

Correct Answer is B - In a CPP, 'Cyber Liability' coverage is important for businesses that handle sensitive customer data electronically. This coverage protects against losses and liabilities arising from data breaches, cyber-attacks, and other cyber-related risks.

92) 'Pollution Liability' coverage in a CPP is specifically designed to address:

Correct Answer is B - 'Pollution Liability' coverage in a CPP is specifically designed to address liabilities arising from pollution events caused by the insured's operations. This coverage is essential for businesses that use or produce hazardous materials or could otherwise cause environmental harm.

State-Specific Regulations (Total: 15 Questions)

Licensing requirements: 5 questions

93) Reciprocity between states regarding property and casualty insurance licensing means:

```
Correct Answer is C - Reciprocity between states regarding
property and casualty insurance licensing means an agent
licensed in one state may qualify for a license in another state
without taking that state's exam, facilitating the process for
agents to operate in multiple states.
```

94) How often must a property and casualty insurance license typically be renewed?

```
Correct Answer is B - A property and casualty insurance license
typically must be renewed every two years. This requirement
ensures that agents remain up-to-date with industry knowledge
and regulatory changes.
```

95) Continuing education units (CEUs) required for license renewal for property and casualty agents:

```
Correct Answer is D - Continuing education units (CEUs) required
for license renewal for property and casualty agents vary by
state and must be completed within the renewal period. This
ensures agents continue their education and stay informed about
the latest practices and laws.
```

96) Which of the following activities generally requires a property and casualty insurance license?

Correct Answer is B - Selling, soliciting, or negotiating
insurance contracts generally requires a property and casualty
insurance license. This ensures that individuals engaging in
these activities are knowledgeable and comply with state
regulations.

97) A property and casualty insurance agent's license can be revoked or suspended for:

Correct Answer is B - A property and casualty insurance agent's
license can be revoked or suspended for not completing
continuing education requirements. This emphasizes the
importance of ongoing education in maintaining professional
standards.

State laws governing insurance practices: 6 questions

98) The 'unfair trade practices' act in state insurance law typically prohibits:

Correct Answer is B - The 'unfair trade practices' act in state
insurance law typically prohibits misrepresentation, false
advertising, and defamation by insurers. These regulations
protect consumers from deceptive and unethical practices in the
insurance industry.

99) State insurance laws regarding 'rate making' aim to ensure rates are:

Correct Answer is B - State insurance laws regarding 'rate
making' aim to ensure rates are adequate, not excessive, and not

unfairly discriminatory. This promotes fairness and financial solvency in the insurance market.

100) 'Risk-based capital' requirements under state insurance laws are designed to:

Correct Answer is B - 'Risk-based capital' requirements under state insurance laws are designed to ensure insurers have enough capital relative to their risk exposure. This regulatory measure aims to maintain the solvency and financial health of insurance companies, protecting policyholders.

101) In terms of insurance, 'prior approval' state laws require:

Correct Answer is B - 'Prior approval' state laws require state insurance departments to approve rates and forms before they can be used. This regulatory measure ensures that rates and policy forms are fair and reasonable before they are offered to consumers.

102) How do state laws typically address insurance fraud?

Correct Answer is B - State laws typically address insurance fraud through specific statutes that define and penalize fraudulent insurance acts. These laws are designed to protect both consumers and insurers from the effects of fraudulent activities.

103) 'Guaranty funds,' as established by state insurance laws, are designed to:

Correct Answer is B - 'Guaranty funds,' as established by state insurance laws, are designed to protect policyholders if an insurer becomes insolvent. These funds ensure that claims are paid even if the insurance company is unable to fulfill its obligations due to financial failure.

Ethical practices and the regulatory environment: 4 questions

104) The regulatory environment in the insurance industry is designed to:

Correct Answer is C - The regulatory environment in the insurance industry is designed to protect consumers and maintain the integrity of the insurance market. Regulation ensures that insurance practices are fair, companies are solvent, and consumers are treated equitably.

105) An insurance professional fabricating a client's application details to secure a policy approval is violating which ethical principle?

Correct Answer is C - An insurance professional fabricating a client's application details to secure a policy approval is violating the ethical principle of honesty. Fabricating application details misrepresents the risk to the insurer and undermines the trustworthiness of the insurance process.

106) What role do continuing education requirements play in promoting ethical practices among insurance professionals?

Correct Answer is B - Continuing education requirements play a role in promoting ethical practices among insurance professionals by providing updates on regulatory changes and reinforcing ethical standards. This ongoing education helps ensure that professionals remain knowledgeable and ethical in their practices.

107) Misrepresenting the terms of a policy to a policyholder is a breach of:

Correct Answer is C - Misrepresenting the terms of a policy to a policyholder is a breach of the principle of utmost good faith. This principle requires both parties to an insurance contract to act honestly and disclose all relevant information.

Insurance Operations (Total: 10 Questions)

Underwriting principles: 4 questions

108) 'Capacity' in underwriting refers to:

Correct Answer is A - 'Capacity' in underwriting refers to the maximum amount of risk the insurer is willing to accept. This term is used to describe the insurer's ability to take on new policies based on its financial strength and reinsurance arrangements.

109) What role does 'reinsurance' play in underwriting?

Correct Answer is B - Reinsurance plays a role in underwriting by providing a way for insurers to transfer part of the risk to another insurance company. This helps insurers manage their risk exposure and maintain financial stability by sharing potential losses with reinsurers.

110) The concept of 'retention' in underwriting refers to:

Correct Answer is B - The concept of 'retention' in underwriting refers to the amount of risk an insurer keeps for its own account without passing it to a reinsurer. This is the portion of risk the insurance company decides to assume itself, indicating its willingness to accept and manage that level of risk.

111) An 'underwriting loss' occurs when:

Correct Answer is C - An 'underwriting loss' occurs when claims paid and expenses exceed premium income. This situation indicates that the insurance company is spending more on claims and operational costs than it is earning in premiums, leading to a financial loss.

Rate making: 3 questions

112) Which of the following best describes 'premium leakage'?

Correct Answer is B - 'Premium leakage' describes the loss of premium revenue due to underpricing or inadequate rating. This can happen when risks are not accurately assessed, leading to premiums that do not fully cover the cost of claims and expenses.

113) 'Underwriting profit' in rate making refers to:

Correct Answer is B - 'Underwriting profit' in rate making
refers to the difference between premiums collected and losses
paid out. This metric is a key indicator of the financial health
of an insurer, showing the profitability of its underwriting
activities before investment income is considered.

114) How do regulatory bodies influence rate making in the insurance industry?

Correct Answer is B - Regulatory bodies influence rate making in
the insurance industry through reviewing and approving rates to
ensure they are not excessive, inadequate, or discriminatory.
This oversight aims to protect consumers from unfair pricing
while ensuring that insurance companies remain solvent.

Risk management: 3 questions

115) 'Risk reduction' in the context of property and casualty insurance can involve:

Correct Answer is B - 'Risk reduction' in the context of
property and casualty insurance can involve implementing safety
training for employees. This strategy aims to minimize the
likelihood and impact of potential losses by promoting safer
practices and reducing the risk of accidents.

116) How does 'diversification' function as a risk management strategy?

Correct Answer is C - Diversification functions as a risk management strategy by employing a variety of risk management techniques to address different risks. This approach spreads risk exposure across different areas, reducing the potential impact of any single risk on the organization.

117) The concept of 'total cost of risk' (TCOR) in risk management includes:

Correct Answer is B - The concept of 'total cost of risk' (TCOR) in risk management includes costs related to risk identification, assessment, and control, including financial losses from realized risks. This comprehensive view encompasses all costs associated with managing risk, not just insurance premiums.

Miscellaneous Coverages (Total: 3 Questions)

Flood insurance: 1 question

118) Flood insurance policies through the NFIP are available:

Correct Answer is C - Flood insurance policies through the NFIP are available to homeowners, renters, and business owners in participating NFIP communities. This program provides coverage to properties in communities that agree to adhere to certain floodplain management practices.

Earthquake insurance: 1 question

119) In terms of earthquake insurance, what is 'loss of use' coverage?

Correct Answer is B - In terms of earthquake insurance, 'loss of use' coverage reimburses for living expenses if the home is uninhabitable due to earthquake damage. This helps cover additional living expenses incurred while the insured property is being repaired or rebuilt.

Crime insurance policies: 1 question

120) How do crime insurance policies differ from property insurance policies?

Correct Answer is A - Crime insurance policies differ from property insurance policies in that crime policies exclusively cover losses from illegal activities, such as employee theft or fraud, while property policies cover a broad range of perils including natural disasters, fire, and vandalism.

Practice Exam 4 (Total: 120 Questions) - Answers & Explanations

Insurance Basics (Total: 14 Questions)

Principles of insurance: 4 questions

1) Which principle is directly concerned with the distribution of loss among multiple insurers?

Correct Answer is C - The principle directly concerned with the distribution of loss among multiple insurers is Contribution. This principle ensures that when multiple insurance policies cover a loss, the burden is shared among the insurers in proportion to their liability.

2) Proximate cause in insurance contracts is important because it?

Correct Answer is C - Proximate cause in insurance contracts is important because it identifies the primary cause of loss for coverage purposes. Determining the proximate cause helps to ascertain whether the loss is covered under the terms of the insurance policy.

3) 'Insurable interest' in the context of property insurance means the policyholder?

Correct Answer is B - 'Insurable interest' in the context of property insurance means the policyholder has a financial stake in the property being insured. This principle ensures that individuals can only insure property if they would suffer financial loss from its damage or destruction.

4) The principle of 'utmost good faith' obligates which party to disclose all known risks?

Correct Answer is C - The principle of 'utmost good faith' obligates both the insurer and the insured to disclose all known risks. It is a legal doctrine requiring complete honesty and disclosure of all material facts relevant to the insurance contract by both parties.

Types of insurers: 5 questions

5) What characterizes an alien insurance company?

Correct Answer is B - An alien insurance company is an insurer incorporated under the laws of another country. This designation differentiates it from domestic and foreign insurers based on the location of incorporation.

6) A cooperative insurance company is unique because it:

Correct Answer is B - A cooperative insurance company is unique because it is owned and operated by its policyholders. Profits are often returned to policyholders in the form of dividends or reduced premiums.

7) Which organization operates by allowing individual underwriters to accept risks on behalf of members?

Correct Answer is C - Lloyd's of London operates by allowing individual underwriters to accept risks on behalf of members. It is known for insuring unique and sometimes unusual risks through a syndicate of members who share in the profits and losses.

8) Self-insurance is a strategy used by which of the following?

Correct Answer is B - Self-insurance is a strategy used by large corporations to manage their own risks. These entities set aside funds to cover potential losses, effectively acting as their own insurer rather than purchasing insurance from commercial carriers.

9) Direct writers in the insurance industry refer to:

Correct Answer is B - Direct writers in the insurance industry are insurers that sell policies directly to the public without agents. This business model eliminates the middleman, potentially reducing costs for the insurer and premiums for the policyholder.

Policy renewals and cancellations: 5 questions

10) What is the primary difference between cancellation and non-renewal of an insurance policy?

Correct Answer is A - The primary difference between
cancellation and non-renewal of an insurance policy is that
cancellation occurs during the policy term, while non-renewal
happens at the end of the policy term.

11) Which of the following is NOT a common reason for the cancellation of an insurance policy by the insurer?

Correct Answer is A - An increase in the frequency of natural
disasters in the insured's area is NOT a common reason for the
cancellation of an insurance policy by the insurer. Cancellation
typically occurs due to reasons like fraud, material
misrepresentation, relocation outside the insurer's coverage
area, or non-payment of premium.

12) How do state laws generally affect insurance policy cancellations and non-renewals?

Correct Answer is B - State laws specify the conditions under
which policies may be canceled or non-renewed. These laws
protect policyholders by ensuring that insurers provide adequate
notice and valid reasons for cancellation or non-renewal.

13) What is the purpose of the notice period before an insurance policy can be canceled by the insurer?

Correct Answer is C - The purpose of the notice period before an insurance policy can be canceled by the insurer is to ensure the insured has adequate time to find alternative insurance coverage. This prevents individuals from suddenly finding themselves without insurance coverage.

14) In the event of a cancellation, what is typically the minimum notice period required by law?

Correct Answer is A - In the event of a cancellation, the minimum notice period required by law is typically 10 days for non-payment of premium and 30 days for all other reasons. This provides the insured with time to rectify the situation or seek alternative coverage.

Property Insurance (Total: 34 Questions)

Dwelling policies: 9 questions

15) Which coverage in a dwelling policy would pay for damage to a detached garage on the insured property?

Correct Answer is B - The coverage in a dwelling policy that would pay for damage to a detached garage on the insured property is Other Structures. This coverage is separate from the dwelling coverage and is specifically for structures detached from the main residence.

16) A 'Water Back-up and Sump Overflow' endorsement in a dwelling policy specifically covers:

Correct Answer is C - A 'Water Back-up and Sump Overflow'
endorsement in a dwelling policy specifically covers damage from
water back-up through sewers or drains or overflow from a sump.
It does not cover floodwaters or other sources of water damage
not specified in the endorsement.

17) The 'Actual Cash Value (ACV)' settlement in a dwelling policy means compensation is based on:

Correct Answer is A - The 'Actual Cash Value (ACV)' settlement
in a dwelling policy means compensation is based on the
replacement cost minus depreciation. This calculates the current
value of the property at the time of loss, accounting for wear
and tear.

18) What does 'open peril' coverage in a DP-3 policy mean?

Correct Answer is B - 'Open peril' coverage in a DP-3 policy
means all perils are covered except those explicitly excluded in
the policy. This contrasts with named peril policies that only
cover the risks specifically listed.

19) A dwelling policy with a 'Replacement Cost' endorsement means:

Correct Answer is A - A dwelling policy with a 'Replacement
Cost' endorsement means the insurer will pay the cost to replace
the damaged property without deduction for depreciation. This
ensures that the policyholder can fully repair or replace their
property after a covered loss.

20) Which statement about 'Loss Settlement' in dwelling policies is correct?

Correct Answer is B - The correct statement about 'Loss Settlement' in dwelling policies is that personal property is covered for its actual cash value, unless otherwise specified. Structural damages to the dwelling are typically covered on a replacement cost basis, while personal property is valued at ACV unless a specific endorsement changes this settlement approach.

21) The 'Earthquake Endorsement' in a dwelling policy:

Correct Answer is B - The 'Earthquake Endorsement' in a dwelling policy is available for an additional premium to cover earthquake damage, which is otherwise excluded from standard dwelling policies. This endorsement expands the policy's coverage to include damage directly caused by an earthquake.

22) Which of the following would be covered under the 'Internal Explosion' peril in a basic form (DP-1) dwelling policy?

Correct Answer is A - An explosion originating from a natural gas leak inside the home would be covered under the 'Internal Explosion' peril in a basic form (DP-1) dwelling policy. This coverage is designed to protect the dwelling from damages caused by explosions that occur within the premises.

23) Under a DP-2 (Broad Form) policy, which of the following is true regarding the 'Weight of Ice, Snow, or Sleet' peril?

Correct Answer is A - Under a DP-2 (Broad Form) policy, the 'Weight of Ice, Snow, or Sleet' peril covers damage to the dwelling but not to personal property inside. This coverage is specific to the structural damage caused by the weight of ice, snow, or sleet.

Homeowners policies: 10 questions

24) Which homeowners policy endorsement would be necessary to fully cover a home-based business?

Correct Answer is B - A Home Business Endorsement would be necessary to fully cover a home-based business. This endorsement specifically addresses the needs of a business operated from the home, covering business property and liability beyond what is provided in a standard homeowners policy.

25) Exclusions in homeowners policies typically include all of the following EXCEPT:

Correct Answer is D - Exclusions in homeowners policies typically include wear and tear, intentional injury or damage caused by the insured, and nuclear hazard, but NOT theft of personal property. Theft is generally covered under the personal property section of a homeowners policy.

26) What is the primary purpose of requiring a 'deductible' in a homeowners policy?

Correct Answer is C - The primary purpose of requiring a 'deductible' in a homeowners policy is to encourage homeowners to prevent losses. By having to pay a portion of the loss themselves, homeowners are incentivized to take measures to reduce the risk of damage.

27) The 'Aleatory' nature of a homeowners insurance contract means:

Correct Answer is B - The 'Aleatory' nature of a homeowners insurance contract means the value received by each party can be unequal. This characteristic of insurance contracts reflects the uncertainty regarding the timing and size of losses, and hence, the benefits that may be received.

28) A 'Waiver of Deductible' clause in a homeowners policy would likely apply in cases of:

Correct Answer is B - A 'Waiver of Deductible' clause in a homeowners policy would likely apply in cases of large losses, where the cost significantly exceeds the deductible. This can alleviate the financial burden on the policyholder by waiving the deductible in situations of extensive damage.

29) What does the 'Coinsurance Clause' in a homeowners policy encourage?

Correct Answer is B - The 'Coinsurance Clause' in a homeowners policy encourages insuring the home for its full replacement value. This clause can penalize the policyholder with a lower claim payment if the property is insured for less than the stipulated percentage of its replacement value, promoting adequate insurance coverage.

30) The 'Mortgage Clause' in a homeowners policy is designed to protect:

Correct Answer is A - The 'Mortgage Clause' in a homeowners policy is designed to protect the mortgage lender's interest in the property. It ensures that the lender can recover the outstanding loan balance in case of a significant insured loss, even if the insurance payment goes to the homeowner.

31) How does an 'Umbrella Policy' supplement a homeowners policy?

Correct Answer is B - An 'Umbrella Policy' supplements a homeowners policy by extending liability coverage beyond the limits of the homeowners policy. It provides additional coverage for claims that exceed the primary policy's coverage limits, offering broader financial protection against liability claims.

32) 'Consequential Loss' coverage in a homeowners policy is designed to cover:

Correct Answer is C - 'Consequential Loss' coverage in a homeowners policy is designed to cover additional living expenses incurred if the home is uninhabitable due to a covered loss. This can include costs for temporary housing, meals, and other expenses during the repair or rebuilding process.

33) In homeowners insurance, 'Actual Cash Value' settlements are calculated based on:

Correct Answer is C - In homeowners insurance, 'Actual Cash Value' settlements are calculated based on the replacement cost minus depreciation. This reflects the current value of the damaged or destroyed property, taking into account wear and tear or obsolescence.

Commercial property policies: 10 questions

34) What role does the 'Deductible' play in a commercial property policy?

Correct Answer is B - The 'Deductible' plays a role in a commercial property policy by reducing the premium by transferring some risk back to the policyholder. It represents the amount the policyholder is responsible for paying out-of-pocket before insurance coverage begins for a claim.

35) 'Peak Season Endorsement' in a commercial property policy is used to:

Correct Answer is B - A 'Peak Season Endorsement' in a commercial property policy is used to increase coverage limits during seasons when inventory levels are highest. This acknowledges the fluctuating value of business assets and provides additional protection when it's most needed.

36) The 'Fine Arts Coverage' endorsement added to a commercial property policy:

Correct Answer is B - The 'Fine Arts Coverage' endorsement added to a commercial property policy provides a higher limit of coverage for specified fine art pieces. This endorsement is tailored to the unique needs of businesses that own valuable art, offering more specialized protection than standard property coverage.

37) In commercial property insurance, 'Valuable Papers and Records Coverage' is intended to:

Correct Answer is D - In commercial property insurance, 'Valuable Papers and Records Coverage' is intended to pay the cost to research, replace, or restore lost or damaged valuable papers and records. It covers the financial impact of losing important documents but does not cover the intrinsic value of the information lost.

38) Which of the following best describes 'Terrorism Coverage' under a commercial property policy?

Correct Answer is B - 'Terrorism Coverage' under a commercial property policy is optional coverage that protects against damage due to acts of terrorism. It must be selected and paid for separately, and it specifically addresses losses resulting from terrorist acts, which may not be covered under standard commercial property policies.

39) The 'Electronic Data Processing (EDP) Coverage' in commercial property policies specifically insures:

Correct Answer is A - The 'Electronic Data Processing (EDP) Coverage' in commercial property policies specifically insures any electronic data processing equipment, software, and data. It covers losses related to computers and electronic data, including the cost to replace or restore lost or damaged data and equipment.

40) What is the 'Debris Removal' coverage in a commercial property policy designed to cover?

Correct Answer is C - The 'Debris Removal' coverage in a commercial property policy is designed to cover costs to remove debris of covered property after a covered loss. This coverage is crucial for businesses to manage the cleanup costs associated with property damage from covered perils, such as fires or storms.

41) 'Pollutant Clean Up and Removal' coverage in a commercial property policy:

Correct Answer is B - 'Pollutant Clean Up and Removal' coverage in a commercial property policy is typically limited to a specified amount per policy period for cleanup costs due to a covered loss. This coverage addresses the immediate need to remove pollutants that have contaminated the insured property as a result of a covered peril.

42) How does 'Inflation Guard' coverage benefit a commercial property policyholder?

Correct Answer is A - 'Inflation Guard' coverage benefits a commercial property policyholder by ensuring that property values are automatically adjusted to keep up with inflation. This coverage helps maintain adequate levels of insurance as property values increase over time due to inflation, preventing underinsurance.

43) The 'Glass Coverage Form' under a commercial property policy:

Correct Answer is B - The 'Glass Coverage Form' under a commercial property policy provides coverage for glass breakage, including windows and doors. This coverage is crucial for businesses with significant glass installations, offering protection against the financial impact of glass damage.

Business interruption: 5 questions

44) What does the 'coinsurance' clause in a business interruption policy encourage policyholders to do?

Correct Answer is C - The 'coinsurance' clause in a business
interruption policy encourages policyholders to accurately
declare their business income to ensure adequate coverage. This
clause aims to make sure that businesses are insured for a
realistic amount of potential income loss, promoting accurate
reporting of business income.

45) 'Named Perils' coverage in a business interruption policy:

Correct Answer is B - 'Named Perils' coverage in a business
interruption policy only covers perils that are specifically
named in the policy. This type of coverage specifies exactly
which causes of business interruption are insured, contrasting
with all-risk policies that cover all perils except those
explicitly excluded.

46) Business interruption insurance is usually effective:

Correct Answer is B - Business interruption insurance is usually
effective after a specified waiting period from the date of the
direct physical loss. This waiting period, often called a
deductible period in terms of time rather than dollar amount, is
designed to establish when coverage for the interruption of
business begins.

47) The 'Payroll Coverage Extension' in a business interruption policy:

Correct Answer is B - The 'Payroll Coverage Extension' in a business interruption policy provides coverage for payroll expenses for a specified period to retain employees during the interruption. This helps businesses maintain their workforce during periods of operational downtime, ensuring that they can quickly resume normal operations once the cause of the interruption is resolved.

48) Which of the following would NOT trigger business interruption coverage?

Correct Answer is B - A voluntary closure for remodeling the business premises would NOT trigger business interruption coverage. Business interruption insurance is designed to cover losses resulting from unexpected events that force a business to suspend operations, not for voluntary or planned closures.

Casualty Insurance (Total: 30 Questions)

Auto insurance: 7 questions

49) 'Single Limit' liability coverage in an auto insurance policy:

Correct Answer is A - 'Single Limit' liability coverage in an auto insurance policy applies the same maximum amount per accident for both bodily injury and property damage. This coverage combines what might otherwise be separate limits into one overall limit for more flexibility in covering the costs of an accident.

50) 'SR-22' insurance is:

Correct Answer is B - 'SR-22' insurance is a form required for drivers with a suspended license to prove financial responsibility. This document, filed with the state by the insurance company, certifies that the driver has the minimum required insurance coverage following a driving violation such as a DUI or other serious offense.

51) The 'Part D - Coverage for Damage to Your Auto' in a personal auto policy includes:

Correct Answer is B - The 'Part D - Coverage for Damage to Your Auto' in a personal auto policy includes comprehensive and collision coverage. This part of the policy covers physical damage to the insured vehicle resulting from a collision or from other covered incidents, such as theft or vandalism.

52) An auto insurance policy's 'Territory' provision specifies:

Correct Answer is A - An auto insurance policy's 'Territory' provision specifies the geographical area in which the policy provides coverage. This defines the locations where the insurance coverage is effective, which can include specific countries or regions.

53) What is the primary function of 'No-Fault' auto insurance?

Correct Answer is B - The primary function of 'No-Fault' auto insurance is to provide immediate medical payments without determining fault. This type of insurance allows covered individuals to receive prompt medical treatment for injuries sustained in auto accidents regardless of who was at fault.

54) 'Agreed Value' coverage in an auto insurance policy is most commonly

used for:

Correct Answer is B - 'Agreed Value' coverage in an auto
insurance policy is most commonly used for high-value or classic
cars where the value is agreed upon at the policy inception.
This ensures that in the event of a total loss, the policyholder
receives the amount previously agreed upon, reflecting the
unique value of the insured vehicle.

55) 'Diminution in Value' claims in auto insurance refer to:

Correct Answer is A - 'Diminution in Value' claims in auto
insurance refer to the decreased value of a vehicle after it has
been repaired following an accident. This type of claim
addresses the loss in resale value that a vehicle may suffer
even after comprehensive repairs have been made.

Workers compensation: 8 questions

56) Which factor is commonly used to determine workers' compensation premiums?

Correct Answer is C - The company's industry classification and
experience modification factor are commonly used to determine
workers' compensation premiums. These factors help insurers
assess the level of risk associated with the company's
operations and its history of claims, respectively.

57) 'Self-Insurance' for workers' compensation means:

Correct Answer is A - 'Self-Insurance' for workers' compensation means the employer sets aside funds to directly pay for workers' compensation claims. This approach allows larger companies to manage and finance their own risk of employee injuries or illnesses without purchasing a traditional insurance policy.

58) What is an 'Independent Medical Examination' (IME) used for in workers' compensation?

Correct Answer is D - An 'Independent Medical Examination' (IME) is used to assess the extent of the employee's work-related injury or illness and to determine if an employee is fit to return to work. This examination can provide an objective evaluation of the employee's medical condition related to the claim.

59) 'Notice of Injury' in workers' compensation is:

Correct Answer is B - The 'Notice of Injury' in workers' compensation is the document an employee files to report a work-related injury or illness. This formal notification is crucial for initiating the workers' compensation claim process.

60) The 'Pay-As-You-Go' option in workers' compensation insurance allows employers to:

Correct Answer is B - The 'Pay-As-You-Go' option in workers' compensation insurance allows employers to pay premiums based on actual, rather than estimated, payroll figures. This method can improve cash flow management by aligning premium payments more closely with actual payroll costs.

61) Under workers' compensation, a 'Permanent Total Disability' (PTD) benefit is paid when:

Correct Answer is C - Under workers' compensation, a 'Permanent Total Disability' (PTD) benefit is paid when the employee is unable to return to any type of gainful employment. This situation arises when the employee's injuries are so severe that they cannot work in any capacity, reflecting the permanent and total nature of the disability.

62) Which of the following best describes the 'First Report of Injury' in workers' compensation?

Correct Answer is C - The 'First Report of Injury' in workers' compensation is the initial claim form that must be filed with the state workers' compensation board or insurance carrier. This document is crucial for initiating the claim process and must detail the injury, how it occurred, and the parties involved.

63) 'Scheduled Injuries' in workers' compensation refer to:

Correct Answer is B - 'Scheduled Injuries' in workers' compensation refer to specific types of injuries that have predetermined benefit amounts or durations. This schedule is part of the workers' compensation law and provides a clear guideline for compensation for particular injuries, such as the loss of a limb or hearing loss.

Liability insurance: 10 questions

64) 'Employment Practices Liability Insurance' (EPLI) covers the business against claims from employees alleging:

Correct Answer is C - 'Employment Practices Liability Insurance' (EPLI) covers the business against claims from employees alleging workplace discrimination, harassment, wrongful termination, and other similar issues. This coverage is crucial for protecting businesses against the financial and reputational costs associated with these types of claims.

65) Which coverage is specifically designed to protect professionals against liability arising from their professional services?

Correct Answer is C - Professional Liability Insurance is specifically designed to protect professionals against liability arising from their professional services. This includes coverage for claims of negligence, mistakes, or failures in the delivery of professional services that result in financial loss or harm to clients.

66) 'Pollution Liability Insurance' provides coverage for:

Correct Answer is A - 'Pollution Liability Insurance' provides coverage for cleanup costs and third-party claims due to environmental pollution caused by the insured's operations. This type of insurance is essential for businesses that handle hazardous materials or are at risk of causing environmental contamination.

67) A 'Business Owners Policy' (BOP) combines which two types of coverage?

Correct Answer is B - A 'Business Owners Policy' (BOP) combines General Liability and Property Insurance into a single package designed for small to medium-sized businesses. This policy simplifies coverage needs by providing both liability protection and property insurance in one policy.

68) 'Cyber Liability Insurance' is designed to cover:

Correct Answer is B - Cyber Liability Insurance is designed to cover liability for data breaches, cyber-attacks, and information security breaches. This insurance is increasingly important as businesses rely more on digital operations and handle sensitive customer information.

69) What is the 'Duty to Indemnify' in a liability insurance policy?

Correct Answer is C - The 'Duty to Indemnify' in a liability insurance policy is the insurer's obligation to pay for damages or settlements up to the policy limit. This duty ensures that the insured is financially protected against claims for which they are liable, up to the coverage limits of their policy.

70) 'Liquor Liability Insurance' is essential for businesses that:

Correct Answer is B - 'Liquor Liability Insurance' is essential for businesses that manufacture, sell, or serve alcoholic beverages. This insurance covers the business against claims arising from damages or injuries caused by intoxicated customers, which are not typically covered under general liability policies.

71) Which scenario is an example of a 'Third-Party Over Action' claim in liability insurance?

Correct Answer is D - A 'Third-Party Over Action' claim in liability insurance occurs when an employee's injury claim leads to a lawsuit against a third party, who then seeks indemnification from the employer. This type of claim can arise when the third party is held partially responsible for the employee's injuries and seeks to recover some of the costs from the employer.

72) 'Products-Completed Operations Hazard' in a CGL policy covers:

Correct Answer is A - 'Products-Completed Operations Hazard' in a Commercial General Liability (CGL) policy covers liability arising from products manufactured, sold, or distributed by the insured. This coverage protects the business against claims of bodily injury or property damage caused by their products or completed operations.

73) In liability insurance, 'Per Occurrence Limit' refers to:

Correct Answer is C - In liability insurance, the 'Per Occurrence Limit' refers to the maximum amount the insurer will pay for a single claim. This limit specifies the maximum payout for damages resulting from a single incident, regardless of the number of injuries or extent of property damage.

Umbrella policies: 5 questions

74) What is the importance of maintaining underlying policy limits in relation to an umbrella policy?

Correct Answer is B - Maintaining underlying policy limits in relation to an umbrella policy is crucial because insufficient underlying limits can result in a gap in coverage before the umbrella policy applies. Policyholders must ensure that their primary policies have adequate limits to cover smaller claims before the umbrella coverage is needed for larger claims.

75) Which of the following scenarios would typically be excluded from coverage under an umbrella policy?

Correct Answer is C - Damages resulting from the policyholder's participation in a riot would typically be excluded from coverage under an umbrella policy. Most umbrella policies exclude coverage for intentional acts of harm or illegal activities conducted by the policyholder.

76) The cost of an umbrella policy is generally influenced by:

Correct Answer is C - The cost of an umbrella policy is generally influenced by the policyholder's driving record and number of vehicles. These factors help insurers assess the level of risk the policyholder presents, which in turn affects the premium of the umbrella policy.

77) How do insurance companies typically handle claims that involve both an underlying policy and an umbrella policy?

Correct Answer is A - Insurance companies typically handle claims that involve both an underlying policy and an umbrella policy by requiring the underlying policy to pay its limits before the umbrella policy contributes to a covered loss. This structure ensures that the primary insurance coverage is fully utilized before tapping into the broader protection offered by the umbrella policy.

78) Which of the following best illustrates the concept of 'drop-down coverage' in an umbrella policy?

Correct Answer is C - The concept of 'drop-down coverage' in an umbrella policy is best illustrated when the umbrella policy's coverage drops down to fill in gaps not covered by underlying policies. This means the umbrella policy can provide primary coverage for certain losses or liabilities that are not covered under the base policies.

Package Policies (Total: 16 Questions)

Business Owners Policy (BOP): 8 questions

79) How does a BOP differ from a 'Commercial Package Policy' (CPP)?

Correct Answer is B - A BOP offers broader coverage in a single package, while a Commercial Package Policy (CPP) allows for more customization of coverages. The BOP is designed for small to medium-sized businesses and combines essential coverages, whereas a CPP is more flexible, allowing businesses to tailor their insurance package to their specific needs.

80) The 'Premises and Operations' coverage within a BOP liability insur-

ance covers:

Correct Answer is C - The 'Premises and Operations' coverage within a Business Owners Policy (BOP) liability insurance covers both the conditions at the business premises and operations conducted by the business. This comprehensive coverage ensures that the business is protected against liability claims arising from its physical location as well as from its operational activities.

81) 'Spoilage Coverage' under a BOP is important for businesses that:

Correct Answer is D (A and B) - 'Spoilage Coverage' under a Business Owners Policy (BOP) is important for businesses that deal with perishable goods and require refrigeration for their products. This coverage helps protect against financial losses when perishable items spoil due to equipment breakdown or power outages.

82) 'Employee Dishonesty Coverage' included in a BOP protects against:

Correct Answer is B - 'Employee Dishonesty Coverage' included in a BOP protects against theft or fraud committed by employees. This coverage is essential for businesses to safeguard against losses due to dishonest acts by their employees, including theft of money, securities, or other property.

83) Which coverage extension is typically NOT available under a BOP?

Correct Answer is B - Professional liability coverage extension is typically NOT available under a Business Owners Policy (BOP). BOPs generally include general liability and property insurance, but professional liability (errors and omissions insurance) usually requires a separate policy.

84) The 'Protective Safeguards' endorsement in a BOP requires the insured to:

Correct Answer is A - The 'Protective Safeguards' endorsement in a BOP requires the insured to maintain specific safety and security measures as a condition of coverage. This can include fire alarms, sprinkler systems, and security systems to help minimize risks and protect the property.

85) What is the 'Automatic Increase in Insurance' endorsement in a BOP?

Correct Answer is A - The 'Automatic Increase in Insurance' endorsement in a BOP automatically increases coverage limits annually based on inflation. This helps ensure that the business's coverage keeps pace with inflation and that the business remains adequately protected as property values and replacement costs increase.

86) Under a BOP, 'Ordinance or Law Coverage' provides protection for:

Correct Answer is B - Under a BOP, 'Ordinance or Law Coverage' provides protection for the increased cost of construction to meet current building codes after a covered loss. This coverage is vital for businesses rebuilding or repairing structures to comply with updated building regulations.

Commercial package policy: 8 questions

87) 'Directors and Officers' (D&O) liability insurance within a CPP is intended to protect:

Correct Answer is A - 'Directors and Officers' (D&O) liability insurance within a Commercial Package Policy (CPP) is intended to protect the personal assets of corporate directors and officers against claims related to their managerial decisions. This coverage is crucial for protecting individuals in leadership positions from personal financial loss due to lawsuits alleging wrongful acts in their capacity as directors or officers.

88) Which is an essential feature of the 'Business Income' coverage in a CPP?

Correct Answer is B - An essential feature of the 'Business Income' coverage in a CPP is compensation for lost net income and continuing expenses during restoration after a covered loss. This coverage helps a business recover financially by covering lost income and ongoing expenses, such as payroll, during the period it takes to repair or rebuild the business premises.

89) 'Umbrella Liability' insurance as part of a CPP:

Correct Answer is A - 'Umbrella Liability' insurance as part of a CPP extends coverage limits beyond what is offered in the primary liability policies included in the CPP. This additional layer of coverage is designed to protect businesses against large liability claims that exceed the limits of their primary liability insurance.

90) Which of the following best describes 'Builders Risk' insurance in a

CPP?

Correct Answer is C - 'Builders Risk' insurance in a CPP covers buildings under construction, including materials and equipment on site. This insurance is essential for construction projects, as it provides financial protection against loss or damage to the structure and materials during the construction process.

91) A 'Business Owners Policy' (BOP) differs from a CPP in that:

Correct Answer is B - A 'Business Owners Policy' (BOP) differs from a CPP in that a CPP is customizable, while a BOP offers standard packages. A BOP combines general liability and property insurance into a convenient package designed for small to medium-sized businesses, whereas a CPP allows businesses to tailor their coverage to meet specific needs.

92) The advantage of including 'Employment Practices Liability Insurance' (EPLI) in a CPP is to protect against claims from:

Correct Answer is C - The advantage of including 'Employment Practices Liability Insurance' (EPLI) in a CPP is to protect against claims from employment-related issues such as discrimination, wrongful termination, and harassment. This coverage is crucial for businesses to protect themselves against claims made by employees alleging violations of their rights or unfair employment practices.

93) 'Liquor Liability' coverage within a CPP is crucial for businesses that:

Correct Answer is D (B and C) - 'Liquor Liability' coverage within a CPP is crucial for businesses that serve or sell alcohol as part of their operations and host company events where alcohol is served. This coverage protects businesses against claims arising from the sale or service of alcohol, including those related to intoxication and accidents.

94) 'Non-Owned and Hired Auto Liability' coverage in a CPP is important for businesses that:

Correct Answer is B - 'Non-Owned and Hired Auto Liability' coverage in a CPP is important for businesses that occasionally rent vehicles for business use or have employees who use their personal vehicles for business tasks. This coverage provides liability protection for businesses when non-owned or rented vehicles are used for business purposes.

State-Specific Regulations (Total: 14 Questions)

Licensing requirements: 4 questions

95) In most states, an individual selling property and casualty insurance must:

Correct Answer is D - In most states, an individual selling property and casualty insurance must pass a licensing exam and fulfill education requirements. These requirements ensure that insurance agents have the necessary knowledge and skills to provide accurate and responsible insurance services.

96) Which of the following is NOT a typical section on a property and casualty insurance license exam?

Correct Answer is C - Personal interview techniques are NOT a typical section on a property and casualty insurance license exam. The exam usually covers insurance policy analysis, state laws and regulations, and insurance terms and concepts, focusing on the technical and legal aspects of insurance rather than interpersonal skills.

97) An individual applying for a property and casualty insurance license typically needs to:

Correct Answer is A - An individual applying for a property and casualty insurance license typically needs to submit fingerprints for a background check. This requirement helps ensure that applicants have a clean criminal record and are trustworthy to handle the responsibilities of an insurance agent.

98) Ethics training as part of continuing education for property and casualty insurance agents is important because:

Correct Answer is B - Ethics training as part of continuing education for property and casualty insurance agents is important because it ensures agents understand their legal responsibilities to their clients. Ethical training helps maintain the integrity of the insurance profession by reinforcing the importance of honesty, transparency, and the protection of client interests.

State laws governing insurance practices: 5 questions

99) State insurance laws governing 'market conduct' focus on:

Correct Answer is B - State insurance laws governing 'market conduct' focus on how insurers and agents market and sell insurance products. These regulations are designed to protect consumers from misleading practices and ensure that insurance products are marketed in a fair and transparent manner.

100) The 'file and use' regulation in some states allows insurers to:

Correct Answer is A - The 'file and use' regulation in some states allows insurers to use new rates and forms immediately after filing them with the state insurance department, without prior approval. This regulatory approach provides insurers with flexibility to adjust rates and coverage options promptly in response to changing market conditions or risk assessments.

101) Under state insurance laws, 'producer compensation disclosure' requirements are intended to:

Correct Answer is B - Under state insurance laws, 'producer compensation disclosure' requirements are intended to inform customers about how agents and brokers are compensated for selling policies. This transparency helps customers understand potential conflicts of interest or the motivations behind the recommendations made by their insurance professionals.

102) The 'surplus lines' regulation under state laws permits:

Correct Answer is A - The 'surplus lines' regulation under state laws permits the sale of excess insurance coverage beyond what is available in the admitted market. This allows for more specialized or higher risk coverage that may not be readily available through standard insurance carriers.

103) In state insurance law, the 'use it or lose it' policy refers to:

Correct Answer is B - In state insurance law, the 'use it or lose it' policy refers to prohibiting insurers from canceling or non-renewing policies solely because a policyholder filed a claim. This regulation is designed to protect consumers from being penalized for using their insurance coverage.

Ethical practices and the regulatory environment: 5 questions

104) Which practice is essential for maintaining ethical standards in the regulatory environment of insurance?

Correct Answer is C - Maintaining ethical standards in the regulatory environment of insurance is essential through transparent communication with clients regarding policy terms and costs. This ensures that clients are fully informed and can make decisions based on accurate and complete information.

105) How does the regulatory environment support ethical practices in handling claims?

Correct Answer is B - The regulatory environment supports ethical practices in handling claims through strict guidelines that ensure fair and timely processing of claims. These regulations are designed to protect the rights of policyholders and ensure they receive the benefits they are entitled to under their insurance policies.

106) 'Twisting' in the insurance industry refers to:

Correct Answer is B - 'Twisting' in the insurance industry refers to the practice of persuading a policyholder to cancel an existing policy unnecessarily for the benefit of the agent. This unethical practice often involves misleading the policyholder about the benefits of switching policies.

107) The principle of 'utmost good faith' in insurance obligates all parties to:

Correct Answer is A - The principle of 'utmost good faith' in insurance obligates all parties to share all known risks and relevant information honestly. This foundational principle ensures that both the insurer and the insured enter into the contract with a clear understanding of the risks involved.

108) What is the impact of non-compliance with state insurance regulations on an insurance professional?

Correct Answer is C - Non-compliance with state insurance regulations can result in possible fines, license suspension, or revocation for an insurance professional. Regulatory compliance is crucial to maintaining the integrity of the insurance industry and protecting consumer interests.

Insurance Operations (Total: 8 Questions)

Underwriting principles: 3 questions

109) 'Automated underwriting systems' are used in the insurance industry to:

Correct Answer is B - 'Automated underwriting systems' are used in the insurance industry to streamline the underwriting process by using algorithms to assess risks. These systems enable faster decision-making and can improve the efficiency and accuracy of the underwriting process.

110) In underwriting, 'loadings' refer to:

Correct Answer is B - In underwriting, 'loadings' refer to additional charges applied to the premium to cover increased risk or administrative costs. Loadings are used to adjust the base premium to more accurately reflect the specific risk profile of the insured.

111) Which statement best describes 'conditional coverage' in underwriting?

Correct Answer is B - 'Conditional coverage' in underwriting refers to temporary coverage provided between the application submission and the formal policy issuance. This provides the applicant with a measure of protection during the underwriting process until the final policy terms are established.

Rate making: 3 questions

112) 'Territorial rating' in insurance rate making is based on:

Correct Answer is A - 'Territorial rating' in insurance rate making is based on the territory or geographic area where the insured risk is located, due to differences in risk exposure. Rates may vary depending on the frequency and severity of claims in different areas.

113) The 'combined ratio' in rate making measures:

Correct Answer is C - The 'combined ratio' in rate making measures the ratio of losses and expenses to earned premiums. It is a key indicator of an insurance company's underwriting profitability, with a combined ratio below 100% indicating an underwriting profit.

114) Which method of rate making involves adjusting the base premium up or down based on individual loss history?

Correct Answer is B - Experience rating is a method of rate making that involves adjusting the base premium up or down based on individual loss history. This approach rewards policyholders with lower risk profiles with lower premiums and adjusts premiums for those with higher claim histories.

Risk management: 2 questions

115) 'Risk concentration' refers to:

Correct Answer is B - 'Risk concentration' refers to the accumulation of risk in a particular geographic area or asset. High risk concentration can increase the potential for significant losses from a single event, such as a natural disaster.

116) In the risk management process, 'exposure analysis' is used to:

Correct Answer is B - In the risk management process, 'exposure analysis' is used to identify and quantify the potential impact of risks on an organization. This analysis helps organizations understand the potential loss exposures they face and prioritize risk management efforts.

Miscellaneous Coverages (Total: 4 Questions)

Flood insurance: 1 question

117) The NFIP defines a flood as:

Correct Answer is A - The NFIP defines a flood as the overflow of inland or tidal waters, unusual and rapid accumulation or runoff of surface waters, or mudslides. This definition encompasses various conditions that can lead to flooding and related damage.

Earthquake insurance: 1 question

118) How does the location of a property influence the cost of earthquake insurance?

Correct Answer is C - The location of a property influences the cost of earthquake insurance, with premiums being higher for properties located in areas with higher seismic activity due to the increased risk of damage. This reflects the higher potential costs associated with insuring properties in earthquake-prone regions.

Crime insurance policies: 2 questions

119) Which of the following scenarios would likely be covered by a 'Forgery or Alteration' coverage in a crime insurance policy?

Correct Answer is B - A 'Forgery or Alteration' coverage in a crime insurance policy would likely cover a scenario where an employee alters checks to embezzle funds from the company. This coverage protects against losses from forgery or alteration of financial instruments.

120) 'Computer Fraud Coverage' under a crime insurance policy protects against losses from:

Correct Answer is C - 'Computer Fraud Coverage' under a crime insurance policy protects against losses from unauthorized electronic funds transfers due to hacking. This coverage addresses the risks associated with cybercrime and electronic theft.

Practice Exam 5 (Total: 121 Questions) - Answers & Explanations

Insurance Basics (Total: 18 Questions)

Principles of insurance: 6 questions

1) Why is the principle of indemnity foundational to insurance contracts?

Correct Answer is C - It prevents the insured from profiting from their loss. The principle of indemnity ensures that insurance contracts compensate for losses up to the actual value of the loss but not beyond, preventing the insured from gaining financially from a claim, which could otherwise encourage fraudulent claims or the intentional creation of losses.

2) What does the principle of subrogation accomplish for the insurance industry?

Correct Answer is D - It allows insurers to recover funds from third parties responsible for losses. Subrogation allows an insurer who has paid out a claim to take legal action in the name of the insured against a third party responsible for causing the loss, helping to reduce the cost of claims and, consequently, insurance premiums for all policyholders.

3) Which principle supports the idea that insurance should restore the insured to their financial position before the loss?

Correct Answer is B - It ensures fair competition among insurers. The principle of subrogation supports the insurance industry by allowing insurers to seek reimbursement from third parties responsible for losses. This process helps keep insurance premiums lower for all policyholders by recovering costs from those at fault rather than distributing these costs across the insurer's entire customer base.

4) In insurance terminology, 'risk pooling' refers to what?

Correct Answer is C - Spreading the financial risk of losses across many policyholders. Risk pooling is the foundation of the insurance process, where the insurer aggregates many similar risks from individual policyholders, spreading the financial impact of individual claims across a larger group, thereby reducing the financial burden of losses on any single policyholder.

5) The principle of contribution applies when?

Correct Answer is A - An insured has multiple policies covering the same peril. The principle of contribution is applied when a loss is covered by more than one insurance policy, and it dictates how insurers share the costs of a claim. This prevents the insured from receiving a payout that exceeds the actual loss, maintaining the principle of indemnity.

6) Which of the following best exemplifies the principle of utmost good faith in action?

Correct Answer is B - A policyholder accurately reports their medical history on an insurance application. This is an example of the principle of utmost good faith in action, where both the insurer and the insured are expected to be completely honest and transparent in their dealings, including the disclosure of all relevant facts that could affect the terms of the insurance contract.

Types of insurers: 6 questions

7) Which of the following insurers operates similarly to mutual insurers but focuses on life insurance for military members and their families?

Correct Answer is D - Service insurers. These insurers operate similarly to mutual insurers but are specifically focused on providing life insurance for military members and their families, offering a unique blend of services tailored to the needs of those who serve or have served in the armed forces.

8) An insurance company that sells policies in states other than where it was incorporated is known as a/an:

Correct Answer is C - Foreign insurer. An insurance company that sells policies in states other than where it was incorporated is known as a foreign insurer in those states, differentiating it based on the location of incorporation relative to where it conducts business.

9) The main difference between a 'foreign' and an 'alien' insurer is based

on:

Correct Answer is B - The location of incorporation relative to
the market it serves. The main difference between a foreign and
an alien insurer lies in where the company is incorporated
versus where it sells insurance. Foreign insurers are
incorporated in one country but operate in another, while alien
insurers are based outside of the country where they offer
insurance products.

10) Excess and surplus lines insurers are important because they:

Correct Answer is C - Excess and surplus lines insurers are
critical because they provide coverage for risks that standard
insurers decline. This flexibility ensures that even
unconventional or high-risk entities can secure insurance,
filling a vital gap in the market.

11) 'Direct writers' and 'independent agents' are terms used to describe different:

Correct Answer is C - 'Direct writers' and 'independent agents'
represent different channels for selling insurance products.
Direct writers sell policies directly to consumers without
intermediaries, while independent agents represent multiple
insurers, offering a wider range of products.

12) A key feature of a reciprocal insurance exchange is that it:

Correct Answer is B - A reciprocal insurance exchange is
distinctive for being managed by an attorney-in-fact. This
structure involves policyholders exchanging insurance contracts
among themselves, under the management of an attorney-in-fact

who handles administration and claims.

Policy renewals and cancellations: 6 questions

13) Which of the following best describes an automatic renewal clause in an insurance policy?

```
Correct Answer is B - An automatic renewal clause in an
insurance policy means the policy will automatically renew at
the end of its term unless either the insured or the insurer
decides otherwise. This ensures continuous coverage without the
need to issue a new policy each term.
```

14) What does 'conditional renewal' of a policy imply?

```
Correct Answer is A - 'Conditional renewal' implies the policy
will renew only if certain conditions are met, such as changes
in premium or coverage terms. This allows insurers to adjust
terms based on new risk assessments or changes in the insurance
landscape.
```

15) A cancellation fee is charged by the insurer to cover what?

```
Correct Answer is A - A cancellation fee is charged by the
insurer primarily to cover the cost of processing the
cancellation. This fee compensates the insurer for the
administrative expenses incurred in terminating the policy
before its natural expiration.
```

16) What is typically required by insurers before reinstating a canceled policy due to non-payment?

Correct Answer is C - Before reinstating a canceled policy due to non-payment, insurers typically require payment of past due premiums and possibly a reinstatement fee. This ensures that the policyholder addresses the primary reason for cancellation before the policy is reactivated.

17) What might an insured expect to receive if their policy is canceled for reasons other than non-payment?

Correct Answer is A - If their policy is canceled for reasons other than non-payment, an insured might expect to receive a prorated refund of the unused premium. This refund compensates the policyholder for the portion of the policy period for which they had paid but will not receive coverage.

18) Which action is NOT a right of the insured upon receiving a cancellation notice?

Correct Answer is B - Demanding immediate reinstatement without addressing the reasons for cancellation is NOT a right of the insured upon receiving a cancellation notice. Policyholders can seek clarification, contest the decision, or find another insurer, but reinstatement typically requires addressing the reason for cancellation.

Property Insurance (Total: 26 Questions)

Dwelling policies: 6 questions

19) Under a DP-2 (Broad Form) policy, which of the following is true regarding the 'Weight of Ice, Snow, or Sleet' peril?

```
Correct Answer is D - Under a DP-2 (Broad Form) policy, the
'Weight of Ice, Snow, or Sleet' peril includes coverage for both
the dwelling and other structures. This broad form policy
provides more comprehensive protection against the weight of
ice, snow, or sleet causing damage.
```

20) What is the 'Liberalization Clause' in dwelling policies

```
Correct Answer is B - The 'Liberalization Clause' in dwelling
policies is a provision that automatically applies any favorable
changes in policy terms to existing policies. This ensures that
policyholders benefit from improved coverage terms or conditions
without needing to renegotiate or update their current policy.
```

21) Which coverage in a dwelling policy applies to medical expenses of guests accidentally injured on your property?

```
Correct Answer is A - The coverage in a dwelling policy that
applies to the medical expenses of guests accidentally injured
on your property is "Medical Payments to Others." This coverage
is designed to offer prompt payment for minor injuries without
the need for litigation.
```

22) How does the 'Inflation Guard Endorsement' affect a dwelling policy?

```
Correct Answer is B - The 'Inflation Guard Endorsement' in a
dwelling policy automatically increases the dwelling coverage
```

amount periodically to keep up with inflation. This ensures that the coverage limits remain adequate over time to rebuild the dwelling in case of a total loss.

23) A 'Scheduled Personal Property Endorsement' in a dwelling policy is used to:

Correct Answer is A - A 'Scheduled Personal Property Endorsement' in a dwelling policy is used to list specific items of personal property for coverage above the standard policy limits. This is particularly useful for high-value items that exceed the typical personal property coverage limits.

24) The 'Non-Occupancy Clause' in a dwelling policy refers to:

Correct Answer is A - The 'Non-Occupancy Clause' in a dwelling policy refers to a provision that excludes coverage if the dwelling is not occupied for a certain period. This clause is based on the increased risk associated with unoccupied properties.

25) What is the effect of a 'Mortgagee Clause' in a dwelling policy?

Correct Answer is A - The 'Mortgagee Clause' in a dwelling policy provides the mortgagee (lender) with certain rights and protections under the policy. It ensures that the lender's financial interest in the property is protected in case of a loss.

Homeowners policies: 8 questions

26) Which of the following would likely NOT be covered by the Personal Liability section of a homeowners policy?

Correct Answer is C - Not covered by the Personal Liability section of a homeowners policy is damages awarded for slander or libel. Personal Liability covers bodily injury and property damage to others, not personal or advertising injury claims like slander or libel.

27) An 'Accidental Discharge or Overflow of Water' endorsement to a homeowners policy covers:

Correct Answer is C - An 'Accidental Discharge or Overflow of Water' endorsement to a homeowners policy covers accidental overflow of water from plumbing, heating, or air conditioning systems. It does not cover flood damage from external sources or intentional acts resulting in water damage.

28) 'Landlord's Furnishings' coverage in a homeowners policy is intended to cover:

Correct Answer is B - 'Landlord's Furnishings' coverage in a homeowners policy is intended to cover appliances and furniture provided by the landlord for the tenant's use. This coverage is for items within a rented property that are owned by the landlord and used by the tenant.

29) Which statement about 'Named Peril' coverage in homeowners policies is TRUE?

Correct Answer is B - 'Named Peril' coverage in homeowners policies covers only those perils specifically named in the policy. It does not cover all possible perils, offering a more limited scope of protection based on the specified risks.

30) The 'Extended Replacement Cost' endorsement on a homeowners policy:

Correct Answer is B - The 'Extended Replacement Cost' endorsement on a homeowners policy pays up to a certain percentage over the insured amount to rebuild the home. This provides additional coverage beyond the policy limits to account for increased costs of construction or materials.

31) What is typically required for 'Personal Property Replacement Cost' coverage in a homeowners policy?

Correct Answer is B - Typically, "Personal Property Replacement Cost" coverage in a homeowners policy requires a separate endorsement and an additional premium. This endorsement ensures that personal property is replaced at its full cost without deduction for depreciation.

32) The 'All Risk' coverage in homeowners policies is another term for:

Correct Answer is B - "All Risk" coverage in homeowners policies is another term for open perils coverage. This type of coverage insures against all risks of physical loss, except those explicitly excluded in the policy.

33) 'Special Personal Property Coverage' in a homeowners policy enhances protection by:

Correct Answer is A - "Special Personal Property Coverage" in a homeowners policy enhances protection by covering personal property on an open perils basis, except for specific exclusions. This offers broader coverage for personal belongings.

Commercial property policies: 7 questions

34) A 'Time Element Coverage' in commercial property insurance refers to:

Correct Answer is B - A "Time Element Coverage" in commercial property insurance refers to protection against losses due to the passage of time, such as business income and extra expense coverage. It covers the loss of income and additional expenses incurred during the restoration period following a covered loss.

35) 'Newly Acquired or Constructed Property' coverage in a commercial property policy:

Correct Answer is A - "Newly Acquired or Constructed Property" coverage in a commercial property policy automatically covers new properties acquired or constructed for a limited time, allowing businesses to protect new assets without immediate notification.

36) Which statement is true regarding the 'Standard Mortgage Clause' in a commercial property policy?

Correct Answer is A - The "Standard Mortgage Clause" in a
commercial property policy protects the mortgage lender's
interests in the insured property. It ensures that the lender
can receive compensation in the event of a loss, even if the
insurance policy is voided by the actions of the insured.

37) 'Outdoor Property Coverage' endorsement in a commercial property policy typically includes:

Correct Answer is A - The "Outdoor Property Coverage"
endorsement in a commercial property policy typically includes
landscaping, signs, fences, and satellite dishes. It provides
coverage for outdoor property that might not be covered under a
standard commercial property policy.

38) The 'Selling Price Clause' in a commercial property policy is beneficial for businesses that:

Correct Answer is B - The "Selling Price Clause" in a commercial
property policy is beneficial for businesses that want to insure
their inventory at the selling price rather than the cost price.
This can be particularly important for businesses that add
significant value to their products through processing or
manufacturing.

39) 'Ordinance or Law Increased Cost of Construction' coverage in a commercial property policy:

Correct Answer is A - "Ordinance or Law Increased Cost of
Construction" coverage in a commercial property policy covers
the additional costs to comply with current building codes after
a covered loss. This can include upgrades required to meet new

environmental standards or accessibility requirements.

40) The 'Electronic Data Processing (EDP) Coverage' in commercial property policies specifically insures:

Correct Answer is A - The "Electronic Data Processing (EDP) Coverage" in commercial property policies specifically insures any electronic data processing equipment, software, and data. This coverage is crucial for businesses that rely heavily on technology and data for their operations.

Business interruption: 5 questions

41) 'Leader Property' coverage in a business interruption policy covers losses resulting from damage to:

Correct Answer is B - "Leader Property" coverage in a business interruption policy covers losses resulting from damage to a nearby property that attracts customers to the insured's business. This can include anchor stores in malls or other key businesses that drive foot traffic.

42) The inclusion of 'fungus, wet rot, dry rot, and bacteria' coverage in a business interruption policy would:

Correct Answer is B - The inclusion of "fungus, wet rot, dry rot, and bacteria" coverage in a business interruption policy provides specific coverage for damage caused by these perils, which are typically excluded. This endorsement can be crucial for businesses in industries susceptible to such risks.

43 How does the 'Monthly Limit of Indemnity' option affect a business interruption policy?

```
Correct Answer is A - The "Monthly Limit of Indemnity" option in
a business interruption policy limits the amount the insurer
will pay out for any single month's loss. It helps manage the
cost of the policy while still providing coverage for ongoing
losses.
```

44) 'Contingent Business Interruption' coverage is particularly important for businesses that:

```
Correct Answer is C - "Contingent Business Interruption"
coverage is particularly important for businesses that depend on
a few key suppliers or customers for their operations. It covers
the loss of income resulting from damage to the suppliers' or
customers' properties.
```

45) The 'Extended Business Income' coverage in a business interruption policy:

```
Correct Answer is C - The "Extended Business Income" coverage in
a business interruption policy provides income coverage after
the business has resumed operations, for a specified period.
This helps businesses recover financially even after physical
damages have been repaired.
```

Casualty Insurance (Total: 32 Questions)

Auto insurance: 8 questions

46) In auto insurance, the 'Right to Appraisal' clause allows:

Correct Answer is B - In auto insurance, the "Right to Appraisal" clause allows the policyholder and insurer to engage independent appraisers to resolve disputes over the value of a claim. This process helps ensure fair compensation for losses.

47) Which of the following typically qualifies for a 'Good Driver Discount' in auto insurance?

Correct Answer is C - Typically, a "Good Driver Discount" in auto insurance qualifies for drivers without any moving violations or accidents for a specified period. This incentive encourages safe driving habits.

48) 'Comprehensive' coverage for commercial auto insurance:

Correct Answer is C - "Comprehensive" coverage for commercial auto insurance protects against theft, vandalism, and other non-collision damage. It offers broad protection beyond just accidents.

49) The primary difference between 'Personal' and 'Commercial' auto insurance is:

Correct Answer is C - The primary difference between "Personal" and "Commercial" auto insurance is the intended use of the insured vehicle. Commercial auto insurance is designed for vehicles used for business purposes, while personal auto insurance covers personal or family use.

50) In auto insurance, 'Permissive Use' refers to:

Correct Answer is A - In auto insurance, "Permissive Use" refers to allowing anyone to drive the insured vehicle with the owner's permission. This provision extends the coverage to occasional drivers not regularly listed on the policy.

51) What does the 'Loss Payee' clause in an auto insurance policy specify?

Correct Answer is B - The 'Loss Payee' clause in an auto insurance policy specifies the party to be compensated first in the event of a loss, typically a lienholder or lessor. This ensures that the financial interest of the entity that financed or leases the vehicle is protected.

52) 'Custom Parts and Equipment (CPE)' coverage in an auto policy is intended for:

Correct Answer is B - 'Custom Parts and Equipment (CPE)' coverage in an auto policy is intended for aftermarket modifications and customizations not originally installed by the manufacturer. This coverage is essential for vehicle owners who enhance their vehicles with custom features.

53) A 'Named Driver Exclusion' in an auto insurance policy:

Correct Answer is A - A 'Named Driver Exclusion' in an auto insurance policy excludes specific drivers from coverage under the policy. This can be used when a household member has a poor driving record that would otherwise increase the policy's premium.

Workers compensation: 8 questions

54) The 'Dual Capacity' doctrine in workers' compensation law allows:

Correct Answer is B - The 'Dual Capacity' doctrine in workers' compensation law allows employers to act as both the insurer and the employer. This doctrine recognizes situations where an employer could be liable in a capacity other than as an employer, such as a manufacturer of a defective product that caused an employee's injury.

55) In workers' compensation, 'Repetitive Stress Injuries' (RSIs) are:

Correct Answer is C - In workers' compensation, 'Repetitive Stress Injuries' (RSIs) are covered as they are injuries that occur over time due to repetitive motions or strain. This acknowledges the cumulative effect of certain types of work activities on an employee's health.

56) 'Death Benefits' provided by workers' compensation insurance to dependents of a deceased worker typically include:

Correct Answer is B - 'Death Benefits' provided by workers' compensation insurance to dependents of a deceased worker typically include reimbursement for funeral expenses and ongoing support payments. These benefits help support the dependents financially after the loss of the worker.

57) What is the significance of the 'Maximum Medical Improvement' (MMI) in workers' compensation?

427

Correct Answer is B - The significance of the 'Maximum Medical Improvement' (MMI) in workers' compensation is that it indicates the highest level of recovery the injured worker is expected to achieve, which may involve permanent disability. It is a crucial point in determining the extent of workers' compensation benefits.

58) The concept of 'Constructive Notice' in workers' compensation implies that:

Correct Answer is A - The concept of 'Constructive Notice' in workers' compensation implies that employers are presumed to know of any hazards that could lead to injuries. This principle holds employers responsible for maintaining a safe working environment.

59) Which is NOT a typical exclusion from workers' compensation coverage?

Correct Answer is B - Injuries that occur during company-sponsored recreational activities are typically NOT excluded from workers' compensation coverage. Such activities are often considered part of employment, making related injuries eligible for compensation.

60) 'Alternative Dispute Resolution' (ADR) mechanisms in workers' compensation are used to:

Correct Answer is A - 'Alternative Dispute Resolution' (ADR) mechanisms in workers' compensation are used to determine the amount of compensation without going to court. ADR aims to resolve disputes efficiently and reduce litigation costs.

61) The 'Waiting Period' in workers' compensation refers to the time:

Correct Answer is C - The 'Waiting Period' in workers' compensation refers to the time before benefits start, typically a few days after an injury. This period helps manage the costs of the workers' compensation system by excluding very short-term disabilities.

Liability insurance: 10 questions

62) 'Motor Truck Cargo Liability Insurance' covers:

Correct Answer is B - 'Motor Truck Cargo Liability Insurance' covers liability for goods damaged or lost while in transit. This insurance is crucial for businesses involved in transporting goods, providing protection against financial loss due to damaged or lost cargo.

63) What is 'Contingent Liability' coverage?

Correct Answer is A - 'Contingent Liability' coverage is coverage for liabilities that may occur, depending on the outcome of an uncertain event. This type of insurance is important for protecting against potential liabilities that are not immediately apparent.

64) 'Hired and Non-Owned Auto Liability Insurance' is particularly important for businesses that:

Correct Answer is C - 'Hired and Non-Owned Auto Liability Insurance' is particularly important for businesses that do not own vehicles but occasionally rent or use employees' vehicles for business purposes. This coverage protects the business against liabilities arising from the use of these vehicles.

65) The 'Care, Custody, or Control' exclusion in a liability policy applies to:

Correct Answer is B - The 'Care, Custody, or Control' exclusion in a liability policy applies to property in the insured's care, custody, or control. This exclusion recognizes that such property should be covered under a different type of insurance, such as property insurance.

66) 'Excess Liability Insurance' differs from an 'Umbrella Policy' in that it:

Correct Answer is A - 'Excess Liability Insurance' differs from an 'Umbrella Policy' in that it only provides additional limits over specified underlying policies without broader coverage. Excess liability enhances the coverage limit, whereas umbrella policies can offer broader terms and fill in gaps.

67) Which of the following best describes 'Premises Liability'?

Correct Answer is B - 'Premises Liability' best describes liability for injuries and damages that occur on the insured's premises. This liability arises from the responsibility of the property owner or occupier to ensure the safety of those who enter the premises.

68) 'Legal Defense Costs' in a liability policy:

Correct Answer is B - In a liability policy, 'Legal Defense
Costs' are covered in addition to the policy limits. This means
that the insurer will pay for the insured's defense costs
without reducing the amount available to pay claims.

69) A 'Named Insured Endorsement' in a liability policy:

Correct Answer is B - A 'Named Insured Endorsement' in a
liability policy adds a person or entity to the policy as an
insured. This endorsement is used to extend coverage to
additional parties as required by contract or circumstance.

70) 'Stop Gap' coverage in a workers' compensation and employers liability policy is intended to:

Correct Answer is C - 'Stop Gap' coverage in a workers'
compensation and employers liability policy is intended to cover
the employer's liability in monopolistic states where workers'
compensation does not include employer liability. This coverage
fills a critical gap in these unique regulatory environments.

71) In liability insurance, the 'Cross-Liability' provision:

Correct Answer is B - In liability insurance, the
'Cross-Liability' provision treats each insured as a separate
entity for the purpose of insurance coverage. This allows for
claims to be made by one insured against another under the same
policy, facilitating coverage in situations where insured
parties may have claims against each other.

Umbrella policies: 6 questions

72) An individual with which of the following characteristics is MOST likely to benefit from an umbrella policy?

Correct Answer is C - An individual with significant assets and potential exposure to large liability claims is MOST likely to benefit from an umbrella policy. Umbrella policies provide additional liability coverage beyond what is offered by standard policies, protecting individuals with more to lose in the event of a lawsuit.

73) 'Excess Liability Insurance' differs from an 'Umbrella Policy' primarily in that:

Correct Answer is A - 'Excess Liability Insurance' differs from an 'Umbrella Policy' primarily in that it only provides additional limits over an existing liability policy without broader coverages. While both types of policies offer additional coverage, excess liability does not expand the scope of coverage like an umbrella policy can.

74) Which activity would MOST likely necessitate additional coverage under an umbrella policy?

Correct Answer is D - Engaging in high-risk sports as a hobby would MOST likely necessitate additional coverage under an umbrella policy. High-risk activities increase the likelihood of incurring liability claims that exceed the limits of standard insurance policies, making umbrella coverage more critical.

75) What typically triggers the coverage under an umbrella policy?

```
Correct Answer is C - The coverage under an umbrella policy is
typically triggered by the exhaustion of underlying policy
limits for a covered claim. Once the limits of the primary
insurance policy are reached, the umbrella policy provides
additional coverage.
```

76) An umbrella policy's coverage for 'Uninsured/Underinsured Motorist' (UM/UIM):

```
Correct Answer is B - In most cases, coverage for
'Uninsured/Underinsured Motorist' (UM/UIM) must be specifically
added as an endorsement to an umbrella policy. This coverage is
not automatically included and provides additional protection in
cases where the at-fault driver lacks sufficient insurance.
```

77) Which statement is true regarding the purchase of an umbrella policy?

```
Correct Answer is B - Purchasing an umbrella policy requires the
purchase of maximum limits on all underlying policies. This
ensures that there is a foundational level of coverage in place
before the umbrella policy provides additional coverage.
```

Package Policies (Total: 14 Questions)

Business Owners Policy (BOP): 7 questions

78) A BOP generally offers which of the following advantages over separate policies?

Correct Answer is C - A Business Owners Policy (BOP) generally offers cost savings and simplicity over purchasing separate policies. By bundling property and liability insurance into one package, businesses can save on premiums and reduce the complexity of managing multiple policies.

79) Which of the following businesses would typically NOT qualify for a BOP?

Correct Answer is C - A large manufacturing plant would typically NOT qualify for a Business Owners Policy (BOP). BOPs are designed for smaller businesses with specific risk profiles, and larger industrial operations often require more customized insurance solutions.

80) The 'Money and Securities' coverage in a BOP protects against:

Correct Answer is B - The 'Money and Securities' coverage in a BOP protects against theft, destruction, or disappearance of money and securities either on-premises or in transit. This coverage is essential for businesses that handle cash or securities, providing protection against financial loss.

81) 'Equipment Breakdown' coverage in a BOP:

Correct Answer is D - 'Equipment Breakdown' coverage in a BOP covers loss due to the breakdown of machinery and equipment necessary for business operations. This includes mechanical and electrical equipment failures, which are not typically covered by standard commercial property policies.

82) Which scenario would be covered under the liability portion of a BOP?

Correct Answer is B - A customer slipping and falling in the store would be covered under the liability portion of a BOP. This coverage protects the business against claims of bodily injury or property damage that occur within the business premises.

83) The 'Personal and Advertising Injury' coverage under a BOP protects against claims of:

Correct Answer is B - The 'Personal and Advertising Injury' coverage under a BOP protects against claims of injury arising from slander, libel, and violation of privacy rights. This coverage is crucial for businesses to protect against lawsuits related to their advertising practices or personal actions that harm others.

84) In a BOP, the 'Business Income' coverage is designed to:

Correct Answer is A - In a BOP, the 'Business Income' coverage is designed to compensate the business for lost revenue during temporary shutdowns due to covered property damage. This helps businesses recover financially during periods when they are unable to operate normally.

Commercial package policy: 7 questions

85) The 'Waiver of Subrogation' endorsement in a CPP:

Correct Answer is B - The 'Waiver of Subrogation' endorsement in a Commercial Package Policy (CPP) prevents the insurer from seeking recovery from a third party after paying a loss. This waiver can be critical in contracts and agreements where the parties agree to limit their mutual liability for losses.

86) Which coverage is NOT standard in a CPP but can be added as an endorsement?

Correct Answer is C - Professional Liability is NOT standard in a Commercial Package Policy (CPP) but can be added as an endorsement. This coverage is essential for businesses that provide professional services, as it protects against claims of negligence or inadequate work.

87) 'Ordinance or Law' coverage in a CPP addresses costs related to:

Correct Answer is B - 'Ordinance or Law' coverage in a CPP addresses costs related to updating a damaged building to current building codes during repairs. This coverage is vital for ensuring that a business can rebuild to current standards without bearing the entire cost.

88) The 'Named Peril' option in a CPP specifies that coverage is provided:

Correct Answer is B - The 'Named Peril' option in a CPP specifies that coverage is provided only for perils specifically named in the policy. This contrasts with 'all risk' coverage, which covers all perils except those explicitly excluded.

89) A 'Monoline Policy' differs from a CPP in that it:

Correct Answer is B - A 'Monoline Policy' differs from a CPP in that it provides coverage for a single line of insurance only. Unlike CPPs, which offer customizable bundles of various coverages, monoline policies focus on a specific area of coverage.

90) In a CPP, the 'Coinsurance Clause' typically requires that:

Correct Answer is B - In a CPP, the 'Coinsurance Clause' typically requires that the property is insured for a certain percentage of its value to avoid a penalty in the event of a partial loss. This encourages businesses to insure their property adequately.

91) Which of the following best describes the 'Aggregate Limit' in a CPP?

Correct Answer is B - The 'Aggregate Limit' in a Commercial Package Policy (CPP) refers to the total amount the insurer will pay for all claims during the policy period. This limit caps the insurer's total liability across all claims made under the policy within the specified period, helping to manage the insurer's risk exposure.

State-Specific Regulations (Total: 16 Questions)

Licensing requirements: 5 questions

92) Temporary licenses for property and casualty insurance agents:

Correct Answer is D - Temporary licenses for property and casualty insurance agents can be granted under special circumstances, such as when an agent is undergoing a lengthy licensing process. This enables individuals to begin their insurance careers or continue working in insurance while fulfilling all necessary requirements for permanent licensure.

93) Non-resident licensing for property and casualty insurance agents allows:

Correct Answer is B - Non-resident licensing for property and casualty insurance agents allows agents to sell insurance in a state where they do not reside, often with reciprocity agreements. This facilitates agents operating in multiple states, expanding their market reach beyond their resident state.

94) The application fee for a property and casualty insurance license:

Correct Answer is B - The application fee for a property and casualty insurance license varies significantly from state to state. Each state has its own licensing fees, which can differ based on the type of license being applied for and other state-specific requirements.

95) What impact does a felony conviction have on obtaining a property and casualty insurance license?

Correct Answer is C - A felony conviction may disqualify the applicant from obtaining a property and casualty insurance license, depending on the nature of the felony and state laws. State insurance regulators assess the relevance and severity of criminal convictions in determining an applicant's suitability for licensure.

96) The 'look-back' period for criminal convictions when applying for a property and casualty insurance license:

Correct Answer is B - The 'look-back' period for criminal
convictions when applying for a property and casualty insurance
license is typically 5-10 years, depending on state regulations.
This period limits how far back an insurance licensing authority
will consider an applicant's criminal history in their
evaluation process.

State laws governing insurance practices: 6 questions

97) How do state laws typically regulate 'captive insurance' companies?

Correct Answer is B - State laws typically regulate 'captive
insurance' companies by allowing businesses to form their own
insurance companies for self-insurance, with specific
regulations and requirements. Captive insurers provide a way for
large businesses or groups to finance their risk in a regulated
and formalized manner.

98) State insurance departments often provide which of the following services to consumers?

Correct Answer is B - State insurance departments often provide
mediation and arbitration services for disputes between insurers
and policyholders. These services help resolve conflicts over
claims, policy interpretations, and other insurance-related
disagreements without the need for litigation.

99) What is the typical state requirement for 'insurance company reserves'?

Correct Answer is B - State requirements for 'insurance company reserves' dictate that insurers are required to keep a certain percentage of premiums to cover future claims. This financial safeguard ensures that insurers have sufficient funds available to pay out claims, maintaining their solvency and protecting policyholders.

100) 'Binding authority' for agents under state insurance laws allows them to:

Correct Answer is A - 'Binding authority' for agents under state insurance laws allows them to bind coverage on behalf of the insurer, within certain limits. This authority enables agents to provide immediate insurance coverage to applicants based on the insurer's underwriting guidelines.

101) In the context of state insurance laws, 'rebating' is:

Correct Answer is B - In the context of state insurance laws, 'rebating' is the return of a portion of the agent's commission to the policyholder as an inducement to purchase. This practice is prohibited in many states as it can lead to unfair competition and may influence the policyholder's decision-making process.

102) State insurance regulations regarding 'data security' typically require insurers to:

Correct Answer is B - State insurance regulations regarding 'data security' typically require insurers to implement measures to protect sensitive policyholder information from breaches. These regulations are designed to safeguard personal and financial data from unauthorized access and theft.

Ethical practices and the regulatory environment: 5 questions

103) Ethical marketing practices in insurance require:

Correct Answer is B - Ethical marketing practices in insurance require full disclosure of policy benefits, limitations, and costs. This ensures that potential clients are fully informed about the products they are considering and can make decisions based on accurate and complete information.

104) In the regulatory environment, the purpose of 'anti-rebating' laws is to:

Correct Answer is B - In the regulatory environment, the purpose of 'anti-rebating' laws is to prohibit the practice of offering inducements to buy insurance that are not outlined in the policy. These laws aim to maintain fairness and transparency in the insurance marketplace by ensuring that all policyholders are treated equally and that decisions are not influenced by unauthorized incentives.

105) The ethical handling of premium payments involves:

Correct Answer is B - The ethical handling of premium payments involves promptly forwarding premiums to the insurer or designated third party. This practice ensures that policyholders' funds are managed responsibly and that insurance coverage remains in effect.

106) A conflict of interest in the insurance industry arises when:

Correct Answer is B - A conflict of interest in the insurance industry arises when an insurance professional has personal interests that could influence their professional duties. Such conflicts can compromise the integrity of the advice provided to clients and potentially lead to decisions that are not in the best interest of the policyholder.

107) The principle of 'indemnity' in insurance ethics is designed to:

Correct Answer is B - The principle of 'indemnity' in insurance ethics is designed to ensure that clients are restored to their financial position prior to a loss, no more and no less. This principle prevents policyholders from profiting from insurance claims and ensures that compensation reflects the actual value of the loss.

Insurance Operations (Total: 10 Questions)

Underwriting principles: 4 questions

108) 'Underwriting profit' is achieved when:

Correct Answer is B - 'Underwriting profit' is achieved when premiums collected exceed the costs of claims and underwriting expenses. This measure of profitability indicates that an insurance company has effectively priced its policies to cover the risks it assumes and the operational costs of underwriting those policies.

109) The 'Law of Large Numbers' is important in underwriting because

it:

Correct Answer is B - The 'Law of Large Numbers' is important in underwriting because it allows underwriters to predict loss occurrences more accurately with larger pools of similar risks. This statistical principle helps insurers to set premiums that are proportionate to the risk, ensuring financial stability and fairness.

110) 'Insurable Interest' must be established in the underwriting process to:

Correct Answer is B - 'Insurable Interest' must be established in the underwriting process to ensure that the policyholder stands to suffer a financial loss from the insured event. This requirement protects against speculative insurance practices and ensures that insurance serves its fundamental purpose of providing financial protection against genuine risks.

111) How do underwriters use 'loss history' during the underwriting process?

Correct Answer is B - As a guide to assess the likelihood and potential cost of future claims based on past claims. Underwriters utilize loss history to estimate the risk level of insuring an individual or entity, helping to determine appropriate premiums and coverage levels.

Rate making: 3 questions

112) 'Judgment rating' in rate making is typically used when:

Correct Answer is A - When there is insufficient historical data to use other rating methods. Judgment rating relies on the underwriter's experience and judgment in such cases, allowing for the assessment of risks that may not be well-documented or are unique in nature.

113) The purpose of 'loading' in the premium calculation is to:

Correct Answer is B - To account for the insurer's operational costs and profit margin. Loading in the premium calculation ensures that the insurer covers its operational expenses and achieves a profit, in addition to the costs associated with the risk itself.

114) In rate making, the term 'actuarial fairness' refers to:

Correct Answer is B - Setting premiums that are proportional to the risk and expected losses. Actuarial fairness involves calculating premiums based on statistical analysis to ensure that they accurately reflect the level of risk being insured.

Risk management: 3 questions

115) Which of the following best exemplifies 'risk mitigation' in property and casualty insurance?

Correct Answer is B - Implementing a business continuity plan to maintain operations after a loss. Risk mitigation strategies like business continuity planning help businesses prepare for and manage the impact of potential losses, reducing the overall risk to operations.

116) The 'risk management policy statement' of a company typically includes:

Correct Answer is B - The company's objectives and guidelines for managing risk. A risk management policy statement outlines the strategic approach a company takes towards identifying, assessing, and addressing risks, including its tolerance levels and mitigation strategies.

117) 'Contingent risk' in the context of risk management refers to:

Correct Answer is A - Risks that are dependent on or contingent upon certain events. Contingent risk refers to potential losses that may occur as a result of specific, uncertain events happening, impacting the company's operations or finances.

Miscellaneous Coverages (Total: 4 Questions)

Flood insurance: 2 questions

118) What is a 'Preferred Risk Policy' (PRP) in the context of flood insurance?

Correct Answer is B - Flood insurance offered at a reduced rate to properties in low to moderate-risk areas. The Preferred Risk Policy (PRP) is designed for properties in areas with lower risk of flooding, offering more affordable flood insurance coverage.

119) How often can flood insurance policies be renewed through the NFIP?

Correct Answer is D - Annually, with no guarantee of renewal if the property's risk level changes. Flood insurance policies through the NFIP must be renewed annually, and changes in risk assessment or flood zone designation can affect the terms or availability of renewal.

Earthquake insurance: 1 question

120) What is typically excluded from standard earthquake insurance policies?

Correct Answer is D - Land subsidence or sinkholes even if caused by an earthquake. Standard earthquake insurance policies typically exclude coverage for earth movement that is not a direct result of the seismic activity, such as land subsidence or sinkholes.

Crime insurance policies: 1 question

121) In the context of crime insurance, what does 'Social Engineering Fraud Coverage' typically insure against?

Correct Answer is B - The manipulation of employees by third parties to transfer money or property based on fraudulent instructions. Social Engineering Fraud Coverage protects against losses incurred when employees are tricked into sending money or assets to fraudsters, a growing concern in today's digital and interconnected business environment.

A Message From Apex Academic Resources

Dear Reader,

Creating this book required dedication, effort, and collaboration from industry professionals, editors, and content developers. Each person contributed their expertise to provide a resource we hope supports your journey in Property and Casualty Insurance.

If this book has helped you, we would appreciate your feedback on Amazon. Your reviews guide future publications and help other readers find valuable resources. Your thoughts matter.

Thank you for choosing our book. We hope it has been valuable and wish you success in your endeavors.

With gratitude,
  The Apex Academic Resources Team

Amazon Review Link

Made in the USA
Coppell, TX
27 March 2025

47598139R30252